Israel/Palestine and the Queer International

Also by Sarah Schulman

NONFICTION
Gentrification of the Mind: Witness to a Lost Imagination
Ties That Bind: Familial Homophobia and Its Consequences
Stagestruck: Theater, AIDS, and the Marketing of Gay America
*My American History: Lesbian and Gay Life during
    the Reagan/Bush Years*

FICTION
The Mere Future
Child: A Novel
Shimmer
Empathy
People in Trouble
Rat Bohemia
After Delores
Girls, Visions, and Everything
The Sophie Horowitz Story

PLAYS
Enemies, A Love Story (adapted from Isaac Bashevis Singer)
Manic Flight Reaction
Carson McCullers
Mercy

FILMS
The Owls (cowritten with Cheryl Dunye)
Mommy Is Coming (cowritten with Cheryl Dunye)
United in Anger: A History of ACT UP (cowritten with Jim Hubbard)

ISRAEL/PALESTINE
and the Queer International

SARAH SCHULMAN

DUKE UNIVERSITY PRESS   Durham and London   2012

"We shall not take others unawares or mislead them, any more than we shall deceive ourselves."

—THEODOR HERZL, *The Jewish State*, 1896

CONTENTS

ACKNOWLEDGMENTS IX

INTRODUCTION: Before 1

PART I Solidarity Visit
   1. Awareness 23
   2. Preparation: Learning from Cinema 40
   3. Maps 48
   4. The Jewish Embrace 58
   5. Solidarity Visit 67
   6. Palestine 77
   7. Finding the Strategy 86

PART II AI-U.S. Tour
   8. Homonationalism 103
   9. Amreeka 133
   10. Backlash 156
   11. Understanding 172

CONCLUSION: There Is No Conclusion 175

APPENDIX: Brand Israel and Pinkwashing:
A Documentary Guide 179

INDEX 187

ACKNOWLEDGMENTS

Thank you to the Corporation of Yaddo. Special thanks to my beloved cousin Marcia Cohen-Zakai. I am very grateful to Tali Shapiro (Israel), Jessie Haycock (United States), and Mikki Stelder (Netherlands) for invaluable research on pinkwashing. Thanks to Nadia Awad for her detailed and engaged feedback.

INTRODUCTION
Before

It was about two weeks after the July 2006 Israeli bombing of Lebanon. I was having dinner with a Lebanese friend, the gay novelist Rabih Alameddine.

"I don't get it," he said. "In the thirteen years that I have lived in this country, many of my friends, maybe most of my friends have been Jews. We usually agree on everything. Sometimes they are more left wing than I am. We agree about the war in Iraq. But, then, Israel invades Lebanon, and suddenly they don't get it. They get it about Iraq, but all of a sudden they are telling me that *Israel has a right to defend itself,* et cetera. And I'm shocked. What is going on? Why don't they get it?"

I have been trying to answer his question ever since, starting with myself. "Getting it." The transformation of my own personal relationship to the state of Israel has been a long, subtle, slow, stubborn journey that has taken a lifetime. One of the strangest things about willful ignorance regarding Israel and Palestine is how often "progressive" people, like myself, with histories of community activism and awareness, engage in it. In this way it somewhat parallels the history of homophobia, in that there are emotional blocks that keep many straight people from applying their general value systems to human rights for *all.* The irony, in my case, of being a lifelong activist and not doing the work to "get it" about Israel is deep and hard to both understand and convey. But I have come to learn that this insistent blindness is pervasive, and I want to use the opportunity of this book to confront and expose my own denial in a way that I hope will be helpful to others. So let me start with the example of my own story.

I was born in 1958, thirteen years after the end of the Holocaust, which is not a long time. It would be like a Rwandan Tutsi being born today. I was born only three years after my maternal grandmother finally confirmed, as postwar chaos subsided, that her two brothers and two sisters had been exterminated by the Nazis and their collaborators ten to fifteen years before. They were not wandering in the Soviet Union or resettled in Israel, but had in fact been murdered. My father's parents were starving, uneducated peasants in Russia who came to the United States before the Russian Revolution, worked in sweatshops (my grandmother actually worked briefly at the Triangle Factory before the fire), and finally opened a clothing store in Elizabeth, New Jersey. My father grew up over the store. He was raised with an adopted sister who had watched her mother and brother be murdered by Cossacks while she hid in the fireplace. My mother's father came to the United States alone as a child from Russia; forty years later his sister was murdered by Nazis at Babi Yar. Both of my maternal grandparents were laundry workers in Brooklyn who spent their lives washing other people's clothes. In other words, my background was typical of my Jewish generation: soaked in blood, trauma, and dislocation.

I think it is fair to say that my parents were afraid of Christians. They never socialized with Christians, which was not that hard growing up in New York City. They found Christians strange, hard to talk to, and hard to read. I had never even heard of Jesus Christ until some kid explained it to me on the playground. There was this guy named "Jesus," and he was "the son of God." When I came home I asked my grandmother, "Who is Jesus Christ?"

"Look," she said as if we were discussing the price of eggs. "There was a girl named Mary, and she got in trouble, so she made up a story."

My mother fervently opposed racism but did not socialize with black people. I think it was because they weren't Jewish. I was brought up to believe that Christians are not trustworthy and are all, at base, anti-Semites. I never heard a bad word about an Arab.

We were raised with two Yiddish concepts about Christians: *kopf* and *punim*. *Yiddishe kopf* and *goyishe kopf*. To say that someone had a *Yiddishe kopf* (a Jewish mind) was to say admiringly that he was a genius. That he was analytical and conceptual and an original thinker. To say that someone had a *goyishe kopf* was to say that he was dull-witted, conformist, and slow. But *Yiddishe punim* (Jewish face) was highly undesirable (by 1958 standards), signaling large features, kinky hair, and dark skin. A *goyishe punim* was what everybody wanted—blonde hair, blue eyes, small nose. My mother, whom I resemble exactly, always thought that she was ugly because she was dark and that her sister was beautiful because she was blonde. In the early 1960s, a female Jewish copywriter with brown hair wrote the two most successful advertising slogans of her era: *If I have one life, let me live it as a blonde* and *Blondes have more fun*.

My grandmother's brother had been recruited from Poland in 1920 by a Zionist pioneer movement called Noye Tsionie (New Zion), which is historically interesting because its name was in Yiddish, not Hebrew, the resuscitated ancient language refabricated for the new Jewish state. Only a few decades later Israel would discourage the speaking of Yiddish. "You're in Israel, Speak Hebrew" signs would command newly arriving refugees from World War II until they drove Yiddish out of existence. "Yiddish was the language of Treblinka" was a common Israeli perception. But at this early date, the Zionist movement enrolled young Jewish men and women, in Yiddish, who knew they had no future in Europe. Zionism had been articulated by Theodor Herzel, a Viennese journalist who was sent to Paris to cover the Alfred Dreyfus trial. After observing the viciousness with which the anti-Semitic French framed poor Colonel Dreyfus, Herzel wrote his book *The Jewish State* attesting that Jews would never be safe in Europe. He was right. What he missed was that Muslims would never be safe there either.

I grew up surrounded by Holocaust survivors. The tailor who sewed in his shop window across the street had a number on his arm. My first girlfriend, when I was sixteen, was the daughter of German Jewish refugees living in Jackson Heights, Queens, where they could buy their German sausages and newspapers from quiet delis on silent side streets. Our family shopped at a children's clothing store in Brooklyn called Borlam's, run by a bunch of friends who had all been in the same camp. They had numbers on their arms and screamed at each other across the store. The kids I went to elementary and high school with who had the most fearful, neurotic parents were the children of survivors. I remember a few who had to go straight home after school; they weren't allowed to go to the park. Some of their homes were anguished, confusing places. My grandmother and I saw a movie based on an Isaac Bashevis Singer novel, *Enemies, a Love Story*. It was about Holocaust survivors living in the Bronx who had been made crazy by their experiences. They yelled at each other for no reason and didn't know how to be happy. I thought it was normal. I'd grown up around people like this all my life.

"We didn't have bread to eat" is the sentence I most frequently remember hearing my father's mother say when talking about her childhood under the czar. Her family, the Glukowskys, had one pair of shoes, which they all had to share. This level of degradation and deprivation was something I considered to be normal, regular, the way things are.

Jews were people who had been arbitrarily violated and could not trust the Other. Israel was a faraway place where pioneers needed money to plant trees and make the desert bloom. America was a scary land filled with palefaces who weren't very bright. New York was home to dark people who yelled when they wanted to and said what they felt. Western Europe was sophisticated and treacherous, while Eastern Europe had gotten what it deserved. If you had told six-year-old me in 1964 that someday Jewish people with guns would go into villages and commit atrocities, I would have thought you were insane. It was unimaginable. I didn't know that they already had.

In 1965, my grandmother's brother came to visit us in New York from his kibbutz Mizrah, a socialist, nonreligious community outside of Haifa. He was so modern that he came by plane, instead of the still typical boat. He had been one of the kibbutz's founders in the early 1920s, and now Mizrah was one of Israel's major producers of pork products. Thus began an occasional stream of visitors from Israel. Some were actually somehow related to us; others knew someone who was somehow related. Given how many had been murdered and scattered, anyone who remained was considered a "cousin." I had never seen Jews like this before. We were soft, and they were hard. They played sports. We barely watched sports. They wore their shirts unbuttoned at the chest and decorated their chest hair with gold medallions. The women were sexy and wore tight shirts. These people were not afraid, they were physical, and they were not polite. My great-uncle complained about everything American. According to him, Israeli family structure was better, and my cousins were lucky to grow up in the kibbutz's "children's house." Israeli juice was better, he was sure of it. American markets were just starting to carry those thick-skinned oranges stamped "Jaffa." I didn't know that Jaffa was an Arab city next to Tel Aviv and that the oranges were actually "yaffeh," which means *good*. These Israelis were arrogant and sensual, and they did not identify with other people.

My mother had raised me to be very aware of the suffering of black people and of how they had been disrespected and denied their rights. I was told to always call black people Mr. and Mrs. and never to call them by their first names. She took us on all-night buses sponsored by the National Association of Social Workers to protest the war in Vietnam and racism. My new relatives did not understand anything about this.

"You, you are too worried about everyone else. First you take care of the Jews," a "cousin" named Eli memorably instructed. His favorite thing about New York? Singles bars.

I'd never heard these kinds of ideas before. My mother, who had not known any of her grandparents, and whose aunts, uncles, and cousins had mostly been exterminated, was so thrilled to have living relatives that she romanticized them. When my parents finally went to Israel to visit, they came back and reported on the euphoria of walking down a street and knowing that everyone was a Jew.

"The policeman on the corner was a Jew," she said, starry-eyed.

This from a woman who had warned us to never run away from a New York City police officer because "he could shoot you." It was a contradiction, but she needed to feel that way. For some reason that was never articulated, Jewish cops meant a better world.

When the 1967 war started, my parents woke us up in the middle of the night. They had panicked expressions on their faces.

"Kids," my father said, terrified. "There's a war that has started in Israel." They worried that it was the end for the Jews, for the streets of Jews, for the newly discovered cousins, for this new reality they had only just experienced. But it was not the end. Instead it was the triumph of the famed *Yiddishe kopf*. Israel showed military supremacy against what we were told were great odds, and my parents were reassured that with all the sports and agriculture and chest hair, these Israelis were still smarter than anyone else around them. Only, unlike in Europe, they applied their smarts to their army. And this was the magic combination. I was nine, and I think I thought that Israel was fighting the Germans. On Steuben Day, when the reconstructed German Americans walked down Fifth Avenue in lederhosen, my grandmother would cry, shake with fear, and look away. But on Israeli Day, she would stand on Fifth Avenue and wave an Israeli flag, clapping to the folk dances and cheering.

I finally became aware of Arabs in 1972 when one Israeli "cousin," actually the friend of a relative, had dinner at our house. A gorgeous Sabra, Tamar was a modern dancer, which many Israelis seemed to be. Some of the first Israeli imports to New York were dance companies performing barefoot, longhaired, physically free, joyful, intense Israeli modern dance. Only later did I learn that the Rothschild family had deliberately sponsored modernists like the Martha Graham dancer Linda Hodes to take these new dance forms to Israel. These Israeli women had the exact same genes that we did, but somehow their skin was olive, their hair was silk, and they were brimming with energy for sex, life, dance, the world. Tamar sat on our couch glued to the television as the Israeli Olympic team was massacred by a group of masked Arab guerrillas. She knew two of the murdered athletes. They all knew each other, and now we knew them too.

Despite being very urban, far from the focused propaganda of suburban temples or country clubs or Jewish centers, without much condensed institutional bombardment of ideology, simply living everyday as a New Yorker, I had never heard, not even once, that Palestinians had had their homeland taken from them by the Israelis. I did not know that they were trying to win this land back. This was never mentioned. I don't even think that my parents were aware of this. Instead, what I now know to be occupation was then presented as one long continuation of the persecution that my grandparents and aunts and uncles had endured. Though my aunts and uncles had been murdered, their children were safely out of Europe, and still someone wanted to kill them. Again. Couldn't the world just leave us alone? "Palestinians" were part of this vaguely articulated surrounding world of people who did what everyone seemed to do to Jews: attack them. For one reason, and one reason alone: we were their scapegoats. We had always been scapegoats. I did not have any idea that Jews were finally in the role of nationalist, dominant aggressors, with state power and the holders of legal and military apparatus. It was impossible to think this. Neither I, nor anyone within earshot, understood or articulated this rapid change of position from truly victimized to refugee to perpetrator within a matter of months.

And yet, somehow, in my community/family/school/city our ("the Jews") fear never fully translated to the Arabs. We still feared the Europeans. When our family went on a trip to France, we went to the Jewish neighborhood and read the plaques. "Fifteen Jewish children were murdered here." "Forty Jewish people were arrested here." We trembled at the French people walking by. They did it. Or they stood by and let it happen. Of that I was sure. And although they might or might not do it again, they wanted to. That was the most important thing. You could see it on their faces. It was clear to me that I had to be aware of this. It didn't have to stop me from living, but I had to face facts.

In 1978, when I was twenty years old, Isaac Bashevis Singer won the Nobel Prize for Literature for his writing in Yiddish. I noticed this. I had grown up going to the Yiddish Theater with my grandmother and was just about to drop out of college to become a writer. So I paid attention. In his Nobel acceptance speech, Singer made a pointed jab at Israel.

The high honor bestowed upon me by the Swedish Academy is also a recognition of the Yiddish language—a language of exile, without a land, without frontiers, not supported by any government, a language which possesses no words for weapons, ammunition, military exercises, war tactics; a language that was despised by both gentiles and emancipated Jews.

To me the Yiddish language and the conduct of those who spoke it are identical. One can find in the Yiddish tongue and in the Yiddish spirit expressions of pious joy, lust for life, longing for the Messiah, patience and deep appreciation of human individuality. There is a quiet humor in Yiddish and a gratitude for every day of life, every crumb of success, each encounter of love. The Yiddish mentality is not haughty. It does not take victory for granted. It does not demand and command but it muddles through, sneaks by, smuggles itself amidst the powers of destruction, knowing somewhere that God's plan for Creation is still at the very beginning.

I felt a lot of recognition when I read this. This was the kind of Jew I was, a diasporic Jew. I didn't need a word for *weapons*. I *sneak by*. Certainly, if I was going to be an openly lesbian writer, as I planned to become, I was going to have to do a lot of muddling. I was never going to be in a position to *command*, if I was honest.

It wasn't until four years later, 1982, that I suddenly realized that something was very wrong in Israel—that it was not simply a matter of my lack of identification. I had already come out as a lesbian, been kicked out of my family, and started my life as an artist living in the midst of a lot of other people who had been kicked out of their families for being gay and artists. I didn't think about Israel. I was trying to live and didn't have any help. I was trying to learn how to be me. I was dating a Christian girl in a left-wing organization, and she said something about the atrocities in Sabra and Shatila, and I said, "Well, that's what they get." I was just ignorantly imitating my parents. Honestly, I had never thought about it for myself.

"No," she said. "What the Israelis are doing is wrong."

This was the turning point really. Looking back, I think the internal mechanism that allowed me to start turning was complex. I had already learned through my own experience of their cruel homophobia that my family was wrong about a lot of things. Why not this? I was not married or getting married; I did not have children; I was not part of any institution that would require a lot of contact with family or Jewish religion or social doctrine. I occasionally attended the Gay and Lesbian Synagogue in Westbeth, but that just furthered the alienation. The Jews didn't want us; that's why we had to have a gay synagogue. So why was I toeing the line of a party that wouldn't let me in? From all third-hand accounts, Israel seemed like an awful place for gay people. I was safely in New York, where my kind of Judaism was as regular as it could ever be. Why was I mouthing unthinking statements of loyalty to Israel, a place I'd never even been? So I started thinking about it all a little differently. Trying to figure something out.

I read a book, popular at the time, by Jacobo Timerman, *Prisoner without a Name, Cell without a Number*. Later I saw him on *60 Minutes*, and I remember the story he told there.

"When I was in Argentina, the fascist police made me get down on my knees and bark like a dog, because I was a Jewish dog," he told Mike Wallace, a Jewish man who had changed his name to have a career in broadcast journalism. "When I came to Israel, I heard that some Israeli soldiers had made some Palestinian youth get down on their knees and bark like dogs, because they were Arab dogs. And I asked myself, are these two incidents the same? And I had to answer yes."

This made a huge impression on me. What he said was incontrovertibly true. And coming from his mouth, a man who had been persecuted for being a Jew, it was not that kind of unsympathetic, uncomprehending, ideological anti-Israel line that I had started noticing in left-wing newspapers and at political events. It was a critique that was rooted in the human, from a place of recognition of his own suffering. I was deeply moved and started to understand. He cared about what was best for the Jews. And this kind of behavior was not good for the Jews.

But every time I thought about Israel, my interest turned to Europe. That same year, 1982, I was part of the first and only American feminist delegation to the German Democratic Republic (East Germany). I provocatively listed the YIVO Institute for Jewish Research, where I was enrolled to study Yiddishkeit, as my institutional affiliation. On the first day, our German hosts whisked us away to visit Ravensbruck, the women's concentration camp. I had never been to a concentration camp before. I had never been to Germany before, East or West. But what shocked me more than the crematorium, which I had spent a lifetime staring at in movies and photographs, was the museum display in the entrance hall, where the East Germans had posted what seemed like hundreds of photographs of murdered women, each with the label "Communist" next to her Jewish name. Sophie Goldberg, Communist. Sarah Kaminsky, Communist. They were taking it away from the Jews. This began a long, heated debate in which the East Germans tried to explain to me that World War II was not "the war against the Jews" as I had been taught, but in fact a "war between Fascists and Communists." I protested so strongly that they sent me off to spend the afternoon with an elderly Jewish couple who were supposed to set me straight. These two had been members of the German Communist Party before World War II, imprisoned by Nazis in camps, and after the war had chosen to live in East Germany. They told me over and over that they did not need Jewish identities, that the important divide between people was class. That they identified with people all over the world regardless of religion. That, in fact, they were not really Jews at all. Later, though, when I came to their spacious house, the kind reserved only for party apparatchiks, I wasn't surprised to see their bookshelves lined with the collected works of Isaac Bashevis Singer.

What I took away was that even the Communist Jews of East Germany were afraid of their Christian comrades. This seemed to be the problem: Europe. While much of what I was raised with was falling away, I was being reaffirmed in my early training that Jews could not trust Europeans. After all, we have every good reason to fear them. Israelis fear "being pushed into the sea." Despite all kinds of racial positioning for political purposes, European Jews don't imagine finding safety in Europe. For them there is the Arab land before them and the angry sea behind. And that is the end of the world. Much contact with European Christians over a long period of time had underlined this. For example, my dear French friends who insist on drawing a casual distinction between "*Les Juifs* et *les Français*."

"*Mais, les Juifs sont Français*," I have repeated over and over again for years.

The reemergence of profound anti-Semitism in the new Eastern Europe and the way it is casually echoed by my immigrant students from Albania, Russia, Ukraine, Poland, Romania, is terrifying. Where I have a professorship, at the City University of New York, College of Staten Island, it is harder to come out as a Jew to my students than it is to come out as a lesbian. Some of my Jewish colleagues never do. In 1984, I went to Belgium on a Fulbright and studied the deportation of Belgian Jews during the occupation. Comparing extant Belgian Jewish literature on the subject to the actual facts was disturbing. Thirty-five years after the Holocaust, Belgian Jews were still afraid to tell the truth about their neighbors, soft-pedaling the history of their own demise. As a New Yorker, I had never experienced a fear so deep as a Jew that I wouldn't tell the truth. But the Belgian Jews' fear was so self-censorious that they didn't even know it. French people thought that the word *Juif* was impolite, so *d'origine Juif* or *Israelite* became the acceptable term. The word *Juif*, after all, was what they made fellow French people sew onto their clothes.

Later, as I started to publish books and have them translated, I had four book tours in West Germany and one in the unified country. These were also informative in this regard. During one visit, *Stern* magazine was conducting a poll: "Who Is Responsible for the Problems in the Middle East?" The options were A. the Israelis, B. the Arabs, and C. both. What happened to D. Europe? Didn't they initiate the series of atrocities that traumatized Ashkenazi Jews into fearful dissociation from other people? At a dinner in Hamburg, my left-wing publisher asked me if I eat pork.

"Yes," I said. "I'm not religious."

"Oh then, so you're not Jewish."

"Of course I am," I said. "With every cell of my body."

She became very upset. "No," she insisted. "You shouldn't use biological terms. The Nazis used biological terms."

But of course, like many Jews, I do think of myself in biological terms, despite how convenient that is for anti-Semitism. There is, after all, a genetic component, since Jewish identity—from the Jewish point of view—is biologically essentialist, dependent on having a Jewish mother. I do, of course, know that there are ways of being a Jew without the maternal biological component, and yet that is an operative factor. I completely understand what my German publisher was reacting to, but that reaction is itself too revealing for comfort. On both sides of the wall, Germans were looking for ways to take away my Jewishness through categorization while thinking they were protecting me. In the European context, my existence was still an anxiety-producing concept fraught with contradiction.

As the years have passed, my perception of European anti-Semitism has not changed, but I now see that Europeans' historic paranoia and acting out against Muslims is as historically consistent. For years I have had arguments with French feminists about French restrictions on the wearing of hijab in public schools or burka on the public streets while simultaneously

permitting nuns in habits to teach and walk. That the third largest contemporary immigration to Israel is French (after Russia and the United
States) becomes comprehensible when one realizes that these are often
French North African Jews, caught between French anti-Arab prejudice
and both French Christian and French Muslim anti-Jewish feeling. As an
American, of course, I hold views about religious "freedom," that is to say
the expression of religious feeling, as sacrosanct. Many of my Muslim students cover to greater or lesser degrees, and — despite all the anti-Muslim
prejudice on Staten Island — this is an integrated and accepted part of the
City University classroom, just as it has always been for religious Jews. No
one would ever argue successfully that they should be banned from class
or forced to disrobe. Yet many Europeans make this argument fiercely, be-
lieving that they are somehow "helping" Muslim women by forcing them
to unveil. What I have come to understand, finally, is that for Europeans,
what they call *laïque* or secular culture is actually a kind of liberal Christian
culture. And so, to them, difference — switching between Jews and Muslims, depending on the historical moment — violates what they believe to
be "secular objectivity" but is really basic Christian aesthetics. One could
argue that American culture is similar in its attitudes, but I didn't grow
up in America. I grew up in New York City. So I don't really know that. I
mean, I did once have a job teaching in Oregon where for some reason the
other teachers and students started calling me "Woody Allen."

"Hi Woody," they'd say when we passed on the gorgeous wooded paths,
me in my black T-shirt and them in their pastel fleece.

But really, I've always felt normal on the subway, and I expect that I
always will. So my changing consciousness about Palestine forced me to go
back and take another look at Europe. After my recognition that the murders at Sabra and Shatila refugee camps were in fact atrocities, I began to
seriously read about the Holocaust. Not just *The Diary of Anne Frank*, but
Hannah Arendt's 1963 *Eichmann in Jerusalem*, in which she claimed that
Israel was manipulating the trial of Nazi functionary Adolf Eichmann not
to get justice but to justify Zionism. For this Arendt was eviscerated by the
dominant apparatus, which over time has proved itself to be consistently
unforgiving of interrogation. Thirty years later, *The Specialist: Portrait of a
Modern Criminal*, a documentary about the Eichmann trial, was finally released, and we could all see for ourselves that she was right. Later I read
Hitler's Willing Executioners, in which Daniel Goldhagen shows that Europeans were not just following orders but went out of their way to com-

mit atrocities. He reveals the pleasure at the root of anti-Semitic cruelty, and he shows photographs of terrified Jews being tortured by laughing, smiling Christians. These photos remind me of those famous photographs of picnicking Americans in Indiana with their happy-go-lucky *goyishe kopfs*, chatting under the body of a black man they have just lynched hanging from a big apple tree. Not a mainstream point of view, perhaps, but one that is organically and honestly my own.

The questions started to form in my mind. How did we get from that to this? Instead of my old questions, such as *How come my Israeli cousins are more beautiful and sexier than I?* I began asking, *How did these soft people with no word for* military tactic *start bulldozing Palestinian houses?* And how did the Europeans, who caused the pain in the first place, get off scot-free, while the Palestinians, who had nothing to do with it, ended up paying the price? What is the psychological equation of this phenomenon?

My first answer was the obvious problem of nationalism. For millennia of diasporic living, Jews were never the majority, dominant oppressor class. Six decades of nationalism, and suddenly everything changed.

Let me stop here and clarify what the word "diaspora" means to me. All my life I have understood the word "diaspora," when applied to Jews, to mean the diversity and variety of Jewish people who exist throughout the world. Intrinsic to this is the understanding that these Jews, everywhere, are by definition a minority living with other cultures that are dominant in size and cultural reach. Because Judaism is not evangelical, Jews are by necessity bound to live as minorities. Christianity, whose heartbeat is evangelical, has as its goal that the world becomes unified in the love of Jesus Christ. Because Jews do not recruit and barely welcome converts, we do not spread. So, to be diasporic, as I have always understood it, is to live globally, as minorities, within other peoples' domains. This means that we, as a people, speak different languages, could be racially dominant or minority, could exist in any financial or social class, and have other components to our realities (Arab, black, biracial, first world, or third world living in Christian, Muslim, Hindu, or Buddhist societies) while being religiously subject to the will of our various dominant cohabitants. As I learned, in my particular generational and geographic diasporic experience, the only alternative to being diasporic was to be Zionist, that is to say to want every Jew to move to Israel and choose to live in a Jewish state instead of the world. While we considered Israel to be part of the Jewish diaspora (i.e., world Jewry), the decision to live there was not a diasporic decision. It meant leaving the diaspora, exiting the experience of being a minority *as a Jew*, and choosing to be dominant. Because my family never considered moving to Israel, we were always self-aware as permanently diasporic. We were refugees from Austria-Hungary and from the Russian Pale of Settlement who currently resided in New York City. Just as our other surviving family members were currently in Russia or Israel. Even though we had lost touch with many of them and often did not know their names, we still had awareness of this scattering of people as being part of the same system: the diaspora. This was a normative, natural part of being a Jew as far as I knew. And I understood it as historically consistent. The desire to leave the diaspora and have our own nationalist state where we make the rules and dominate other people was an alien paradigm shift with rapid, profound consequences on Jewish self-perception. That mine was the transitional generation is partially why it took me so long to understand what these changes ultimately meant. It is hard to comprehend the meaning of change on an identity rooted in the very recent past, as lesbian, gay, bisexual, and transgender (LGBT) people well know.

Then there is the question of Zionism itself, and how it came to be successful. Zionism has always been a minority position among Jews. Even today, 58 percent of world Jewry prefer to live in the diaspora rather than to move to Israel. Increasingly, Israelis are refusing Zionism by moving back to the diaspora, to the United States and to Europe, where they are choosing to again be minorities. Even the *Jerusalem Post* acknowledges that seven hundred thousand to a million Israelis are living outside of their country, as emigration has outpaced immigration since 2007. At no time in history has Zionism ever been the dominant trend among world Jewry. Before the Holocaust, Zionism was a small tendency, like the Back to Africa faction of the Black Power Movement. But the Jews murdered in the Holocaust were diasporic Jews, not pioneers to Palestine. Many of the murdered were Yiddish speakers. After the war, large numbers of traumatized, starving, diseased Jewish refugees were living in displaced persons' camps. No one wanted to absorb them. They couldn't go back to such places as Poland, and the United States didn't want them. The United States and the Allies needed a strong military base in the Middle East, and there was widespread guilt about the lack of global aid during the genocide. So creating the state of Israel as a place to dump the refugees and build a military footing in the region for the West served everybody's needs. Of course, Arab Jews were indigenous to the region. In the post-1948 period, the European refugees were joined by large numbers of Sephardic Jews, including Arab Jews—some of whom were expelled from their homes, some of whom were recruited by Israel and were required to abandon their millennial Arab identities. These were followed by refugees from the Soviet Union, the first wave of whom were Jewish and the subsequent waves vaguely or just officially Jewish—many of whom had acquired anti-Muslim sentiment from the long war with Chechnya. In this way Israel accrued an 80 percent Jewish population with imposed and transported anti-Muslim or anti-Arab sentiment, or a learned rejection of one's own Jewish Arabness that enhanced its Jewish nationalism and racial supremacy.

Ironically, from the founding of the state of Israel in 1948, of all the various parties supporting Zionism, Jews have been the smallest and least powerful faction, outweighed by Western military interests, countries not wanting to absorb Jewish refugees, nations feeling pressure to account for their inaction, oil interests (of course), and, more recently, powerful fundamentalist Christians like George Bush who had apocalyptic religious investment in the region. Had these other interests not predominated, there would be no state of Israel. So there is an emotionally and psychologically confusing relationship between Zionism and Jews—one that creates paranoia. Does America support Israel because it loves Jews and wants to protect them, or because it just needs a military base in Israel from which to conduct wars and control resources? It's a naïve question. All military alliances are strategic in nature. But the blurring gives both the illusion of independence and the illusion that the United States is a "friend" of Israel. The result is a lot of instability, false fronts, fear, and pretending. Israel exists simultaneously as a colonial settler state in relationship to Palestinians, and as a semicolonized project of the Christian West, the very people who caused the Jews' suffering to begin with.

It is this toxic mix that has created the pathological state policies that we are grappling with today. It has always been clear to me, emotionally, though entirely unarticulated—that Israel does not represent "the Jews," only some Jews. That in fact the dialogic nature of the Jewish religion, the analytical roots of secular Jewry, and the disparate cultural, linguistic, and historical experiences of global Jewry make any agreement among "the Jews" impossible, undesirable, and culturally counter-indicated. Forcing Jews into a consensus about Israel's current policies of occupation and separation can only cause splintering, pain, and chaos. Even asking for consensus on the question of the need for or desirability of a Jewish state reliant on occupation with global diasporic support seems impossible. We are simply too diverse.

Impossible to overstate are the long-range consequences of the trauma of genocide on the European Jewish psyche and how this has been expressed through Israeli culture and policy. Through this process African Jews, Sephardic Jews, and especially Arab Jews have been created as implementers of the consequences of a trauma they did not experience. Yet their own authentic historic trauma of displacement and Israeli racism is never discussed. It is common knowledge that after the Holocaust, little was known about post-traumatic stress disorder, and few survivors of torture and genocide received treatment. Most simply did not talk about their experiences. The trauma became played out in all kinds of pathological ways, as is natural. There are deep emotional consequences to oppression. And especially to oppression without resolution. But what constitutes resolution? Because of the Jewish religious requirement to tell the story of one's people, Jewish culture has led the Holocaust to be simultaneously both the most well-documented and yet dramatically denied genocide. Apparently there is more to healing than having your victimization be known. There is also the process of response to that knowing, called justice.

What is justice? And did the European Jews get it?

In Christianity, I believe, one is supposed to forgive others whether or not they know they did something wrong, whether or not they stop doing it. Jewish forgiveness is not this way.

Maimonides wrote in the late twelfth century:

Repentance and Yom Kippur only atone for sins between Man and God. Sins between one man and his fellow are never forgiven until one pays up his debt and appeases his fellow. Even if he returns the money he owes he must still ask for forgiveness. He must appease and beseech until he is forgiven. If his fellow refuses to forgive him then he must bring a group of three of his friends (presumably the injured party's friends) and go to him and ask him [for forgiveness]. If he still does not forgive him he must go to him a second and third time (with a different group of three people). If he still refuses to forgive him he may cease and the other is the sinner. If [the injured party] is his teacher (rebbe) he must go to him even a thousand times until he is forgiven.

It is forbidden to be cruel and difficult to appease, rather, a person must be quick to forgive and difficult to anger and when the sinner asks for forgiveness he should forgive him willingly and wholeheartedly.

In other words, justice requires that the person causing the pain say that he caused it, take actions to undo it, and start an amends process. He must directly ask the harmed person for forgiveness *three times*. Like a lot of things in traditional Jewish culture, justice requires frank, truthful acknowledgment, recognition, and overt accountability on the part of the person who caused the pain. This is in strong contrast to a culture of passive forgiveness. "Father, they know not what they do," Jesus said. The desire to "let things go and move on" because accountability is uncomfortable, troublesome, and difficult is very *goyishe*. This stark contrast proves, yet again, that the idea of "Judeo-Christian culture" is a fantasy. Jewish and Christian cultures are distinct, and they are motivated by very different value systems.

Today, on those occasions when leaders are wise, there is public effort through a truth and reconciliation process to evoke some acknowledgment by the killers, the torturers, of what they have done. At Nuremberg, of course, a handful of leaders were tried, and a few were executed. But the average European genocidal maniac? His life basically returned to normal. His nation was rebuilt, and he went on with his personal concerns. There was no individual accountability. Western culture is not structured to facilitate individual accountability, and, as we all know, all cultural structures benefit some people at the expense of others. They are kept in place by reward-and-punishment systems that falsely naturalize the enforcement.

My own story had its own predictable ironic outcome. In 1996, after an unbearably pathological homophobic incident in my family, I decided to go to Israel to see if I had any gay relatives. I desperately needed some kind of support and love from someone I was related to. I wrote to an array of cousins on both sides, ranging from pig-raising kibbutzniks to Lubavitcher Hasidim. My letter said, "I am thirty-eight years old. I am not married, and I do not want to get married. Would you like to meet me?"

I just did not want anyone to think that I was going to Israel to find a husband. One contact on each side of my family wrote me back, and thus began my discovery of a whole new family of loving, caring, supportive cousins. Not "cousins" but actual cousins. None of whom, by the way, are gay. And just as war separated us two generations ago in Poland and Russia, war reunited us when three of my cousins subsequently immigrated to New York, Miami, and Los Angeles. They have become central people in my life. And through them I have met other Israelis whom I love and admire and consider to be family. We do not agree about Israel, how could we? Our experiences are so different. It's their home, and no one wants to leave his home unless he has to. They've all served in the army, and they feel an ownership of their government, police, and military that American Jews very rarely experience. We still see ourselves as separate from our state, as diasporic. And this diasporic alienation from the police and military is as strong as the Israelis' sense of identification with their state. I am still emotionally diasporic, and they are emotionally nationalistic.

So, this is *why*, to answer my friend Rabih the novelist, Jews have such a hard time facing facts about Israel. Because we understand the roots of the pathology. We see how brutality bred brutality, and there is no higher moral model to point to. We see Europe continuing its lack of accountability and anti-Semitism, and we see no alternative that feels safe. So we lie to ourselves, because the truth is so much more frightening. The truth is that Israel's policies do not make the world a safer place for Jews or anyone else. To be a responsible government is to act as though other human beings are real and have lives that matter. In this regard, both the U.S. and Israeli governments have deteriorated into rogue states causing pain and inflicting suffering from a delusional place. The problem that stopped the evolution of my own thinking was that I thought that opposing Israel meant putting faith in the hands of Europe, an entity that has shown no reliability for Jews, and America, a country whose policies and norms are influenced by fundamentalist Christians, the world's most powerful Zionists.

One experience that helped prepare me for the events of this book was the experience of teaching at the College of Staten Island, where students so regularly and comfortably express vulgar anti-Muslim prejudice that it inhibits the ability of the Muslim students to learn. I quickly perceived that Muslim students were having alienating, demeaning experiences in the classroom and that it was my responsibility as their professor to disrupt that whenever possible. This involved refusing to allow Christian students to implicate me in some kind of fantasy alliance between Jews and Christians against Muslims. I had to correct them every time they used the word "we" to articulate anti-Muslim viewpoints.

"Don't look at me," I'd say. "I'm not Christian."

I had to create a status quo assumption in the classroom that there were no weapons of mass destruction, that Palestinian people deserve and must have self-determination, that Israeli policies were as inhuman as U.S. poli-

cies, and that Muslim students must have the right to articulate their experiences openly in the classroom. The payoff came when I was assigned
one year to teach freshman composition and ended up with a large number of Muslims in a class—though of every race and nationality. In one
room I had a Muslim kid from Azerbaijan who wanted to be a firefighter,
two sisters from Kosovo who were sales reps at Bloomingdales, three white
students from Albania, a guy from Nigeria, two cousins from Egypt (both
in hijab), one religious guy from the Philippines, a fully covered Yemeni
woman who worked in her father's deli, a middle-aged man from Palestine who sold clothes on Fourteenth Street, and two fully covered Nation of Islam young women from Brooklyn. The conversation in class was
an incredible privilege for me. Because there was a critical mass of Muslim students, we got to have a public conversation about passing, harassment, profiling, job discrimination, religious interpretation, family, dating,
women's liberation. I learned very quickly that part of Americanization for
some of my students was recognizing gays and lesbians. One of my Egyptian students wrote stories about transsexuality and same-sex marriage set
in her home country. I heard about gay life in Kosovo, you name it.

By the time of the Israeli assault on Gaza, it was obvious that I had to
make my position known in personal relationships, in the classroom, on-
line, and in public. I started posting notices on Facebook about Israeli
demonstrations against the assault on Gaza. I was shocked by the nasty,
vicious responses I received by some Jewish intellectuals, known writers,
people my age or even younger. A man I was trying to do business with
joined a Facebook group called "People Who Hate People Who Hate
Israel." Joel Kovel, the prominent psychiatrist and psychoanalyst, was fired
from his Alger Hiss Chair (how ironic) at Bard College for his anti-Zionist
activities. Turns out that Martin Peretz of the American Israel Public Affairs Committee was on Bard's board.

I started joining public protests. The first time I ever marched in a pre-
dominantly Arab demonstration was very easy—it was the week after 9/11,
and Brooklyn Arab American Family Service held a march against retalia-
tory street violence. I went with Nuar Alsadir, Kris Knudson, and Jonathan
Lethem (an Iraqi, Norwegian, and Jew, respectively). It was a simple, appropriate action committed with great clarity. This time, though, demonstrations against Israeli attacks on Gaza were very difficult. They took place
at the Israeli embassy. The problem was not the rabid, screaming nationalist Jews across the street. It was, rather, the signs carried by some of my
fellow protesters. It was here that I sussed out my new layers of discom-

fort, dominance, and positionality. The first had to do with Hamas. I considered the current Israeli government and Hamas to both be craven, and by being in demonstrations with pro-Hamas signs, I felt compromised. I talked this over with my few like-minded Jewish friends and finally had to face facts. The first truth was that I did not know or understand enough about Hamas outside of what was fed me on American television to evaluate intelligently. I certainly did not know what Hamas meant to Palestinian people. Second, I realized that I have spent my life marching in coalition with people I profoundly disagreed with, even people who opposed my basic existence. I have marched in the same gay pride parade with gay Republicans for decades, and I once marched with Hasidic and Orthodox Jews in Brussels when a synagogue was bombed, even though I knew that they opposed my freedom and existence as a lesbian. I have been in antiwar demonstrations with Catholics who actively fight against abortion rights, which I consider to be essential to female autonomy. So the only reason that sharing a common outrage with Hamas at the killings in Gaza disturbed me more than all the other religious fundamentalists I had had some moment of common ground with in the past was my own prejudice. Once that conceptual gap was faced, I examined the specifics. Hamas was democratically elected. It doesn't matter what I think about Hamas. What matters is that *my* country, the United States of America, is providing military aid to Israel, who in *my* name is committing war crimes. So, consistent with my lifetime of work for justice, *my* responsibility regarding Israel is to speak out against what is being done in my name with my tax money. Period. It's not always so clean, these decisions, but they still need to be faced.

Personally, I think that the best place in the world for Jews is New York City. You can be culturally normative without keeping other people down and still be a healthy remove from identifying with the army, the cops, or thinking you can win the presidency. And the rabbis can't get you either. Also, I am free from the sense of impending doom that plagues European Jews, and I can actually mix freely with people from other cultures who are not anti-Semitic. I am lucky to have been born in a multicultural city, and this privilege breeds responsibility. Responsibility to think, to speak, to act.

This is the journey I had undergone from birth in 1958 to middle age in 2009, and where I started when the events of this book first presented themselves. These are the experiences of transformation that prepared me only to begin.

PART I SOLIDARITY VISIT

1. AWARENESS

Like many queer people, I first imagined that BDS stood for bondage/domination/submission. But actually it stands for boycott/divestment/sanctions, a strategy chosen in 2002 by Palestinian academics and intellectuals in the occupied territories. Later the Palestinian Campaign for the Academic and Cultural Boycott of Israel (PACBI) was founded in Ramallah in April 2004 to create boycott, divestment, and sanctions as an international movement. Theirs is a nonviolent strategy, modeled on the South Africa divestment experience, to change Israeli policy through economic and cultural pressure.

Although I considered myself to be a well-informed participant-citizen, I had not heard the word "boycott" in relationship to Israel until 2009. That March my straight but pro-gay Jewish friend and colleague, Professor Dalia Kandiyoti, forwarded a series of emails from Toronto about the Canadian queer filmmaker John Greyson's withdrawal from the Tel Aviv LGBT Film Festival. John had initially submitted his new film before the assault on Gaza, and it had been accepted. But he was deeply troubled by the subsequent brutality and decided to remove his film. As far as I know, this was the first time a queer person deliberately withdrew from a queer event because it was funded by the Israeli government. I come from a time when LGBT events had no state funding or corporate funding, and the concept of state sponsorship is one I am still getting used to. In 1986, Jim Hubbard and I cofounded MIX: The New York LGBT Film and Video Festival (now celebrating its twenty-fifth anniversary) with no funding. All of the expenses were paid by the community through the box office. The idea that LGBT organizations could be extensions of governments had been a reality for a while, but I had not realized the level of dependence that many LGBT groups have on government money. I had to update my thinking to make a realistic evaluation. I didn't know much about queer life in Israel beyond the most common generalities: queer people serve in the military, Tel Aviv has a thriving gay community, and the religious domination of Jerusalem made Gay Pride events there shaky, fraught, and obstructed. Yet I hadn't put together that the Israeli government was giving money to LGBT cultural events. And, naïvely, perhaps, I found it surprising. I associated religious right-wing governments with lack of support for gay people. I had not yet understood that by financially supporting Tel Aviv's LGBT community, the Israeli government was investing in something other than equality.

When Dalia and I talked about Greyson's decision to apply BDS standards to a queer event, I briefly thought about boycott as a strategy, but I did not bother to actually find out about it. Like most ignorant people I conveniently decided *without evidence* that it would not be effective. But I did take in that it seemed a way for people frustrated by the lack of progress in Israel to show their opposition to the occupation of the West Bank and the siege of Gaza. It was a *new* action, and that was appealing. What made me pay even this much attention was my own knowledge of John Greyson's work and the respect I had long held for him as an artist and as an activist for South Africa. John belongs to a category of gay and lesbian artist that I call "credible." By this I mean that they have consistently produced artistically engaged work with authentic queer content *and* that they treat other openly gay thinkers and artists with a recognition and respect denied them by the straight world. Given how many queer artists pander to mainstream approval by closeting, watering down, or coding their content—or who turn away from the community at the first sign of mainstream recognition—those who have regularly chosen truth over power are people I take very seriously. The professional price one pays for authentic LGBT subject matter is life changing. So when these individuals take a stand, I pay attention.

The following August, Dalia started sending me emails again, this time because John Greyson had withdrawn his new film *Covered* from the Toronto Film Festival when it announced a "Spotlight" program on Tel Aviv. In his public letter, John cited as the reason for his withdrawal the Israeli Consul General Amir Gissin's announcement in *Canadian Jewish News*, which had described "Spotlight Tel-Aviv" as the culmination of the yearlong "Brand Israel" campaign. This was the first time I'd heard about Brand Israel. A well-funded and highly orchestrated marketing campaign to sell Israel to tourists and cultural consumers, Brand Israel promotes Israel as a modern, liberal society with open values while whitewashing its human rights violations and dual citizenship systems. Gissin described bus, radio, and TV ads, a traveling Dead Sea Scrolls exhibit, and "a major Israeli presence at next year's Toronto International Film Festival with numerous Israeli, Hollywood and Canadian entertainment luminaries on hand." Gissin said that Toronto had been chosen as a test city for Brand Israel by Israel's Foreign Ministry, and he thanked sponsors for donating the $1 million budget. In other words, the Israeli government openly bought $1 million worth of programming at the Toronto Film Festival as part of a marketing campaign to normalize its policies.

"We've got real products to sell to Canadians," Gissin said. "The lessons learned from Toronto will inform the worldwide launch of Brand Israel in the coming years."

Greyson's letter went on to cite the one thousand civilian deaths in Gaza, the election of right-winger Benjamin Netanyahu as prime minister, the extension of settlements, the growth of the "Security Wall" and further enshrining of the checkpoint system. While the Toronto Film Festival's program described Tel Aviv as "a vibrant young city . . . of beaches, cafes and culture ferment," Greyson noted that Naomi Klein, a Canadian writer, had called it "a kind of Alter-Gaza. The smiling face of Israeli apartheid." Klein, author of a best-selling analysis of modern capital's growth apparatus, *Shock Doctrine*, then followed up with a piece in the *Toronto Globe and Mail*, "We Don't Feel Like Celebrating with Israel This Year." She did not call for boycott of the festival, but she said that she and others would not go, and that their principled absence was a small way of showing support for Palestinians living under occupation and siege. I noted how important Klein was to John's decision and started to pay a bit more attention to her as well.

That fall, Jim Hubbard and I exhibited the ACT UP Oral History Project (www.actuporalhistory.org) at Harvard Museum. There, a visiting queer Israeli law professor, Aeyal Gross, asked me if I would like to go to Israel for a speaking engagement. "Sure," I said. "You would come?" he asked. "Sure," I said, feeling uneasy but having no idea why he asked the question. Two weeks later, in November 2009, I received an email inviting me to give the keynote address at the Israeli Lesbian and Gay Studies Conference at Tel Aviv University.

Staring at the message on my computer screen, I realized I had agreed to something that I did not fully understand. And that I had to now face and learn about the very questions I had long been avoiding. But how to proceed? I started with a person I trusted; I phoned my friend Dalia.

"I don't know," she said. "Is it being held at Tel Aviv University?"

Yes.

"They're under the boycott," she said. "Have you read Naomi Klein?"

In those first few moments I didn't have a sophisticated analysis, but I knew the fundamental fact that when it comes to Israel, no one comes out of it clean. Whatever I did, someone would be angry, and there would be repercussions and accusations. I pictured myself filled with conflict, fending off other people's anger and constantly scrambling to catch up. I did not even know the terms of the boycott. Did it apply equally to LGBT events? How could that be possible? That very week I had published a new book, *Ties That Bind: Familial Homophobia and Its Consequences*, which was resonating broadly with readers. I certainly looked forward to talking about this most painful and fundamental subject with other queer Jews. Since LGBT people faced familial homophobia in Israel, they did not have full human rights. I assumed and hoped that the invitation to speak to people who are demeaned mitigated the terms of the boycott. So I started by looking for a way out.

But where did I begin ideologically? The Israeli oppression of Palestinians was wrong, horrifying, and unjustifiable on all fronts. This I had long understood. In my book on familial homophobia, I called for third-party intervention. That is to say, I made very explicit my belief that when people are victimized and ask others to intervene, those others should help them. In this case, I was talking about gay people being violated by their families, their partners, the arts and entertainment industries, and the state. Third-party intervention is certainly a principle I believed in across the board. In my book I called it "the human obligation." What circumstance better called for third-party intervention than that of Palestinians?

On the other hand, I very much wanted to accept the invitation, and I didn't even know what the boycott really was. Did I believe in boycotts? Yes. One of the first political movements I became aware of as a child was the United Farm Workers boycott of nonunion produce in the 1960s, which led to the creation of the union. In the 1970s, before dropping out of the University of Chicago, I witnessed the South Africa divestment movement, which would become even more popular in the 1980s. I had long boycotted Coors beer for its opposition to gay rights. My parents boycotted German goods all of their lives. Even in 1968, they would not drive Volkswagens or drink German beer, and they would never visit Germany. My mother refused to get on a plane because it was operated by Lufthansa. But I didn't know if the long boycott of South Africa ("Don't Play Sun City") had actually contributed to the fall of the white supremacist government there. Was it a key factor in regime change, or was it just encouraging to people on the front lines? And wouldn't that be enough of a reason? Were South Africa and Israel in any way comparable situations? Did that matter? Was there any other way for things to get better in Israel? Was there any other strategy that was preferable? And here was one of my biggest questions: Was this for me to decide? Wasn't it more important that victimized people received the intervention they were asking for?

This last question was a new one for me, for in my lifetime of political commitments, I had never worked in solidarity. I had asked for solidarity: asked for straight people to support queers and people with AIDS, asked men to stand up for women. I had always worked directly with oppressed constituencies. That is to say, when I was in the abortion rights, gay liberation, and AIDS activist movements, "we" were the people "we" were fighting for. I had observed others in solidarity movements where "they" were the people "we" were fighting for, and I had seen many errors. Most present in my mind was the movement of Americans in support of the Sandinista revolution that overthrew the Somoza dictatorship in Nicaragua in 1979. Supporters were told to restrain their North American values as culturally inappropriate and not bring up abortion. Only later did we learn that a major cause of death of young women in Managua at the time was illegal abortion. Today, despite Northern assumptions about Catholic countries' cultural alignments, Mexicans, Brazilians, Portuguese, and South Africans have gay marriage, whereas Americans do not. The left-wing negation of the humanity of gay Cubans was a bitter lesson, not to be forgotten, despite advances in that country. Gay people historically have been asked to subsume their desire for freedom to support other rebellions only to eventually realize that there is homosexual desire and practice under many different conceptualizations, wherever there are humans. Our willingness to accept that we are secondary had resulted in the abandonment of queer people in other places. This was simply something I did not want to replicate. I could never accept a politic that sacrificed gay people for Palestinians or the other way around, since these two categories, like all human categories, are never mutually exclusive. There had to be a path that represented a freedom vision for all.

"Read Naomi Klein," Dalia said.

I found and read the PACBI declaration on-line and then explored

Naomi Klein's website. When I finally decided to ask Klein's advice as well, I wrote to her assistant, carefully spelling out my credentials and my situation. I hoped to avoid the disrespect problems that plague minority leaders by making clear to Klein's staff that my condition spoke directly to their agenda and that I was someone worth responding to. I made it known that I needed her advice for a reason larger than myself.

That same day I also wrote to Berkeley professor Judith Butler, who is at the top of my list of credible LGBT people. I had heard Butler speak at the City University of New York on Israel a few years before. Knowing I was looking to her for guidance, Butler got back to me in four hours with many concrete leads and suggestions. Read this, read that, find out about this person, find out about that. I was getting my own personal reading list in classic professor mode. She never told me what to do, but sent me further down the rabbit hole.

"Talk to people in Israel." *Like who?* "Write to Dalit." *Who is Dalit?* "If you accept," she said, "Omar is going to ask you why." *Who was Omar?*

It was the beginning of Sarah-through-the-looking-glass. I was entering a world of people, acronyms, and organizations that were entirely unfamiliar to me. Anything else? "Read Neve Gordon's article 'Boycott Me.'" *Who is Neve Gordon?* "Read Naomi Klein," she said.

I started reading and wrote back to the LGBT Studies Conference hosts that I very much wanted to come and was trying to make it work. I still thought that would be the inevitable outcome. Then I started following up on Butler's contacts, beginning with the Israeli academic and activist Dalit Baum.

The title of Dalit Baum's 1996 doctoral dissertation in mathematics from Bar-Ilan University is "Skew Algebraic Elements of Simple Artinian Rings." She coordinates the organization Who Profits from the Occupation (www.whoprofits.org), was a member of Black Laundry (an Israeli LGBT group against the occupation), and is the recipient of a Facebook fan page celebrating her utter butchness. These commitments plus Butler's recommendation were enough credential for me to trust her. In other words, like Greyson and Butler, she is accomplished, community oriented, and out in her work. *Credible.* Still no word back from the Klein camp, but Dalit Baum wrote me right away.

After much thought and some conversations, my recommendation to you is to decline the invitation and to do it publicly. It seems odd that of all the rich conferences in Tel Aviv University, it would be our little queer studies conference that would suffer the loss. . . . [The boycott] represents a clear and valid request from a wide range of groups representing a people under extreme and violent repression. . . . A solidarity visit should be organized. You can have alternative events, in grassroots or Palestinian venues and use your visit to learn and teach by meeting the communities and speaking about it later abroad. Naomi Klein has just visited here in such a manner, it was a learning experience for all. One thing I was thinking about today was how much the academic boycott is really an educational tool. It is making you and us, for example, examine the implications of this visit by asking a lot of questions and contacting more people. Thank you for taking the time to think this through.

Honestly, this was not what I had expected. There would be no more hedging now, no easy way out. I reviewed my path thus far and was surprised at what I saw in my own behavior. I had gone only to other Jewish people for guidance. I had not gone to Palestinians for advice. Nor had I even reached out to John Greyson, who is not Jewish. Without realizing it, merely on impulse, I had set out to make this decision Jewishly. And yet the safest of all possible paths — the one most likely to lead me to accept the invitation — had instead brought me to this moment. Like every matter involving Israel, the divisions are profound, and one simply, at some point, has to decide. Plenty of Jews had realized this before me. And this was where I would join them.

I had never in my life turned my back on queer people. But this idea Dalit proposed — of a *solidarity visit* — appealed to me. A picture started to form in my mind: I could still meet the same folks and talk to them, just in a different building, under different auspices. To stay home and do nothing, to literally "boycott" seemed absurd. What would that accomplish? But to go to Israel and to Palestine and meet and talk and listen, that felt reasonable. In fact, it felt productive, like a positive active step. I started to imagine that an action that felt right might, after all, be possible.

Strangely, at that moment I received a disturbing phone call from my editor at the University of California Press. My book *Gentrification of the Mind* had come back with one very hostile review. The editor seemed shocked. When I read the letter, I, too, was shocked. Although my book is about the confluence of AIDS and gentrification, and its expression in systems of domination, the extremely angry reviewer, anonymous to me, never mentioned either subject. She or he did not even mention AIDS. The reviewer's problems were mainly with my long chapter on coming to terms with Israel as an example of how a person can face her own supremacy ideology. She or he cited a handful of observations about my own personal intellectual process regarding Israel, which clearly generated great offense. This reviewer put quotation marks around statements that did not appear in my text and misrepresented my ideas. The reviewer was enraged. Was this person really going to be able to stop my book about AIDS and urbanity from being published because she or he disagreed with me about Israel? My editor suggested that I write a response and said that he would follow up. As I worked on the answer document, there was something about the review that seemed vaguely familiar. The more I looked at it, the clearer the identity of the author was. It was Professor F. A very important and esteemed lesbian intellectual in her seventies, who—I suddenly realized—was the daughter of a Holocaust survivor, she clearly was unable to step out of her position on Israel as a place of response so visceral, and she was willing to abuse her power and stop my book. My suspicions were confirmed later when the same Professor F emailed me a conservative article defending Israeli policies. Why that provocation of contacting me? She couldn't contain her glee at having stopped the book. I confronted her about abusing her position of power. She then both acknowledged and defended her actions. That she would be the person to do this was tragic. But I already knew that the subject of Israel made people irrational. I completed my response and began the long wait.

The combination of Dalit's compassionate, reasoned letter and Professor F's irrational, inappropriate use of power clicked in my mind, and I made my decision. Two months after initially receiving the offer, after daily engagement, conversation, introspection, and research, I decided that I would decline the invitation to keynote the Israeli LGBT Studies Conference and instead would travel to Israel and Palestine on a solidarity visit.

December 3, 2009

Dear Friends,
Thank you so much for the great honor of being invited to keynote the LGBT Studies Conference in Tel Aviv. I respect and admire you and all LGBT people around the world courageously trying to build awareness and knowledge about our history and points of view. Very sadly and with great concern, I unfortunately must decline because the conference's university sponsor is included in the PACBI guidelines for Academic and Cultural Boycott of institutions that are not actively and explicitly anti-occupation.

This is not a boycott of LGBT people, but rather of Israeli institutions that normalize the occupation. There are increasing numbers of Jews committed to social justice who are being forced into this position by Israeli government policies and, may I add—the role of the United States in supporting these policies. I hope, instead, to come on a solidarity visit in the near future and would love the opportunity to meet with Palestinian and Israeli queers to discuss the pressing issues of our survival in the context of an anti-occupation movement. This is an awful situation and I deeply apologize for any problem it may cause you personally.

Yours Sincerely, Sarah Schulman

Because Dalit had asked me to decline publicly, and I understood that this was part of the political process, I sent the letter to everyone who had answered my emails and to Omar, whom I by then knew was Omar Barghouti of PACBI. He seemed to be the contact preferred by Jewish and Israeli LGBT people. I wrote to Dalit that she had my permission to use the letter publicly "to the degree that it will be helpful without exploiting the gay people of Tel Aviv." On December 11, I received a note from Omar writing from Ramallah: "I warmly thank you for your principled position in applying the PACBI Guidelines for the International Academic Boycott of Israel. It is quite inspiring! We in PACBI hope that such a courageous position will become more common in the US academic and intellectual circles."

I was surprised to discover that I was still so acculturated to a visceral Jewish identification that being praised by PACBI made me uncomfortable. It was disturbing to face, but even though Omar and I agreed about the responsibilities of human beings to each other, I discovered that I still experienced him as "other." And I felt, in some deep way, that I was being treacherous. There was no logical reason for these feelings since I had no illusions about Israel and had zero religious feeling. And I knew that Omar was doing something positive, essential, and courageous and that he deserved my support. Yet there it was, my racism. Thankfully, I had long before heard the insight that "feelings are not facts." Through all kinds of therapy and a lot of listening in a twelve-step program, I have come to understand that just because I feel something doesn't mean it is true or right. A feeling is just the first step in a process of awareness. And just because I fear something doesn't mean that it is dangerous or that I am endangered. I know that a great deal of people's emotional or instinctive or impulsive reactions to events come not from the truth of those events, but rather as projections from past experiences to which the events in question are unrelated except as triggers. I was doing something right, and yet somehow I felt wrong. I resolved to live with this feeling.

However, this decision, too, was not a free pass. I had to learn, right then, what fears to sit with and which ones to face and deal with. For there was something nagging at me that was real and important to engage. And it had nothing to do with Jew versus Palestinian. In my letter, I had been so clear about the queer aspect of my decision and the conflict of turning my back on an LGBT event. But in Omar's letter this had not been acknowledged. I wasn't sure why.

I was starting to think of my own actions as more in the "sanctions" category, since I would be going to Israel, spending money there, talking to Israeli as well as Palestinian people, but avoiding the state institutions. "Boycott" seemed more like a metaphor than an actuality in my case. But I was constantly reassured that "boycott" meant exactly what I was intending. Avoiding state-sponsored institutions. One could "boycott Israel" and still go. And I just couldn't see the point of staying home. Therefore, the preparation for the solidarity visit was of paramount importance.

Again I turned to Butler for guidance, and she put me in touch with another credible, Zohar Weiman-Kelman, a queer Israeli doing graduate work at Berkeley. Zohar would soon be in New York, and we made a plan to meet up for coffee. Zohar turned out to be very young, very smart, learned, super-energetic, and filled with information and ideas. I desperately needed someone in Israel who would be willing to make arrangements for the trip since I had no contacts and knew nothing about the political landscape. I had enough frequent-flyer miles for the ticket and just wanted to meet as many people as possible. Zohar promised to find someone in Israel who had the time and energy to take this on.

At this point I started realizing that I needed to tell people in my life about the actions I was taking and the reasons why. I knew that many people would be angry and would disagree, but I didn't want this to be something I conveniently didn't mention in order to avoid conflict. After all, these kinds of moments exist to create honest conversations. As Dalit had suggested in her letter, in many ways that is their purpose.

The first encounter came some weeks later when I was contacted on Facebook by an Israeli film director, NW, visiting New York. She came over to my apartment and brought along a male friend. Her gift to me was a set of Sabbath candles, something I have never used in my life. Both of my guests were queer, born in the diaspora, and had chosen to spend extended periods of time in Israel. She had actually exercised the Jewish right of return, "made aliya" (literally "going up"), and become an Israeli citizen, even though she was not traditionally religious. In fact, her mother was Catholic. I could see right away that she was kind of a hustler. She got a lot of perks for immigrating. Free language lessons, job placement, and so on. Any Jew, even half-Jew, can become a citizen and enjoy the goodies that Palestinians cannot touch. She called herself "post-Zionist," but I didn't exactly understand what that meant. Since these two were unusual in their commitments to Israel and were part of my queer artists' diaspora, I did not want to hide anything from them. So I laid out the whole story and my plans for a solidarity visit.

"You got advice from *who*?" the guy asked.

I repeated the list.

"*Israelis? Jews? Queer Israeli Jews?* That's who you went to, and *they* asked you to do this?"

"Yes," I said.

"Okay," he said. "That's who you should be listening to."

Actually it was more complicated than that. I had been guided by queer Jews who were responding to a "call" or request by presumably straight Palestinians for our participation in the boycott.

I was relieved by their supportive responses, but I knew it wasn't always going to be that easy. I set up a lunch date soon afterward with one of my straight Israeli cousins who was temporarily living in New York. I didn't know her well, but I loved her. Her grandfather, Shimshon, and my beloved grandmother, Dora, were brother and sister in Poland. Dora came to America in 1921 and, despite being able to speak five languages, became a laundry worker. Shimshon went to Palestine in 1920 and founded one of the early kibbutzim, where my cousin was born. Four of Dora and Shimshon's brothers and sisters stayed behind in Europe and were exterminated. Their names were Solomon, Shmul, Mina, and Adela. My cousin and I wanted a relationship and authentically liked each other. I respected her and found her to be straight ahead and kind. If there had been no anti-Semitism, we would have grown up down the street from each other in Rohatyn, Galicia, and spoken Yiddish together with our crowds of cousins. But that's not how it played out. Those cousins were never born, I don't speak Hebrew, and she can't understand my fifty-word Yiddish vocabulary. Ironically, we now lived two blocks away from each other in the East Village—as it was meant to be—and treat each other with respect. Yet we rarely talk about Israel in any depth. We know that we disagree, and that's that.

This time I had to break the silence.

"What do you think of the boycott?" I said.

"It's bullshit," she said. "Everyone is criticizing Israel. This Goldstone Report, the Spanish bringing war crimes charges. No one else faces that. Israel should only be criticized when everyone else is criticized."

This was an argument that I was to hear over and over again, a position that I didn't know how to take in. Was it true? I knew that the World Court was prosecuting fallen leaders from the former Yugoslavia, Rwanda, and Liberia who committed war crimes. *So was it true that sanctions were not brought against any government besides Israel? And did that matter? If the world doesn't respond, what is the solution? Is what we do a problem only if other people do it too?*

But I asked none of these questions. They seemed diversions. Too large to be helpful. Instead I focused on the small.

"But what about Jews who support the boycott?"

"They don't live in Israel," she said.

"I think some of them do," I suggested quietly.

By then I had learned that Neve Gordon, an Israeli professor brought to my attention by Judith Butler, was part of the "Boycott Me" movement. I had read his plea in the *Guardian* in August 2009 for an international boycott to "save Israel from itself." I thought (and still think) that his argument is profoundly moving and would be very persuasive if allowed to be amplified. It would be much easier for American Jews to practice sanctions if they were allowed to know that there are Jewish Israeli academics asking them to do so. In some ways this is the most potentially powerful piece of information in the whole BDS phenomenon. For after all, "Boycott Me" is a compelling argument for people concerned with what is best for the Jews. Not exclusively, but still deeply. And, as Gordon says, the current policies of the Israeli government are terrible for all people and for the Jewish people—for our integrity, our relationship to self and others, and our future. He helped me understand that we need to be saved from ourselves.

"Yes," she said. "My mother told me about it. But you know, we have to solve our problems ourselves. We can't go crying to the world to solve them for us."

My cousin's *we* is a different one than mine. It is common wisdom that Israelis identify as Israelis and not as Jews. And I reciprocate by not identifying with them. So is there a *we* larger than a nation-state?

"Have you read Naomi Klein?" I heard myself say.

I was stunned. I had stunned myself. Was "Read Naomi Klein" now going to be my fallback mantra as well? Why? Having now read and learned from her pieces on the Toronto Film Festival and other Israel-related subjects, I knew she was persuasive. But it was more than her power of argumentation. It was her normalcy that made "Read Naomi Klein" the easiest thing to say. What should I have said instead? Why didn't I reference the queer people—the ones who called me back—Dalit Baum and John Greyson? Because I was looking to use normativity to sway my cousin. Something was off-balance in the way I was thinking. Something needed to be faced.

Soon I heard from Zohar. She kept her promise and hooked me up with Sonya Soloviov, a lesbian activist in Israel who kindly offered to organize the trip. She proposed that I come from March 30 to April 7, which coincided with my Passover/Easter break from work. This was really happening.

Some weeks later I was watching TV at the gym and saw Naomi Klein on CNN. I had never seen her before. She was on a panel of pundits talking about the economic crisis. She was articulate, intelligent. Her point of view on capital was enlightened and interesting. And of course she was conventionally heterosexually attractive. *If only our people could get on CNN,* I thought. They could integrate homophobia and heterosexism into the issues that Klein raises. But of course, that's why they're not on CNN. The unspoken—perhaps unconscious—agreement about heterosexual neutrality implied by silence is a requirement for inclusion. I went home and for the third time reread the website of the organization Dalit was affiliated with, Black Laundry: "Our own oppression as lesbians, gays and transpeople enhances our solidarity with other oppressed groups." This is so easy for queers to understand and yet impossible for so many others.

Then something clicked for me. There was a key conversation I had been unconsciously avoiding, because a potential transformation lay within. I telephoned John Greyson in Toronto.

John kindly listened as I poured out all my trepidations and concerns. Even though we had never spoken in person before, he made time for me and recognized what I was grappling with. My concern became clarified as I spoke my anxieties out loud to him. If he hadn't listened, I wouldn't have been able to understand what was bothering me. My concern was thus: if he and I were turning our backs on gay events and organizations for the larger principle of solidarity, we had to be careful that it was not a one-way street. The people we work with, whether straight North American intellectuals or representatives of PACBI, had to—in some way—reciprocate. Why was I invoking Naomi Klein's name to my straight cousin to validate my own actions? Why wasn't the fact that John Greyson took this stance enough for me? Why do queer people often need to invoke straight people for justification? While not necessarily agreeing, John certainly understood what I was saying. He immediately put me in touch with another credible, Elle Flanders. This was an introduction that would change everything. Again.

Elle, also Canadian, is a Jewish queer filmmaker responsible for the gorgeous feature *Zero Degrees of Separation*. The film contrasts home movies of her Zionist philanthropist ancestors, posing like tourists in front of "exotic" Arab villagers in the early days of the state of Israel, with contemporary documentary footage about a lesbian couple, Samira and Edit, and a gay male couple, Ezra and Selim; in both couples, one partner is a Jewish Israeli and the other is a Palestinian. The connection between the two tropes is the historical irony that the Jewish man in the relationship is Ezra Nawi, a renowned warrior for Palestinian rights but also a former gardener for Flanders's ancestors.

Elle had just returned to Toronto after a year of living in Ramallah. Though we had never met, Elle immediately made time for a long phone conversation and offered guidance and engagement on difficult questions. This willingness to communicate, which I had by then also experienced with Butler, Dalit, Zohar, and John, comes from the mutual recognition and respect among queer credibles. The lack of mainstream currency does not diminish "importance," does not render the person unworthy of respect and engagement. In fact, because we understand the reasons for our marginalization, we know what it proves about our integrity or true value. I explained my concerns to Elle. She offered to talk to people in Israel, help Sonya set up events, and basically help me understand better where I was going and whom I was going to meet. I explained very clearly my trepidations, conflicts, and desire for queer reciprocity on all fronts. She promised to talk to people in Israel and Palestine and get back to me.

By January 21, 2010, I had a response from Elle, just as she had promised: "There is a lot of support in full for your decision with queers from the conference." This was an enormous relief, but it also revealed to me the generosity of anti-occupation queer Israelis. They want to have a gay life too, but if you can't do it with them, they understand. There is something so heroic here, to have so little queer life and be gracious about giving it up. These Israeli activists live between the three monsters of militarism, religion, and racial supremacy, yet they were actively fighting for their like-minded counterparts around the world to isolate them. This was an attitude I would learn much more about as time went on.

Elle's next idea was even more unexpected: "I have a query out . . . about Barghouti's response and a statement from PACBI recognizing the queer voices who are supporting them." That I found this shocking was quite revealing. I had never imagined that PACBI could be approachable on the queer question. Obviously I had been harboring stereotypes about Arabs that were simply not true. Of course he would be approachable. He couldn't be worse than a U.S. theater producer who refuses to do a lesbian play or a U.S. publisher who refuses to publish lesbian novels. The worst that could happen is that he could say no. I caught myself internalizing ridiculous false stereotypes that depict whites as more pro-gay than Arabs. This had to change, and it had to change now. To make a contribution, I had to think everything through for myself. And Elle was one of many who were standing there to help me.

Elle also had some suggestions for venues and for people to meet. There was a radical café in Tel Aviv that hosted readings and talks. She mentioned some Palestinian queers whom she thought I should know. Aside from the appearance of Samira and Selim in Elle's film, as far as I knew, I had never seen or heard a queer Palestinian. I wrote down her contacts' names.

Next I heard from Sonya that she had been out of touch for a while because of a series of demonstrations and arrests in Jerusalem. She suggested I give a talk in Haifa as a guest of Aswat (Voice), which she explained was a Palestinian lesbian organization (and the only lesbian organization in Israel), and of Isha L'Isha ("Woman to Woman," a feminist group that shares the Haifa Women's Center with Aswat). She also mentioned El Kaus (Rainbow), another queer Palestinian group, and proposed a solidarity visit to a demonstration in Bil'in. Finally I was familiar with something. Bil'in is a Palestinian village that was separated from 60 percent of its farmland by the Israeli Separation Wall. The inhabitants have held weekly protests since 2005 asking to have the wall moved to the other side of their land. It is hard to understand how Israeli officials could justify refusing a demand that is so reasonable, but they have chosen to bring out troops every Friday for five years to oppose the villagers' request. Elle had some other suggestions, a group she now called "Al-Qaws" instead of "El Kaus" and a visit to a university in the West Bank. Elle and Sonya started preparing a press release to send to various journalists. Included on their list was Isabel Kershner, who reports from Jerusalem for the *New York Times*. This scared me. I felt very underprepared.

"I don't know if I am informed enough to handle that at this point," I wrote them. "I am sure that when I come back I will be in a better place."

I'd had an interesting life and been a participant witness to some very dramatic political moments, but rarely had I done something this bold when I was not sure of what I was doing. It would be impossible for me to summarize my political history here, but suffice it to say that my life has been filled with actions that have contributed to social transformation. I've seen and helped along great paradigm shifts in the lives of women, queer people, and certainly people with AIDS. While refusing any kind of progress narrative (not a fan of "It gets better"), I have witnessed over and over again how focused, committed concrete actions can produce positive change. Usually I really process my thinking and take actions that make profound, clear sense. But in this case, that just wasn't going to be possible. I made the decision to trust trustworthy people who knew more than I. In this way I chose being uncomfortable and unsure over being complicit. Doing nothing, and thereby taking a passive negative action, would have been far more uncomfortable. In fact, it would have been so wrong that I would not have been able to live with it. I note fear, but then I grapple with it, and I have never understood people who use it as a crutch to avoid facing the thing that is scaring them. I have spent my life being simultaneously afraid and yet going forward anyway. And this was the ultimate application of that practice.

On January 30 a friend forwarded an announcement from the Queer Theory Listserv announcing that Heather Love, a respected young professor from the University of Pennsylvania, would give the keynote address at the Tel Aviv LGBT Studies Conference, scheduled for May 23–25. I wondered if she knew about the boycott. On February 4, my editor from the New Press forwarded another post from the Queer Theory list. Heike Schotten, a professor from the University of Massachusetts in Boston, wrote a long post about what she called "queer imperialism." This was what some people call the equating of a nation's "gay friendliness" with its tolerance or level of democracy. Professor Schotten's post helped me to understand why Israel funds things like the LGBT Film Festival while denying democratic rights to Palestinians. She explained that this was a tactic that Israel has used (in, for example, its inclusion of gay people in the army) to somehow nullify the violation of Palestinian human rights and its own rampant homophobia. The United States does it all the time, as if having a black president means we are not racist and are not committing war crimes in Afghanistan and Iraq. Schotten went on to talk about how anti-gay policies by some Muslims are used to further pathologize Islam. This happens, for example, in Holland, where Muslim homophobia is used to justify racism. I saw this in myself, in my surprise at Elle's suggestion to approach PACBI about queer support. Anti-Muslim racists can express some concern for the well-being of gays only when the homophobia is Islamic — and not, for example, Catholic. And Muslim homophobia is considered far more destructive than Jewish, Hindu, or Christian homophobia. And by extension, U.S. war crimes against Arabs and Muslims are ignored. Professor Schotten then alerted readers to the existence of the PACBI boycott, specifically in relation to the very same Tel Aviv conference.

Heike's posting was my first exposure to the broader conceptual questions about queers and occupation. But it would not be my last. Nope. Again, my own ignorance was illuminated. Obviously these conversations have been going on for some time, and I had not been paying attention.

I decided, for the time being, not to intervene either with Heather Love or this conversation. I didn't want to grandstand, just to be effective. And I believed that this situation would evolve without my provocation. I simply continued to go about planning my trip and sharing the information on a one-to-one basis with the people with whom I came into contact. I feared the inevitable polarization; I anticipated the anger of right-wing Jews as well as the exploitation by people who do not have Jewish interest at heart. I knew that the time bomb would eventually fizzle or explode, but it didn't have to do it that afternoon.

2. PREPARATION

Learning from Cinema

By February 2010, I had still not heard back from the University of California Press. The editor did not answer emails or return phone calls. My book was mired in sludge, and so I did a rewrite in which I eliminated every reference to Israel. The word no longer appeared. I took that content and used it to start writing this book; the ideas would have to be separated. Manuscript revised, I sent it off and hoped that somehow this concession would permit my ideas about the relationship between gentrification and AIDS to be heard.

My anxiety about being censored was displaced, however, by the joyful and surprising news that the Panorama section of the Berlin Film Festival had accepted *The Owls*, the movie I had cowritten with the director, Cheryl Dunye. I had written film scripts before, but they had never been made into a movie. To be invited to such a prestigious and fun event on my first time out was an experience not to be missed. So I got a writer friend to cover my classes on Staten Island, cashed in the last of my frequent-flyer miles, and set off for ten days in Germany. In the cab to the airport I got a phone call from a Naava Et-Shalom, a Jewish grad student at the University of Pennsylvania who had heard a rumor that I was boycotting an Israeli film festival and wanted me to sign a petition to end the Jewish right of return. I declined to sign because, at the time, I saw petitions about the Law of Return as futile, and I was not interested in acts of futility. And yet our conversation made me realize that I needed to think more about the Law of Return — something I had honestly never evaluated. I needed to take in all points of view, face them honestly. Consider everything, and then choose strategies that seemed alive and viable.

When Judith Butler spoke at the City University Graduate Center in 2006 on "Jewish Ethics under Pressure," I heard, for the first time, the phrase "Palestinian right of return." Because of the limited and prejudiced way that I took in information about Israel and Palestine, I was hearing ideas primarily from Jewish thinkers, and not directly from Arab thinkers. So it took a talk by an out Jewish lesbian, Butler, for me to get it together to go. When Butler argued for the Palestinian right of return, I at first imagined Israelis giving up their stolen homes to the original inhabitants, only to wander again perpetually unstable and alone. After all, Israelis are the only colonialists in history who do not have a motherland from which to plunder and retreat. I learned about such emblematic ironies as Edward Said's ancestral home being taken over by Martin Buber when the Saids were forced to leave. However, I came to understand over time that although specific families have claims on specific properties and houses, the larger idea behind Palestinian right of return has to do with compensation, citizenship, and autonomy (i.e., power). It's not about sending Israelis back to Poland, Yemen, and Ethiopia begging for readmittance. I wondered if there was any faction that supported one nation of equal citizens in which all Palestinians and Jews in the two diasporas would have the opportunity to return. Something I am sure most of them would not want to do. After all, more Jews are leaving Israel than are "returning," and I assume that some Palestinians in their own diaspora are not interested in going back to live, only in being able to. As the cab approached the airport, I told the woman on the phone that I needed to think more about return, and I thanked her for her call.

Berlin in February. From an American perspective, the Berlin Film Festival's security system was surprisingly lax. No one searched bags, and there were no metal detectors. The elaborate bureaucratic systems at the film festival were easy to subvert. *The Owls* was a backdoor production, made by a collective. Sixty people worked for free, and the film, which runs for an hour and ten minutes, was made for $22,000. As the founder of a film festival, I know that films can change people's lives, help us learn how to see and therefore how to live. I was excited to watch so many works about Palestine and Israel on the roster—films that I would never get to see in New York. I was counting on these films to bring me further along to a place of clarity and resolution in preparation for my trip.

That first morning I went to meet friends in Kreuzberg. Berlin, in the 1980s, *was* Kreuzberg: a Turkish neighborhood with a lot of Nan Goldin characters (including Nan Goldin) drinking coffee, shooting heroin, smoking thick cigarettes. It was a continuation of the East Village in New York. Today, it is like the West Village minus the chain stores: charming, cute, and child friendly, with restaurants, wine shops, and outlets for

Mommy Yoga. Still absolutely lovely, and, if I had to live in Berlin, which I can't fathom, that's where I would live. Almost immediately, over the first cup of coffee, the five Germans and I get into "the Turkish question," which drives me crazy. I hate seeing smart people, especially German ones, spout this crap. The two gay men at the table were so "concerned" about the Muslims and how they don't assimilate. But they had no desire to change anything about German society so that multiculturalism can actually occur. Multiculturalism is a two-way street, and Germans don't want to reciprocate. I argued a little, but I knew it was futile. They started complaining about women wearing the veil—the typical European line. It was the millionth conversation I had had with Christians who want me to bond with them around some unexamined assumption that their own culture is neutral and that Muslims are threatening. I am threatened by Christians so I will never feel this way. We went two more rounds, and then we dropped it.

Back at the festival, I sat in auditorium after auditorium losing myself in Israel, Palestine, and the work of artists committed to these arenas. I started off with the Israeli documentary *Black Bus* by Anat Zuria. It's about two women, Samit and Sarah, who are escapees from ultraorthodoxy in Israel. Sarah, a divorcee with two children, has an illicit blog where other people from her sect, the Ger Hassidim, write in secretly about the increasing repression of women and sexuality in their group. Sarah still lives with her parents, but she blatantly walks around Bnei Brek and the religious areas with a camera, violating the modesty code by taking photos of women, girls, and men, many of whom wince and hide when they finally notice her. The two women, by the way, are classic Jewish beauties. Samit is light, and Sarah is dark. The thing that has provoked them both to this dangerous transformative place is a new edict by the head rabbi that men and women must ride segregated buses. So now men have the front two-thirds of the bus, where they leisurely read their holy books. The women—young, old, or pregnant (and a lot of them are pregnant)—are crammed into the back third, where they have to stand, watching the men recline. Apparently there is no Jewish religious law that justifies this, and it brings both women to the point of explosion. What I found so amazing about the film was not only its insistence on the inherent corruption of all fundamentalism, but its larger message: that some individual women in this world, in every kind of circumstance, just have to be free. Even if no one has described this freedom to them, they know instinctively what it is, and they have to have it. At any cost.

In the question-and-answer session afterward, someone asked Zuria why the Israeli religious are upping the ante at this moment in history. The filmmaker answered that it is part of the global rise in fundamentalism. But I was not happy with this answer. There is a human impulse, when consciousness is regressed, to shut down when something deep has to be faced. That's the way many people roll when they don't want to know, and there is something in Israel, whether it's the secularity or it's the immorality of occupation or a million other factors all interreacting, that is inflaming the oppressive instincts of the ultraorthodox. Nothing could have been more relevant to these concerns than the film I ran to catch immediately after, *Still Alive in Gaza* by Nicolas Wadimoff.

This was the second Palestinian film I ever saw. The first was Cherien Dabis's *Amreeka*, which I watched at the Sunshine Cinema in New York, a representationally groundbreaking, character-based family drama about Palestinian immigrants in America. *Still Alive in Gaza* is entirely different from *Amreeka* and has a different goal. It is a very quiet film. Gaza is covered in rubble, and everyone lives on top of it. People are smoking in rubble. Families are picking up the scattered, splintered wood of 650-year-old olive trees that have been destroyed. The lion in the zoo died during the bombing, and Gazans can't get another, so they stuffed him. Badly. Men everywhere sit with nothing to do. No one can get through the Egyptian checkpoint regardless of how badly he or she needs a hospital. The children play grown-up and act out scenes of their bereaved relatives and countrymen.

"I had ten children," a cute eight-year-old mimics an adult neighbor, in his version of playing house. "Now only two are still alive." That's what it means to him to be an adult—describing the murder of one's children.

Clowns make jokes to kindergartners about bombs that continue to go off in the background on occasion. Five men get together to cook and eat one small fish. A young girl draws pictures with crayons of funerals, bombings, and dead people in the street. There is nothing to do. They are trapped. There is the beautiful sea; Gaza could be a luxury resort. They can't leave, and they can't live. They call the Israelis "the Jews." *The Jews* bombed, *the Jews* killed. "*The Jews* don't want me to get an education." Over and over, people counsel each other to get educated. Children want to get educated, their parents want them to get educated. Why would the Israelis not want this?

In my classroom, I scrupulously differentiate between Jews and Israelis. But here, the word "Israeli" is never mentioned. I find this particularly strange because the Israelis I know rarely think of themselves as Jews. Their identity is a nationalist one. The longer I watch the details of daily life in this level of chaos and pain and, most of all, waste, the more I understand that every time the Israelis do something like this, they create a century of historical trauma. I am still uneasy around Germans, and the Holocaust has been over for almost seventy years. How long will this have to be over before anything can heal? Longer than any one person's life. I already know how the children inherit the pain and pass it on.

I have never been one for comparisons. I refused to compare AIDS to the Holocaust, and I don't compare slavery or genocide to occupation or apartheid. Each person's historical context is unique and needs to be seen in its own detail. And yet there are associations that are almost irresponsible to avoid. I was riding the Berlin U-Bahn to the next film and looked at the young man sitting across the aisle. This happens to me occasionally, and this is the first time on this trip. His face. He has that classic German face that I have seen in endless black-and-white photographs of men wearing SS uniforms or saluting "Heil Hitler" in Leni Riefenstahl movies. Only this guy is just reading a newspaper. Amazing, isn't it? How the same people can do good, destroy, or be benign. Almost as if it's arbitrary. I realize then that every person who suffers from the Israelis is going to have this experience, and so will their grandchildren—seeing a facsimile of the torturer riding, unknowing, on the same subway car. And that facsimile could easily be me.

I arrived at the theater to see *A Film Unfinished* by a very young Israeli, Yael Hersonski. She found a roll of German propaganda film called *The Ghetto*, shot by Nazi film crews in the Warsaw Ghetto three months before the deportation and liquidation of the quarter. For some reason I told the blonde German woman sitting next to me that I am a Polish Jew. I felt very hostile. The film opened with a bird's-eye shot of the teeming, crowded ghetto on one side of the wall and, on the other, the empty, spacious Christian sector of Warsaw, with people leisurely gallivanting. The first association I made was between the prison of the ghetto and the prison of Gaza in the previous film. The comparison is unavoidable when the two works are viewed one right after the other. I won't go beyond that observation aside from saying that I am absolutely bewildered how Israelis can justify this. This will be the hardest thing of all for me to understand.

The original Nazi-produced footage of *The Ghetto* constructs a false image of a luxury class of Jews living in spacious apartments and wearing high-quality clothes who were indulged by benevolent Nazis with full markets, restaurants, and theater performances while other Jews starved in front of them. It's a fake documentary of manufactured good conditions and similarly manufactured depraved indifference of wealthy Jews in the ghetto. Hersonski juxtaposes the diary entries of Adam Czerniakow, the head of the Judenrat—the titular Jewish leader of the ghetto who collaborated in selecting the names for various deportations until he committed suicide in 1943. He writes long descriptions of the filmmaking process. He describes how the Nazis brought in well-fed, robust actors to play the wealthy Jews and how they brought in props, including an ornate silver menorah, to decorate the shots. Hersonski also intercuts scenes of survivors of the ghetto watching the footage and commenting. Old Jews in Israel look through the footage of teeming crowds for a sign of their mothers' faces. This is again intercut with multiple takes of crowd enactments ordered by the Nazi filmmakers, until we in the audience start to understand how and what they were constructing. Cumulatively we realize that the starving, traumatized people in the ghetto were forced to perform false scenes of excess, in multiple takes. And because they had no option, they obeyed. Some outtakes show ghetto inhabitants being physically beaten into the roles of extras, being forced to smile, being forced to enact panic. Being forced to enact greed.

The second stunning detail is that the handful of elderly survivors whom Hersonski amassed to view and comment on the original footage call the Nazis "the Germans." And some of them speak their commentary in heavily accented Hebrew. They are speaking Hebrew, in Israel, talking about "the Germans" just as the people of Gaza are talking about "the Jews."

That same night I saw *Budrus*, directed by a Brazilian, Julia Bacha. *Budrus* is a Palestinian/Israeli/U.S./international production about the West Bank town of Budrus, faced with the Israeli Wall of Separation (the Palestinian name for "the Security Wall"). As with the village of Bil'in, the Israelis have decided to build the wall between the town and their farmland. A Fatah member and experienced community figure organizes a nonviolent multifaction coalition including Fatah, Hamas, Palestinian women, Palestinian children, Israelis, Americans, and internationals to oppose the placement of the wall, and eventually they win. It's a very upbeat and hopeful film about the ideal of nonviolent coalition work and the responsibility of Israelis to join these protests. Afterward, I talked to one of the Jewish coproducers, a British guy living in Brooklyn. I asked him what he thought about the boycott.

"We're not for the boycott. We're not against the boycott."

This was the first time I heard someone who was breaking the boycott (by using Israeli state funds) tell me that he was neutral. It is a trope that would reoccur. I told him where I'm coming from. That I turned down Tel-Aviv University for the Haifa Women's Center, and so on.

"So you are violating the boycott?" he said.

"No, I'm not."

"Yes, you are!"

"Are you Israeli?" I asked, because I knew I was not violating the boycott.

"I lived there for seven years," he said.

I explained again what I was doing. For the first time I explained that one can go to Israel and still maintain the boycott. That it is about Israeli state funding.

"You're not violating the boycott," he conceded, disappointed that he didn't catch me being wrong. "You're doing what we're doing."

Well, not exactly, but I loved his film and the people it documented. Then I told him about the whole queer side of this trip — my forthcoming meeting with Omar and with Palestinian queer activists.

"Oh, they're not real Palestinians," he said.

"Yes, they are!" I said, having no idea what the phrase *real Palestinian* actually means. I'd never heard anyone make this accusation, and while I do not know what I am talking about, I am instinctually sure that gay Palestinians consider themselves to be *real*. I just feel it.

"If they're gay, they give up being Palestinian."

"No," I said. "There are Palestinian lesbian and gay organizations." I was thinking of Aswat in particular and trying to figure out what I now know of as "Al-Qaws" is.

"Oh," he said, thoroughly depressed at now having lost the entire argument. "I didn't know that. Well," he says, "good for you. It would make a great film project."

By the end of the film festival, my friend Alex Juhasz, one of the *Owls* producers, and I were exhausted. We'd spent the last day together going to see the Holocaust memorial by the Brandenburg gate. Alex has a big Jewish nose, kinky Jewish hair, and she is loud, pushy, smart, and dialogic. But she's from Colorado, so, even with a Holocaust survivor Hungarian father, she doesn't have the same Jewish self-perception that we continue to hold in New York. Normalcy. We get to the installation—a city block of rows of gray squares rising, looming, and falling in a maze, blocking and letting in light. I am walking it, actually thinking of the names of my exterminated ancestors. And little German children are playing hide-and-seek, giggling, their parents are smoking, drinking beer, and talking on cell phones.

"Well," I said to Alex, "it's great public art, but it has nothing to do with the Holocaust."

"I think it's perfect," she said. "The Germans smoke, play with their children, and drink beer, just like they did during the Holocaust. It's very accurate."

I went back to New York feeling much surer that I was on the right track regarding Palestine and Israel. I was grateful to filmmakers, film festivals, and the medium itself—how it hypnotizes us into receiving knowledge privately, deeply, emotionally, through the communion with image in a quiet, dark place. Much more confident now, convinced that my earlier wavering was a consequence of my own self-imposed lack of awareness, I was excited and looking forward to being part of the change that has to come.

3. MAPS

Back in New York and back to work, I could feel how much I had grown. Still jet-lagged, I stumbled from teaching on Staten Island to give a reading at Dixon Place on the Lower East Side with my friend Charles Rice-Gonzalez to celebrate his new book, the first gay Puerto Rican novel set in New York. I decided to take advantage of this small venue and celebratory opportunity to give my first exploratory public talk on boycott/divestment/sanctions. As I was speaking, I felt very clear. The little that I said had been thought through. The audience seemed both attentive and supportive, and I finally felt comfortable with my own commitments. Only later that night, scanning the friendly, encouraging faces, did I realize that I was one of the few Jews in the room of mostly Latinos and friends. This is something I have rarely measured or noticed in my half century as a New Yorker. I am becoming hyper aware of myself as a Jew in a place where that is not necessary.

A couple of days later, February 24, I heard from Elle, who had been working overtime to make my upcoming trip meaningful. She continued to propose ideas and create experiences for me, and her trust was enriching. Again we discussed my meeting with PACBI to talk about the group's acknowledgment of "queers in solidarity." She wrote that my "meeting with them might get some of that started." This was becoming one of my greatest hopes for the trip. Elle also suggested that I meet Ezra Nawi, the man from her film, now active in Ta-ayush, an organization working in villages in the southern Hebron Hills. I did a Google search for a map of Hebron Hills. I realized, in doing this, that watching the film *Budrus* had prompted my first efforts ever to look at a map of Palestine. I spend the next hour trying to find a cohesive map of the West Bank on-line. My own ignorance continues to astound me. This is not the person I thought myself to be, someone who has never looked at a map of the West Bank. Googling for a map of Palestine has to be my low point for lack of awareness on this journey. Perhaps ten different options come up. The range of ideological answers is more depressing than overwhelming. Finally, I found a map of Jewish settlements in the West Bank. It looked like a diseased cell.

I was beginning to see how much actually grappling with BDS can provoke learning and depth of understanding. At the same time, I started to wonder what I had to offer the various groups and individuals with whom I would be meeting. I did understand that the primary purpose was for me to get information that I can think about and convey. I understood clearly that this is how this sort of thing works. But there is also the emotional bond among queer people, and I wanted to enrich that relationship mutually. One contact suggested that "the folks in Ramallah are just beginning to deal with what it means to be queer in a place not all that friendly toward them/the idea. I wonder if you could offer them some historical perspective of your work back in the day fighting similar battles."

That is something I certainly do have to offer: hands-on strategic experience with basic organizing. In the abortion rights movement, gay and lesbian liberation, direct action groups like ACT UP and the Lesbian Avengers, I had learned how to think through and complete tasks in a productive way that could have an effect. Through the founding and maintenance of cultural institutions such as the MIX Festival, through failed efforts (including the five-year thwarted campaign to get Irish lesbians and gays to march in the Saint Patrick's Day parade), and through successful efforts (such as forcing the pharmaceutical industry to change research agendas to find treatments for AIDS), I had also learned a great deal about the emotional and familial obstacles that queer people have to face in effecting change. This is what I had to offer: knowledge of how to be effective.

The next day, February 25, 2010, *Haaretz*, a progressive Israeli newspaper, published an interview with Judith Butler conducted by the journalist Udi Aloni. It was carefully and somewhat humorously titled "As a Jew, I Was Taught It Was Ethically Imperative to Speak Up," with an overtness more characteristic of Tevye's "dream" than a typical newspaper headline. What followed was a highly articulate conversation explaining Butler's position on boycott to Israeli readers. As far as I know, this makes her the most high-profile American intellectual to come out for boycott. I felt overwhelmed with pride and gratitude that someone with the integrity to be so out as a lesbian was taking the leadership that the rest of us needed, not just emotionally but practically. It had been a long time since I felt real leadership before me that I could rely on. I experienced a great feeling of relief to see and hear that other voice, that other face literally creating a context one day, for me, whereas the day before there was none. The example of her throwing the weight of her considerable credibility behind Palestine was very comforting.

Butler also seemed to be trying to understand what Israelis were thinking. She clearly has had a much more Israel-oriented life than I have and has gotten much further than I in this regard. My impression is that she grew up with more religious education and a Zionist context. This has brought her closer to Israel, and the intimacy is expressed by her focus in that direction. In the *Haaretz* piece, Butler articulates how the Israeli government and media represent murdered Palestinians as "war instruments" instead of as people who are suffering. In this way, she writes, they are

> understood no longer to be lives, no longer understood to be living, no longer understood even to be human in a recognizable sense, but they are artillery.... So when a people who believes that another people is out to destroy them sees all the means of destruction killed, or some extraordinary number of the means of destruction destroyed, they are thrilled, because they think their safety and well-being and happiness are being purchased, are being achieved through this destruction.

What is so life-giving about leadership like Butler's is that it instantly allows one to leap forward. And because I am dialogic, as is she, I immediately started to discover myself more acutely in reaction to her ideas. One of her principal selling points in this piece directed toward Israelis is the idea of Jewish ethics. And I grapple with this. Butler, generously, attributes her own integrity to the very thing that the people she opposed attribute their actions to: Jewishness. Butler says clearly that "as a Jew one is under obligation to criticize excessive state violence and state racism." Of course I understand what she is trying to do, to define Jewish values as social justice values. But is that really still a viable position? Don't all religious and cultural moral frameworks offer justifications for peace and justifications for war? Justifications for shunning and justifications for facing and dealing with problems? After reading her, I asked myself if the kind of Jewish traditional thinking about justice that she ascribes to can ever coexist with nationalism. Perhaps we are coming to the moment when another historical shift in Jewish consciousness about how we want to exist in this world is about to take place.

"The Israelis are so crazy," my Lebanese friend Rabih said to me on the phone. "It is strange to watch."

"They are self-destructing," I said. "And taking everyone else along with them."

I decided that I had to come clean with the straight Israelis in my life. I wrote to my cousin again. I told her for the first time, directly, that I was supporting the boycott. "When we talked about Neve Gordon, you said, 'They are asking the world for help.' This comment made an impression on me." She was very kind, and we made a date for lunch.

I also, finally—and I had been dreading this—wrote to my friends Yehudit and Tal, a straight Israeli couple living in Brooklyn. We had met through my cousin about five years before, and we just clicked. In fact, I can honestly say that we love each other. They, however, are very Israeli. We just don't talk about politics, but how long can I have an authentic relationship with them and not bring this up? I wrote Yehudit a breathless summary of the previous four months, and she answered with characteristic warmth and humanity. "I hope you will be enriched by this journey. I can't wait to hear about it and be there with you and for you." She sent me her brother's and sister's phone numbers in Israel, in case I needed anything. Something profound was happening to me. I was connecting and receiving immense love, engagement, and respect from many corners.

I heard from Sonya, who was spending her weekends at demonstrations in the West Bank. She started to fill me in on the schedule. I would speak in Tel Aviv and Haifa and spend two nights in Ramallah. She asked me to speak on BDS. I resolved to do the best I could.

After reading Butler's piece, I asked Elle about going to Birzeit University in the West Bank. She suggested that I ask "Judy," but I had a feeling that would be overstepping. Butler and I were not friends, despite how much she was helping me. There was a distance there of style, position, and self-perception, and I didn't want to ask for too much. Elle responded characteristically with an introduction to Professor Sonya Nimr. Jailed at age nineteen for three years for belonging to a Palestinian student group, she is in her fifties and married to a filmmaker. I looked up Birzeit and saw that it had a women's studies program. Excited, I wrote an email to Professor Nimr.

I am coming to Ramallah on a Solidarity Visit, having declined an offer to keynote the Lesbian and Gay Studies Conference at Tel-Aviv University. I am a novelist and playwright, and a Professor of English at the City University of New York, a fellow at the New York Institute for the Humanities at New York University, and on the Advisory Council of the Carr Center for Human Rights and Social Movements at Harvard University's Kennedy School. If there is some capacity in which I can visit Bir Zeit or meet with you or anyone you suggest during my short time there, that would be wonderful. I would be happy to offer a one time Fiction writing workshop in English if any of the students are interested — or do anything that would be engaging. Please let me know what you think would be best.

As with Naomi Klein, I was trying to play both sides of the street. I approach, coming out directly from the top letting them know that I assume this won't be a problem. But just in case it is, I attempt to mitigate this somewhat with my mainstream credentials. And, again, with Nimr as with Klein, it did not work. I did not hear back from Professor Nimr. I did, however, get a sharply worded rebuke from Sonya, to whom I'd copied the email. "I want to remind you that on all your talks," she wrote back, "you should mention the reason for the solidarity visit, and the boycott, in order to not violate its terms. I've been told that to stay within the terms of the boycott, when you speak in Israel, you have to also talk about PACBI's request for sanctions." This is when I go into my "instructions from Moscow" mode. Of course I wondered if it was my offer to teach a fiction workshop that provoked this. And I really wanted to know what "I've been told" meant. But regardless, I did now understand why so many people were putting so much effort into my trip and that there was a lot of information sharing going on behind the scenes with people I did not know.

To strengthen my arguments, I gave small public lectures in New York.

The second one of these talks was at Sidewalk Café on Seventh Street in the East Village. I was reading with Peter Schjeldahl, the *New Yorker*'s art critic. And again there were only about thirty people in the audience. In a sense it was a rehearsal for invited guests, a number of Peter's friends, and some of my friends and students. I saw Vani Natarajan, a young, queer woman who had been in my private writing group for the previous two years. She wrote fiction about her involvement with Palestinian solidarity and the reaction of her Hindu father. I was glad she had come to the talk and looked forward to her suggestions. I gave the same reading I gave at Dixon Place, but this time, for the first time, I faced some opposition. My Jewish lesbian neighbor from Ninth Street raised her hand. "I appreciate your struggle," she said. "But why should Israel be judged by a higher standard than everybody else?"

It struck me immediately that this was exactly what my cousin had said, almost word for word. My instinct told me that this must be one of the standard responses that people hear and repeat. So, based on my lifetime experience as a political organizer, I thought through the question. As I stood there, thinking aloud on the stage, I realized that it was a false question. Israel was not being judged by a higher standard. In fact, Israel and the United States were judged consistently by a lower standard. When we oppressed people, occupied their land, took away their futures, and destroyed their human potential, we acted as though it hadn't happened or didn't matter or was somehow justified. But when this behavior was enacted by other governments, we roundly protested.

I told myself to be vigilant in the future—to look at the structure and assumptions of questions so I don't get trapped into arguing against something that doesn't, in fact, exist.

The next day I received an email from Vani. She was very supportive and gently pointed out that I was mistaken in my assumption that the a in PACBI stands for "authority." The Palestinian Authority was not running the boycott; an independent group was. My grasp of basic information was still so below par. She then offered to get together to talk it all over.

This delighted me. I absolutely loved the women in my private workshop. I felt a joy being among them as though luxuriating in a succulent garden. I was so joyful to have the opportunity to learn from Vani about Palestine, for this would further enrich our very precious relationship. We made an appointment for dinner, our very first meeting outside of the writing sessions.

On March 6, the Israeli filmmaker who had made aliya, NW the "post-Zionist," wrote me that when I came in through Israeli customs, I needed to identify someone whom I could say I was coming to visit. Customs officers opened her brother's laptop and looked at his Facebook and emails, she said. She made clear that I couldn't use her name, even though she is a citizen. She was afraid. I phoned my cousin in Tel Aviv and explained honestly and clearly exactly what I was doing. Then I asked if I could give his name. He said yes. I became a middle-aged Jewish teacher from New York going to Israel to see my cousin during Pesach.

Vani and I got together, and I asked her a lot of questions about the local organizing effort. Ours is the first talk I have had with anyone about the actual organizational structure of Palestine solidarity movements in the United States. From what I could tell, the movement seemed factional:

invisible, with an agenda not known to the general public. We talked
about the need for visible leaders with some kind of credibility. Of course
I understood the problem: "credibles"—people who are accountable to
disenfranchised communities instead of to the apparatus of power—are
denied visibility. So real leaders with inspired visions about Palestine immediately become marginal. There was no Palestinian in the United States
in a firm leadership position and with access to mainstream media to articulate a way forward. There were inspirational journalists such as Ali
Abunimah and his Electronic Intifada, but he is not on CNN. Progressive people with mainstream media access simply weren't speaking out on
Israel. So there was no guidance. There was also no visible agenda; almost
none of the Americans I discussed this with had ever heard of the boycott,
and that includes active intellectuals and progressive figures: professors,
curators, artists, writers. A friend of mine who is a very sophisticated museum curator and an articulate political person was invited on a free trip
to visit artists' studios in Israel. "Brand Israel?" I suggested. She had never
heard the term. In the United States, the question of boycott/divestment/
sanctions is barely known. Most Americans have never heard of it.

Vani believed that the size of the Israeli economy makes boycott and
sanctions a viable strategy, but I didn't see how this would work. And she
couldn't fully explain it to me, or else I couldn't fully understand. Finally,
we talked about the actual agenda for change. In ACT UP, we instinctively
used the same strategy that Martin Luther King articulated in his amazing
"Letter from Birmingham Jail." First: educate yourself to your own condition. Second: make demands that are reasonable and doable. When those
demands are refused, move to the third step: purify yourself; it's a kind
of spiritual preparation in which your values are put to work toward your
goals. Fourth: engage in nonviolent civil disobedience until the goals are
met.

I asked Vani, in her understanding, what the most important goals for
Palestine are. She said: "End the occupation, Palestinian right of return,
rights for refugees and exiles." I asked, What is the strategy for achieving
these goals? We looked at each other. The answer was clear: boycott/di-
vestment/sanctions.

On March 9, I heard from Sonya that my first two events would be
on April 1. At 5 P.M. I would meet with a private group that she had not
named. More mystery. At 7, I would speak at the Rogatka, a queer anarchist café in Tel Aviv. The stated subject was "Ties That Bind." I realized

that I would have to bring over about twenty copies of my books. Would it be hard to get them through customs?

The plans regarding the West Bank were more elusive. It had been decided that I would stay for three nights to avoid having to go back and forth through the crossing. The plan was for me to go to Bil'in on Friday, April 2, and then on to Ramallah. There, on Saturday, I would meet with PACBI for an hour and a half. This would be the most important conversation of the trip. Afterward, an informal gathering with activists was planned for the evening. Someone named Sami Shalami, whose gender was as yet unknown to me, was part of the queer community in Ramallah. Sami asked me for books for the group's newly created Queer Library. Sami asked for a gathering on Saturday during the day "as we have women who cannot attend the general meeting that takes place in the evenings." I would meet with PACBI, the Stop the Wall Campaign, the BDS Campaign, and queer activists, all in Ramallah. Then I would return to Israel and speak in Haifa with Aswat, the Palestinian lesbian organization, and with Isha L'Isha, the Jewish feminist organization that shares Aswat's office.

Sonya wrote to say that the "private" group I will be meeting with is called Mesolelot, which means "Tribads." "It's a phrase taken from the Talmud. This is what the Talmud tells the husband: if you find your wife *mesolelet* with another woman you can banish her. It's basically the only thing in Judaism relating to lesbians." She said that the intent of the organization is to show the relationship between LGBT "struggle to equality and the Palestinian struggle." I read this statement with understanding and concern. I fully grasped what she wanted to convey: supremacy ideology, the practice of dominance, its consequences on the lives and potentials of individuals and communities. This is something many of us have been articulating all of our lives. But it has to be done with complexity, or it simply won't be true. Of course I agreed to meet with Mesolelot.

Sonya forwarded me a message from Sami responding to the initial schedule. "Tell me what Mesolelot and Isha L'Isha are," Sami wrote. "As PACBI asked if she was visiting Israel and what she will be doing there." Interesting. I think I am starting to see the structure more clearly. I now think that Sonya is organizing the trip for PACBI. And they are not familiar with the Israeli anti-occupation queer organizations. Two very important pieces of information.

On March 9, 2010, U.S. Vice President Joe Biden was embarrassed on his visit to Israel by Netanyahu's announcement of more Jewish housing being built in East Jerusalem. This prompted a "crisis" in which Secretary of State Hillary Clinton condemned settlement expansion and Israel's obstruction of negotiations. Could Hillary Clinton end up being the "leader" we are all looking for, to turn the attitudinal tide? Israel had given the United States an opportunity to make the relationship more accountable. Certainly, this shift is well recognized by Americans and broadly acknowledged in the media. Is this the start of a change, or will it soon be forgotten?

On March 13, Sami wrote a short note: "I just realized that I forgot to mention that the house we are meeting in on Saturday with Al Qaws activists is underground and top secret. It virtually does not exist. . . . So, it would be appreciated that you do not mention that part of the program, or at least where it's happening, and if you can keep the meeting with the West Bank group as low profile as possible, as we are also an underground group."

On March 15, I heard from Sonya.

Just to inform you of the latest developments:
Last night at 2 A.M., the Israeli army entered Bil'in village. A document was posted around the whole village of Bil'in. This document declared that Israeli and international activists were strictly prohibited from entering Bil'in between the hours of 8 A.M. and 8 P.M. on every Friday, the day in which the weekly demonstration takes place. Every Israeli and international activist must leave the village during this time, or else he or she will be deported or arrested by Israeli soldiers. The head of the police, Benjamin, ordered that this action be taken. The permit declares Bil'in to be a closed military area until August 17th.

This action is another step of the Israeli government to kill the struggle. We all know that if there will be no internationals and Israelis in the village, the army is going to arrest the Palestinians.

Although I think that you should go there anyway, I will totally understand if you choose not to. If you choose not to go, we will find another way to get you to Ramallah.

I wrote back: "My instinct is to go with you. Lets re-evaluate when we see each other at 5 P.M. on the 1st and have a more up to date sense of events." Sonya wrote back one word: "Great."

The day for my lunch with my cousin finally came. I couldn't believe how loving and straightforward she was. She didn't agree with what I was doing, and she had many different kinds of reasons. She thought that I could have a larger audience if I spoke at the university, "not just ten people in some café." I knew that this was true. She felt that universities are the main place in Israel where progressive things happen. She wondered why I focused on Israel and not other countries with human rights problems. She told me very frankly that I simply "cannot understand." Which I am sure is true, as there is already so much I don't understand. I learned a number of things from her. She had been in the West Bank twice: once in Bethlehem to see the Christmas stuff, and once in the army. I know, of course, that every Israeli I meet and love has been in the army, and I will never know what they did there. This is a given. I took in, for the first time, my beautiful cousin's contradictions — ones she cannot resolve. I so recognize the experience of being an American in her conundrum — of knowing what one has at the expense of others, knowing this on some very deep level, and also acquiescing to it in some way, so as to have a sense of self along with one's advantages.

Then it happened. In the middle of our conversation I understood, suddenly, that I had to do this trip as an American, and not as a Jew. As a Jew, it's not my country. As an American, it's my tax dollars. How's that for a capitalist perspective? But I internalized it and held it quietly. At the end, she offered to send me her parents' email address and phone number at the kibbutz where she was born and where they still live. In case of emergency. And a few days later, she did exactly that.

4. THE JEWISH EMBRACE

The unequivocal goal of BDS is to force Israel to abide
by international law. —NAOMI KLEIN

Opposition is an intense and intimate relationship. It makes the contested
object important, relevant, and dynamic with one's own growth. In other
words, I was getting sucked into Israel.

As a second-generation New Yorker, I have long held a de facto Jewish
identity. I have had nothing to prove. I can be normal and Jewish without
even trying. As a result I have never belonged to a Jewish organization. In
fact I have avoided contemporary Jewishness almost entirely. No knowledge or interest in Israel, religious questions (ordination of women, de-
genderizing the liturgy, gay marriage), Jewish advocacy organizations, or
ongoing developments in Jewish culture. My interest in Jewishness went
from Emma Goldman to Ethel Rosenberg, with Noam Chomsky and Amy
Goodman as icing on the cake. Hence the privilege of being a New Yorker.

At this point, I was thinking about Israel every day and speaking Jewishly with Jews about Jewish things. I had to admit that the relationship
was finally starting to take hold, but under very rigorous terms. Of course,
being an American has provided many years of practice for this. As an
American I have insight into the Israeli conundrum, as I have spent my life
as a citizen of a country that consistently violates international law, defies
standards of human rights, and financially supports oppressive regimes
(including Israel) while regularly killing civilians in different places on
earth without justification or reason. Even today, I live in a country that
regularly murders people in Iraq and Afghanistan under the orders of a
president I voted for. If anyone should have practice understanding what
it is like to be an Israeli, it would be an American.

Elle put me in touch with Udi Aloni, the man who conducted Judith
Butler's interview for *Haaretz*. Of course that is the wrong way to describe
him. Actually, he is an artist, philosopher, filmmaker, and journalist. While

researching his work I came across a startling statement: "We must cleanse Zionism of its nationalistic elements without relinquishing its Messianic fervor for liberty, freedom, and equality." This profoundly interested me. I felt that I did not understand what Zionism is. What did Udi mean? Is this really redeemable? Is Israel to Zionism as the Soviet Union was to Marxism? This is a conversation I wanted to have. That same day, a friend independently sent me a video of Udi. I see a man my age, smiling while serious. The next day we had our first Skype conversation. I'd just gotten Skype, as apparently nothing can be done in the Middle East without it.

The first thing he told me, as the video came into focus, was that since he will be in New York during my trip, I can stay at his apartment. I'm grateful. We talked for a while about the queer angle to the story, which he immediately grasped as interesting new territory. I told him that I hadn't heard of the boycott until August, and he warmly invited me to become part of Jewish Voice for Peace. I immediately experienced that old recoil. I couldn't imagine joining a Jewish organization, but I didn't say that. Who knows, maybe this too will change. Someday.

"Come," he said. "Tony is on the board. Judy is on the board. I'm the hetero on the board."

Tony is Kushner, Judy is Butler, and I knew that I would not join Jewish Voice for Peace, although I increasingly read the group's e-letter, *Muzzlewatch*, which documents retribution by the right-wing Jewish community against anti-occupation Jews. I also started reading the Electronic Intifada, the on-line go-to source for news about Palestine. Udi and I would overlap one night before I was to leave for Tel Aviv, so I invited him over for a drink. Only then did I realize that my date with Udi would be the first night of Passover, something I had entirely forgotten and for which I had made no plans. So seder would be spent drinking in my apartment with Udi Aloni. I knew five people in Israel, and they all knew each other. Is it the Jewish embrace, or is it the *Bitzah*, one of my newly acquired Hebrew words? The swamp.

Muzzlewatch mesmerizes me. Its stated function is to "track efforts to stifle open debate about U.S.-Israeli foreign policy." In every realm, human beings who try to transform supremacy ideology are met with degradation, diminishment, indifference, dismissal, distortion, and outright persecution. I have experienced this sort of thing most of my life as a writer of primarily lesbian content, and when it happens you basically have to grin, bear, and keep moving on. But the Jews of *Muzzlewatch* have been able to systematically document this experience in a way that no other group of dissidents can. They have a confidence about their right to dissent that allows them to *expose* the punishers. Implied in that action is the assumption that someone will care. I think back to Butler's approach to Israel from the position of "Jewish values." As long as Jews think we have "Jewish values," the violation of them can be *exposed*. The person you are revealing has to want to be seen as other than he really is for that tactic to work. This is a new understanding for me of the political realm into which I have fallen: it's one in which exposing the other is a viable strategy.

During this time, I came across a March 15 posting on *Muzzlewatch* about an attack by Eran Shayshon of the Reut Institute on Naomi Klein. To Shayshon's assertion that Klein "opposes Israel's right to exist," Klein responded:

> Once again, I challenge him to find one single example in anything I have said or written that would in any way support this claim. He won't find it. This lie could just be slander, and attempt to inflict more "shame" on BDS advocates. . . . But I suspect that if challenged, Shayshon would simply claim that to support BDS is to oppose Israel's existence, a claim I have heard before. This is interesting. Since the unequivocal goal of BDS is to force Israel to abide by international law, what Shayshon seems to be saying by implication is that Israel cannot exist within the confines of international law. I would never make such an argument.

I took this in very deeply. "Existence" is a word bandied about quite often in this conversation, and it has become code to me that the person using it isn't thinking for himself. Israel exists. The accusation that one doesn't hope for Israel to exist or the defense that one does hope for it are both avoidance techniques obscuring the more pressing question of what "we" are going to do to move that existence away from violation of international law.

That week, Netanyahu arrived in Washington. I saw him on CNN, speaking to AIPAC, while I was at the gym. Normally, I would have watched long enough to register his affect, then changed the channel. But I was by then sucked into all things Israel/Palestine, so I watched. He listed specific actions by the Palestinians as proof of their lack of interest in peace. He talked about their naming a street after someone who had committed public violence that killed Israel civilians; he seemed to think this was the grand crime, not the occupation and domination of an entire people. I noted his physicality as he spoke — his lips, eyes, facial demeanor. He was not sincere. He was playing a game. I thought through the situation he described: the creation of Palestinian desperation. Then I realized that he is a perpetrator who pretends to be a victim. He blames his own victims for the consequences of his actions. I thought back to my earlier question, the one that came to me in Berlin as I watched *Still Alive in Gaza*. What do the right-wing Israelis think their actions will accomplish? Just from a practical point of view, how could they believe that their actions will produce their stated goals? It didn't make sense before. Now it does. His goal is not peace, even though he says it is. His goal is land-grab. He wants it all. But he won't say this out loud. He's a liar. And so I watched him continue to lie. And then I listened to AIPAC applaud.

Muzzlewatch had become my second read of the morning, after Hollywood's *Variety*. The March 23 edition addressed a number of instances in which U.S. consulates kept Palestinian activists from coming to the United States. Mohammed Omer, the 2007 winner of the Martha Gellhorn Prize for Journalism, had to cancel his U.S. speaking tour because he couldn't get a visa. Mohammed Khatib, founder of the Bil'in Popular Committee against the Wall, could not get a response for his visa request from the U.S. consulate in East Jerusalem. I wondered if I would see him in Bil'in, if I got there. Over and over I asked myself how I could have closed my eyes to all of this for so long. I was ashamed, but I also really understood. The process of coming into understanding is mesmerizing and magnetic. The degradation of Palestine and the waste of its people's human potential, the destabilizing of the eight million Palestinians in the global diaspora, was one of the starkest, clearest examples of injustice in my contemporary world. And even though it was being done with my money and in my name, and in a sense by the people I know, love, and am related to, it was kinetically easy to avoid. There was simply no one who could be heard on any coherent mass level, no one to insist on our attention. Palestine was not branded and could not compete in media culture. It was too real, and we were too false.

Thinking about the question of marketing and branding put a lot into perspective. Ben Yehuda, the founder of modern Hebrew, was, I now realized, a genius marketer. David Ben-Gurion was the first proponent of Brand Israel. Choosing new Zionist names was part of branding. My cousin's name is no longer Liebling, but Avivi. No longer Jerushalmi but Zakai. I wanted to find out more about the geniuses who conceptualized and marketed Zionism and if they were the same people who originally theorized it.

On March 27, *Muzzlewatch* reported that Mohammed Omer got his visa and it thanked "everyone for your letters." I wondered how many were sent. What is the size of this critical mass? That same day, Omar Barghouti wrote to confirm my meeting with him and Hind Awaad of the Boycott National Committee for Saturday, April 3, at 1 P.M. in Ramallah. Since I had never seen my schedule and had no idea how I would be getting anywhere, I copied the email to Sonya, whom I was counting on for full disclosure when I arrived. If someone told me where to be and how to get there, I would go. This much I knew. The meeting with PACBI was emerging as the centerpiece of the trip as far as I could understand the itinerary from my still-in-NYC vantage point. I didn't know if this would just be Omar, or others as well. I knew nothing about Palestinian cultural mores: how people communicate, what is appropriate. I only knew that my task was to ask them to openly acknowledge queer support for the boycott. My meeting with Al-Qaws would probably be after the meeting with PACBI, so no opportunity for prompting there. I was nervous. From what I could tell from my Internet searches, Omar was a bit wordy, so I expected to listen a lot, and I wanted to. But my fear was that I would get nowhere or, even worse, have no idea if I got anywhere or didn't. I didn't know how much of this was pre-decided, or if the meeting itself would just be a theatrical gesture.

I found the announcement on-line of my engagement at the Rogatka on April 1 at 7:30. Sonya described it as "the queer anarchist café." Mookie, a friend from New York, said, "As a good leftist, I of course know the place." Amit Kama, a longtime friend and fellow academic, had never heard of it. The announcement of my lecture on familial homophobia mentioned that the talk would be followed by a party with "DJ Leila Khaled." I'd better get some sleep. And then I found it: a leaflet printed on-line from an organization called Boycott!

The log line for Boycott! read: "Supporting the Palestinian BDS Call from Within. A group of Palestinians and Jews, citizens of Israel, who join the Palestinian call for a BDS campaign against Israel, inspired by the struggle of South Africans against apartheid." The headline below: "BOY-COTT! Supports Sarah Schulman's Boycott of Israeli Universities." *Whoa.* I thought I was supporting *their* boycott, not the other way around. And I was still thinking of my actions as "sanctions."

I took a deep breath.

Here we go. The chess game had begun. And I had agreed to be a pawn. The open letter to me read as follows:

Dear Sarah Schulman,

We at BOYCOTT! would like to praise you for your important decision to boycott state-run and apartheid-complicit Tel-Aviv University and Ben Gurion University of the Negev, who invited you to their "Sex Acher 10" conference in Israel this year. By engaging in the academic institutional boycott of Israel you are helping to raise the oppressed Palestinian voice instead of adopting a "business as usual" attitude towards the Israeli apartheid.

As you know, policy makers in your country and elsewhere fail to truly pressure Israel, they back its policies bluntly or abstain from even criticizing Israel for the full scale of its crimes and human rights violations. In such conditions it is up to conscientious individuals like you and to civil society organizations and groups to join in solidarity the popular Palestinian struggle for justice and freedom. Boycotts and calls for divestments and sanctions against Israel are legitimate non-violent means by which everyone around the world can make a difference.

Indeed, Palestinians need all the support they can get. This is evident by the years-long Israeli inhuman siege that has rendered Gaza the world's largest open air prison; the 2008/9 Israeli massacre in Gaza that has left more than 1400 Palestinians dead and terrorize the lives of 1.5 million people; further deadly and destructive attacks that the Israeli army has carried out against the Gazan population to this day; and the ongoing Israeli occupation segregation and colonization of the West Bank, including East Jerusalem, by separate legal and administrative systems, the apartheid wall, apartheid roads, Jewish-only settlements, checkpoints and the Israeli army's unrestrained and often murderous violence.

Acting as a colonizing force in the region, Israel still denies responsibility for the Nakba and rejects the right of return and the compensation of the Palestinian refugees that it has expelled and robbed. Through over 3 inequality laws, as well as informal policies and practices, it further discriminates systematically against its Palestinian citizens in almost every aspect of social life. All of these forms of injustice constitute the Israeli apartheid that organizes itself on a clear separation between the state's treatment of any Palestinian, on the one hand, and of any Jew, on the other hand. To perpetuate itself, the Israeli apartheid conceptually and physically divides the Palestinian people into more controllable parts and Bantustans. It has to be resisted in its entirety, as done by the BDS movement.

Your act of solidarity will be added to your already longtime activist and cultural work on LGBT/queer issues and your undeterred pursuit for just peace and freedom. We share with you these values and support you in your decision to boycott Israel as long as it continues to function as an apartheid state and to oppress the Palestinians.

In Solidarity,

Nitzan Aviv, Ronnie Barkan, Lilach Ben-David, Matan Cohen, Adi Dagan, Hamutal Erato, Yael Kahn, Dorothy Naor, Ofer Neiman, Yeoshua Rosin, Adv. Emily Schaeffer, Ayala Shani, Tal Shapira, Sonya Soloviov, Ruth Tenne, Yossi Wolfson, Moni Yakim

Wow. Not that I necessarily disagreed with the facts, but I never would have used this language. No sign of my "public" letter to the LGBT Studies Conference saying how honored I was to be invited, how much I respected them, and how sorry I was for all the trouble I was causing. And most important, the issue driving my visit was not even broached in this open letter: namely, that if people like me are going to turn our backs on queer events in support of the boycott, then we must be assured that the boycott both recognizes queer support and acknowledges Palestinian LGBT organizing. I am occupying a very tiny zone in between many worlds, none of which I know anything about.

I was supposed to spend my Pesach that night with Udi Aloni. The following morning, March 30, I would catch an 8:30 A.M. flight to Tel Aviv.

After a twelve-hour flight to New York, and a shower, Udi Aloni climbed the six floors of my apartment building to our version of a Passover seder: a bottle of good wine, an array of treats—olives, marinated onions, sweet peppers, cheese, grapes, and chocolate—and a conversation about liberation. This was my chance to finally discuss my trip in person (not email/Skype/chat/text) with a human being who actually knew what he was talking about, and it was incredibly helpful. The question on the table was: Is there a bridge—current and future—between boycott and queer that makes sense? Or was my pursuit of this some kind of folly? I presented my plan to ask PACBI about acknowledging queer participation in the boycott.

"I support you," he said. "But let me ask you a few questions."

Thus began a two-hour dialogue and commentary about all the ups and downs, pitfalls, benefits and possible strategies of bringing together the

U.S. LGBT and Palestine. He started with some arguments I'd already heard or had considered. The first was the question of "imposing" Western values on Palestinians, who already have enough problems. Of course this is both a real and false concern. And it raises other questions. One is whether there is an assumption that homosexuality—not just the sex part, but the love, the desire, the bonding, the longing, the building of lives, the human transformation through love and sex that heterosexuals are expected to have—whether this most basic human possibility is in fact Western. To answer this, I take the following into consideration: we are all now grown up enough to know that the reasons for and consequences of two women having sex with each other are both universal and culturally specific. So I can respond that homosexual desire is Western and also not specifically so. Since Udi and I already knew that Palestinian queer organizations existed, it was clear that there are Palestinian people who imagine themselves in this realm. Even though I had not yet met them beyond my emails with Sami, the way they constructed themselves politically already pointed to both the globalized gay model and the culturally specific model. But queer people coexist, sometimes with ourselves. Therefore to then acknowledge their activism reflects both desire for something imagined to be fully realized, simultaneous with the acknowledgment of what already exists. Palestinian queers exist and are organizing. Denying that would be stupid. However, any politic that does not fully acknowledge the profound destruction of the occupation and the even deeper desire for autonomy that Palestinian queers share with their fellows/families/larger community, would also be stupid. Keeping these two conditions—Palestine and queer—linked is not only the job of queer Palestinians, but of the global LGBT, of Palestine itself, and of the world.

Now that I have entered into a relationship with Palestine, I am a citizen of what I am thinking of as "the queer international," a play on history, words, and movements past and present. "Queer Nation" was an LGBT activist organization created in the early 1990s by people in ACT UP who wanted a venue to act on queer issues that were not AIDS related. The word "nation" was used tongue in cheek, since queer nationalistic patriotism was unimaginable to people at the epicenter of the AIDS crisis. It implied instead a kind of spiritual place, a queer place with no land or borders that hovered above straight people's geography. Then there is the word "international," well known to communists of all stripes as an identity to strive for, in which nationalist boundaries would be defeated by larger similarities among workers, where the bonds should lie. "The International" was the theme song of world communism, whose lyrics began "*Arise ye prisoners of starvation. Arise ye wretched of the earth.*" The Bolsheviks led the Third International—the global coalition of world communist organizations, but Leon Trotsky's concept of permanent revolution led to the idealism of "the Fourth International," in response to Stalin's corruption of revolutionary principle. In his book *Desiring Arabs,* Joseph Massad, a professor at Columbia University and a Palestinian, describes the "Gay International" as a Western apparatus imposing concepts of homosexuality on Palestinian sex between men. All of these factors converged on my use of the "queer international," a worldwide movement that brings queer liberation and feminism to the principles of international autonomy from occupation, colonialism, and globalized capital. The newest, broadest movement for freedom for all on this earth.

"It's my job," I said to Udi. "This is what I do, and this is what I have to give."

He received an email just that moment, indicated by a light *ding* from his handheld phone. Like all Israelis and Palestinians, the cell phone takes priority over the human. Every call has to be answered no matter what is happening in real time.

"Look," he said. "It's about you."

I looked at the phone. Just that second, Sonya had sent an email announcing "Sarah Schulman to go to Bil'in." News to me, but I was glad that someone had made the decision. We went back to eating olives.

"What about honor killing?" he asked. "What about women? What about feminism?"

I surprise myself by blurting out and realizing in the same moment that "right now, that is not my job."

"Okay," he said as his jet lag finally set in. "I support you." Then he laughed. "It's your job." He lay back on the couch. "But what if you fail?"

Good question. What if I am inappropriate, incoherent, egotistical, bourgeois, and too American? What if I am overstepping, failing to listen, and operating under the wrong assumptions?

"Then at least I tried," I said. "Maybe the fifth person after me who tries will succeed."

"Okay," he said. "But if you fail, don't be upset."

I thought, He means that politically, not personally. Don't make a scene if it doesn't go your way.

I took it in. And I nodded my promise.

5. SOLIDARITY VISIT

My second night of Passover was spent on the El Al red-eye from London to Tel Aviv.

"We wish you all a very happy holiday," the pilot said over the loudspeaker. "And assure that that all your food is kosher for Pesach."

Then the flight attendants handed out the matzoh. Getting through security in London brought back the same feelings I'd had on my first visit to Israel twelve years before. There is something about the sight of young Jewish people in these military, police, and security positions that repulses me. It makes me feel afraid, not secure. In fact, I realize perhaps again, that Jewish authority, Jewish police, Jews in uniforms, Jewish governments, all these things bothered me. I am truly an American Jew in this way. I prefer to be one of many.

"What are you doing in Israel?" the Israeli security agent in London asked; she could have been a social worker from Brooklyn had she been born in the diaspora. But since she was born in Israel, she was carrying a gun.

"I am going to visit my cousins," I replied with a sentence I had practiced repeatedly in preparation for this moment.

"What are their names?" I gave full names to AZ in Tel Aviv and LA in Kibbutz Mizrah, knowing that they sound perfectly Zionist.

She laughed. People also laughed twelve years ago when I said "Kibbutz Mizrah." I guess fewer and fewer tourists go to visit family members on a kibbutz, although I wasn't sure that's why she laughed. It could be a trick of some kind, I thought. Or she might be human. I wasn't sure.

"Do you speak Hebrew?" she asked.

"No."

"Nothing? You didn't even go to Hebrew school when you were little?"

"*Ahnee lo medeberate eevreet*," I said in my horrible nonaccent. It wasn't the complete truth. I could also say *good morning, good evening, the pencil is on the table,* and *Hear Oh Israel, the Lord our God, the Lord is One.* She let me go by.

I arrived in Israel at 5:30 A.M., had no problem getting through customs, and took a cab to Udi's generously lent apartment just blocks from the beach. Outside was what seemed to be the movie set of an idealized Tel Aviv. The most beautiful streets, the most intelligent architecture, the loveliest plazas, the most attractive cafés, the gorgeous beach where one could walk for hours past the religious people enjoying Pesach. Gay people can hold hands, and the religious just look away. This is the theater set of liberated Tel Aviv: beautiful, sophisticated, tolerant.

Thursday night at 5, I went out to meet with the Mesolelot (Tribads). I arrived at an airy apartment to find four women waiting for me around a large bottle of iced tea. One of them was Sonya, the organizer of my solidarity visit. Sonya turned out to be a very likeable young butch woman, a Russian immigrant, whose commitment to the community is continually revealed through the course of the evening. She explained that she not only works as an activist in the anti-occupation movement but also is a master's student in modern British literature at Tel Aviv University and works with LGBT kids in one of two government-funded service organizations. Next to her was Tal, a pansexual, slightly manic, extremely articulate, and smart, hardcore politico; she had that "dangerous femme" aura, evidenced by the fact that her blouse was open two buttons too many throughout the conversation. Also in the room were a self-described "Moroccan" woman, J, whose English was not strong enough for us to communicate much, and a bisexual daughter of South African immigrants. They all seemed to be between twenty-five and thirty-five.

Before this trip, I, having entirely ignored Israel, knew nothing about a good many things, among them the Ashkenazi/Sephardic/Mizrahi breakdown in Israel. I quickly learned that it permeates everything. I grew up aware of some friends of my mother's who spoke Ladino. They were described to me as "Sephardic." I knew that there were Sephardic Jews and Ashkenazi Jews, but I never had any inkling that there was any conflict between the two groups. I certainly did not know that there were many Arab Jews who were not descendants of Spanish escapees of the Inquisition, but were instead indigenous to the Middle East, going back two thousand years. In the very Ashkenazi world that I grew up in, the number one division between Jews was between Germans and Russians. German Jews were cultured, spoke languages (Yiddish didn't count), and played instruments, and Russian Jews were *grubayink* (common) and trying to make a living. In fact, I had never heard the word *Mizrahi* (except to know that the name of East Germany in Yiddish was "Mizrach Daitchland") until I came to Israel. My friend and colleague Dalia Kandiyoti, who had started me off on this journey, had helped me to see the Ashkenazi dominance of Judaic studies. I was also vaguely aware of the work of Ella Shohat and the interest some Arab Jews had in reconnecting as part of the Arab people, but I had no idea that Arab Jews, Sephardim, and Mizrachis were discriminated against by Ashkenazis in Israel or that the enactments of this discrimination were highly racialized. In a way, I didn't even know enough to wonder. It was part of knowing nothing about Israel. It was just ignorance. Once again I have no excuse. J was the first of many Israelis to introduce themselves to me as "Moroccan." At first I didn't know why, but then finally understood that this was reclamation of a demeaned category. I started to hear nightmarish stories of marginalization: Ashkenazis who won't date Mizrachis, the diminishment of Mizrachis as crass and tacky. Stories of Mizrachi parents keeping their children out of the sun so their skin won't darken. These are paradigms right out of American white supremacy.

I asked the small group what their goals are, what they need. Their answers: "Visibility" rearticulated in many different ways. Parity with gay men, some recognition from society, a chance to be seen, to exist. Simple existence, integration, basic acknowledgment. These desires poured out of them. In fact, their answers to my short questions were long, passionate, and filled with the need for change, for a place to be. Even in liberated Tel Aviv.

When we talked about the occupation, they said they wanted to make the "connections between struggles"; I noted their use of this kind of old-left language, and their clearly hard-won acceptance of the wrong that is the occupation. But they didn't have political visions, they didn't know how to develop strategies. They were filled with a longing for some kind of liberation but lacked the experience and training to be able to imagine it. They didn't have a concrete goal or an understanding of how to work toward a goal. It had taken every ounce of drive, personal integrity, intellectual honesty, and personal truth that each of them could muster just to get this far: to be out as queer *and* as anti-occupation. In other words, they were smart, they were brave, they had integrity, they knew the difference between right and wrong, but they didn't have the experience or opportunity necessary to build an effective and mature political movement.

At one point the conversation moved to this curious link between the occupation and lesbian life in Israel. This is a new variation on the theme of bringing together queer and Palestine, but it enriched and enhanced my understanding of this intrinsic relationship. They spoke of Israelis as "post trauma." They said that everyone is shut down in part as a result of their experiences in the army. And then they said something that I will hear over and over again — that in Israel everyone lives as though "it" could all end at any time. "It" meaning life itself, the land of Israel, the beach, Tel Aviv Gay Pride, the beautiful cafés. To me it sounds more like a vision for apocalypse rather than reality, but then I remember that the men running this country would rather be destroyed than compromise. Given their circumstances and their path, Israel could actually drive itself to its own destruction. Since they are the ones in control, annihilation is actually possible.

Suddenly the conversation shifted, and this room of lesbian women turned into a gathering of ex-soldiers. Lesbians are quasi-out in military training, they said. But sometimes this disappears by the time of active duty — even though the government, in its need for soldiers, has no anti-gay restriction on who can serve. It needs every soldier it can get. But the culture of lesbians in the army includes those with an inclination toward combat units, with a competitive desire to achieve in the military, and with a hope that having done military service can somehow normalize them in Israeli society and mitigate the stigma of their being queer. Some-one makes a joke about the "crush on the commander" as something that bonds women soldiers in general, something even the straight ones like to talk about.

"That's why motherhood is everything here," Tal said. "You can't ever have a real role here unless you have children, because mothers produce soldiers, and that is what the country wants."

"Even more," J said. "Mothers are valued because they create soldiers, but also because they create Jews."

Suddenly Tal started to talk about her military service in Gaza. How she saw a Palestinian man, his shirt torn off, on his knees, hands handcuffed behind his back. How she, based on who she was at that time, simply assumed that he had done something wrong and deserved to be treated that way. But by the time we were talking, she realized that he could have done nothing. Or that he could have done something that was an action to free himself from the occupation. Now, looking back, she asks herself, "How did his shirt get torn off his body?" — a question she never asked herself then. There is a haunted quality to this story. She didn't say it, but it was apparent that her activism in the anti-occupation movement is an attempted corrective to the pain she caused Palestinians unjustly in the past. But how many Israelis come to the understanding that they can turn poison into medicine? Not many.

"They relive the trauma," one woman said. "People tell their army stories over and over again." She worked in intelligence and knew about an assassination days before it occurred, she said. She went to America and, when she returned, was called back again into the reserves and fought in the most recent war in Lebanon. At the time she did not question her own role. Now she knows.

These women carry this knowledge into not only their current political activities but also into their love relationships.

"Is it possible," I asked, "for lesbians to have a healthy relationship in Israel today?"

They all shook their heads no. Then they all said "no" at the same time. And then there was an almost palpable sadness. "No."

Later I found a blog post from one of the women at the apartment.

I met *Sarah Schulman* yesterday in Tel-Aviv.

I and a few other lesbian identified (boy this is complicated for me) women are trying to get together a grass roots movement off the ground, aimed at creating lesbian visibility which is *lacking* in the gay community and generally speaking (my aim is also to weed out biphobia and bisexual erasure with in the lesbian community) and make feminism accessible to young women — feminism is very much perceived to be a high brow theoretical thing, something that only the educated can be and something that doesn't actually help women, or anyone, from a lower socio-economic base.

Sad, but true. We're very backwards here when it comes to feminism on the street.

Any way. Ms. Schulman came to speak with us and it was a really wonderful experience. We were five women in a Tel-Aviv apartment lounge and Ms. Schulman. It was very intimate.

I had no idea who she was until my fellow group member told me she was coming to Israel on a solidarity trip to Israel/Palestine. We spoke the structure of oppression, the disinformation, the fact that we are such a teeny-tiny minority (radical queers, anti-Occupation activists — I should do more), how the IDF [Israeli Defense Force] stratifies class mobility, how class is tied with ethnicity, what it means to have served, what it means to not have served, the PTSD mentality that's infected people here, that is and how LGBTQ rights are used as propaganda to the outside world to show how fucking liberal Israel *really* is.

When we're not.

At all.

Hence the fact that the murderer of the gay youth club shooting is still at large. Fuck, I can't believe it's been *eight months* and still nothing. There are kids who are still in rehab wards in the hospitals and they're not going to be getting social security welfare because this shooting doesn't count as an "Act of Terror" when it fucking *was*!

Yes. Okay. The past year was a big kick in the ass for me when it came to treatment of queers in Israel, *by* the State and from society at large.

I asked her about her book *Ties That Bind: Familial Homophobia and Its Consequences*, which I've just ordered. She was very informative and made me feel better about the fact that I don't actually *want* an "alternative" family.

My family has enough estrangement and I can't bear the thought of not having them in my life.

Homophobia in the family, like everything else, isn't a personal thing. It's a political thing. And it really needs to be exposed for what it is and not just focus on the fact that "oh, parents, siblings etc. just need to *get used to the idea.*

I don't have time for people to get used to the fact that I fucking exist.

Any way, it was fascinating and we spoke about being gay, radical and how we want to include women from every where and be more direct action, which we should have asked more about because of Schulman's involvement in ACT UP and Lesbian Avengers.

I think I'll email her at some point.

This was a bit angry, a bit not. Well, mostly angry. But it was a really good meeting. It's a real privilege to meet people like her.

feeling: moody

hearing: David Bowie (feat. Trent Reznor) — I'm Afraid of Americans

Of course, reading this is moving, but it is also informative. Not only about how she is struggling with the contradictions, her desire to know what's true — but also the very stark admission that the Israeli government is using the hard-won gains of the LGBT community to, in her words, "show how *fucking* liberal Israel is." And how Nine Inch Nails inspires across borders.

After I've met with the women of Mesolelot for a couple of hours, I realize it is time for my second event in Tel Aviv. Our small group walks over to the industrial district where the venue is situated. My cousin in New York had told me, "If you speak at Tel Aviv University you will have a full room, if they put you in some café you will speak to ten people."

At first it seemed that my cousin was correct. We arrived at the Rogatka Veggie Bar, an entirely under-the-radar queer anarchist vegan café. "Rogatka" means "slingshot," as in David and Goliath. Basically, the café was a room with a stage and a makeshift bar with an abbreviated cook stove. The event was scheduled for 7:30, and when we got there at 7:20, there were four people waiting: three professors and my friend Mookie from New York. The profs were three of the organizers of the LGBT studies conference that I had declined. I thought they were wonderful to come to attend my talk and to connect. Two were women I did not know previously, one a gender studies professor whom the Mesolelot girls had lovingly praised.

"I have been thinking," she said. "Maybe there is a way to move our conference out of Tel Aviv University. Right now they pay our speakers fees, but maybe there is a way."

I was so moved by her honesty and again concerned that queer people find it increasingly hard to imagine events without government funding. ACT UP never asked for government funding; the Lesbian Avengers never sought any corporate underwriting and wouldn't even ask for permits to demonstrate. This was just not in my mind-set.

Another professor, an out lesbian who was born into a religious family, was also supportive. "We totally understand," she says. "We agree with you. We don't want people to think we are the bad guys." And of course this has been one of my fears since the beginning, that the queer professors would get scapegoated somehow. The third conference organizer was my dear old friend Amit, who had come only out of friendship to me, which was deeply moving.

"You are going to speak to ten people," he said, both as a provocation and a confirmation. "There has been no publicity."

However, by the time we started the event, an hour and ten minutes late ("Israeli time"), there were about sixty people in the room, ranging in age from twenty to seventy, lesbian, gay, bi, trans, perhaps straight, anarchist, feminist, militantly anti-occupation, as well as lesbians who just came to hear me speak on the advertised subject, "Familial Homophobia and Its Consequences." So, my greatest fear about participating in the boycott, the fear of not being heard, was put to rest.

"It's the same people," one of the conference organizers said, looking around. "The same people who would have heard you at the conference. You would have had a bit more of an audience, but many of the same."

That evening I met many "queerim" and "queerite" — Israeli queers who do not identify with the nationalist and assimilationist Israeli LGBT movement. I also briefly met Haneen Maikay, a young woman in her early thirties with long brown hair and a pierced eyebrow, who, someone explained to me, is one of the Palestinian queer leaders. Our first encounter was brief and uneventful but Haneen would later become one of the most significant political partners of my life, and we would collaborate together profoundly and effectively for a long time to come.

Finally, two hours late, Sonya introduced me to the audience at the Rogatka, and I began my talk by explaining briefly why I was at the vegan café and not at Tel Aviv University. Then I briefly summarized some of the key arguments in my book about familial homophobia, principally the idea that familial homophobia is *not*, as queers have been told, a personal problem, but that it is a cultural crisis. That the stigma needs to be shifted from homosexuality to homophobia, with the latter being acknowledged for what it is: an antisocial pathology that causes violence and destroys families. And that to accomplish this we need a range of third-party interventions that can include speaking to one another's families. I talked about taking on the authority that some of us now have to normalize the idea that homophobia, not homosexuality, is the problem. Many of us in secure positions, me included, are people who are entirely out of the closet, yet we still hedge on certain occasions and privilege the prejudice. Perhaps someday we could actualize the belief that society, maybe even the state, should be acting on our behalf instead of against us. I spoke for fifteen minutes and then opened it up to questions.

Immediately it was clear to me that the audience understood my argument. Their criticisms and comments were on point and helpful. There is a kind of classic style of critique that certain kinds of queer audiences engage that is also quite Jewish. They look for flaws, not for strengths, which is fine, because when they do compliment something, you know they really mean it. The first comment was that "the family *is* the problem," meaning, of course, the nuclear family, and I, of course, agree. Yet, while I hope for a better future, I still recognize that the world of the family is the world in which we live today and in which gay people are punished even though we haven't done anything wrong.

One of the things I found myself offering to the audience was how much I understood their situation. "I have spent my life as an American," I said, "with a government constantly violating international law. A government consistently killing civilians. Today I have a president, *whom I voted for*, who is running wars in Iraq and Afghanistan that I oppose." I saw the nods.

The next dependable reaction from a queer audience is the one asking for broader representation. We are a very ambitious gathering of people, attempting to include a wide range of experiences and backgrounds. LGBT people very much want to be in relationship to each other, to know and acknowledge, and they will predictably try to expand any presentation to include a wider range of concerns than the ones the presenter has mastered. This was evident in two comments criticizing any attempt to globalize or universalize one approach to homophobia based on one idea of family. A grad student in gender studies, Yael Mishali, introduced herself as "Moroccan" and then warned me not to think there was one model of family or of homophobia, or of appropriate response. I accepted this, of course. But I did sort of insist that there *is* a universal reality, which is that in every country and every ethnicity group, the perception of heterosexuals as "neutral, natural, objective, value free, and just the way things are" is a problem for queers however they are constructed. To this, the whole room agreed. It was an extension of the conversation Udi and I had had about homosexuality being dismissed or acknowledged as "Western." As the LGBT movement unites across racial and ethnic borders, the need to both acknowledge queers and not contain them in one method of acknowledgment is ever under discussion.

There also were comments by some transgender people. An older transwoman therapist, perhaps in her sixties, and a younger transman in his twenties, stated that homophobia in the family has overlap with but is not equal to transphobia in the family, which is also right. What I have found consistently over the decades with queer audiences is that the wish to be seen and acknowledged is predominant. There is a denunciatory style, in which a person insisting on something sounds accusatory. But I have learned over time that the tone of insistence is not a condemnation of what the addressed speaker does not yet understand. Instead, it becomes a way for the excluded person in the audience to still connect, without giving up himself or herself. It's an acquired manner and could be seen as generous.

Then, finally, the conversation turned to the boycott. For me the most valuable moment of the evening was when my friend Amit, who was clearly more mainstream than the vast majority of the Rogatka audience, talked about the consequences of the boycott on him personally. He said that it affected him as an academic. That he felt the pressure. When he travels abroad or goes to conferences, he finds himself under a specific kind of scrutiny as an Israeli. He is put in a position he is uncomfortable with, one in which he finds himself confronted and could even end up defensively defending the Israeli government. Some of the audience was rude to him, wanting to disassociate from his comments. One articulate transman, Yotam, explained that boycott is "against institutions, not individuals," which was helpful. "Boycott me!" Yotam said. "You are doing the right thing. Boycott me!"

I decided to start posting short reports from my visit to Facebook—starting with the information that one could boycott and still communicate. Over the course of the trip, I would post repeatedly on my experiences in Israel and Palestine and on my process of revelation. Although I received many positive and encouraging messages and comments publicly, I also received a large number of private messages expressing doubts and even anger. In every case, it was "Boycott Me" that critical people found the most compelling. That Israelis, and especially Israeli academics, were asking this from us was enormously powerful. "Boycott Me" had the potential to be the most potent element in the sanctions process. If only it could become better organized and more visible.

Yet, at the same time that Yotam's comments were reassuring, I was interested in how informative Amit's reaction was. He was giving us honest, crucial information that needed to be heard. Not only was the boycott affecting academics who did not endorse it, but it was placing these people in a position of having to have conversations that they didn't want to have and didn't know how to have. Perhaps it was because this is where I had started five months before, and here it was April 1, and I was in an entirely different reality, that I found his comments particularly relevant. Certainly, in my case, having to face the boycott was an opportunity for enormous growth and understanding. As Dalit Baum had pointed out earlier, it created an opportunity to educate and learn.

In the end, I felt very clearly that I had been heard and that I had listened. I had talked with and to the people I had hoped to meet initially, and I had done this without violating the boycott. This was an enormous relief to me. My primary concern about participating in the boycott had been the question of cutting off dialogue and abandoning Israelis who are in my community. Now, I knew that one could boycott and still communicate. It became clear to me that solidarity visits should be institutionalized, with a kind of Underground Railroad of venues set in place. In this way it would become much easier for people to participate in sanctions. The rejection and then rapprochement with Israeli queers had been a success.

Next stop: Palestine.

6. PALESTINE

It was a gorgeous Friday morning in Tel Aviv. I was eating homemade gourmet matzoh brie. It was still Passover, after all. Only the Arab stands had bread. Sonia, Tal, and two friends picked me up for the ride to the West Bank village of Bil'in. They asked me, twenty-five years older than they, to sit in the front seat to make us more palatable to checkpoints. I was the middle-aged beard. The story, in case we got stopped, was that we were on our way to visit friends in the settlements. The driver had prepared a "Friday demonstration tape" that he plays every week as they make this voyage. It starts with Israeli songs that contain the Hebrew word for "Friday," then plays some transitional Beatles tunes. Finally, the soundtrack switches over to Arab music just in time to make it into the West Bank. We took a roundabout way to avoid smaller, more direct checkpoints that may have this license plate on record, and traveled the mainstream highway into Palestine.

The first sign that we are arriving, of course, was the "fence," the "security wall," or the "wall of separation" purposely visible on both sides of the modern highway. In some places the highway is Israel, and the fenced-in areas are the occupied lands. Occasional signs indicate turnoffs to various settlements, but none indicates access to the Arab villages, often with the same names, sitting quietly across the street. The landscape is stunning: rocky hillsides filled with olive trees, and eclectically developed villages. The Arab villages look older and are more mixed in size and style of buildings. From the highway, the settlements look like cookie-cutter gated communities, a kind of nationalist Levittown with signature homogenous red roofs. There is still a lot of open space visible from the highway. Is this someone's home, or is it empty land waiting to be filled by the settlements? We started to see settlers hitch-hiking. They seemed so confident. Even this woman, in her long skirts, hitch-hiking alone.

"No way," the driver said, zooming past.

Strangely, I feared for her, as I consider religious men to be very dangerous.

After taking an hour to complete a normally half-hour drive, we pulled into Bil'in, a village of sixteen hundred people who have been holding weekly demonstrations against the wall every Friday for five years. The physical distance from the beach chairs on the sands of Tel Aviv is small, but the psychological and emotional distance is incalculable. Many people here will never see that beach.

There is trash along the streets and the slight smell of open sewers. Young children quickly approached us, offering to sell crocheted wristbands with the Palestinian flag and a heart.

"No thanks."

"What is your name? What is your name?" They insisted, fearless. And why should they have been afraid? Bil'in is their village.

We went to a community house for internationals to use the toilet. It was covered with posters, and the front door had clearly been bashed in, the lock ripped off by Israeli soldiers. Sometimes the demonstrations were tiny, sometimes they were quiet, but sometimes there was violence, and people got seriously hurt. But whatever happened, week after week the demonstrations continued. The spiritual and psychological strength it takes to protest an entrenched wall defended by soldiers was part of daily life to the people of Bil'in.

We walked down the road to the home of W, a villager who offers breakfast and tea to this handful of activists every Friday morning before the demonstration. His son's wife had just had triplets, and they were on happy display. His other son was arrested at a weekly demonstration two months before, and W had no idea when he would be freed. His wife shook our hands upon arrival and then disappeared into the kitchen. We sat with the men, and a half hour later a daughter appeared with a tray of mint tea. One of the demonstrators, an Arab man from Jaffa with his Jewish wife, poured it out for all of us. An hour later, it was time for Tal to give new demonstrators their orientation: what to do about tear gas, what to do about violence, but W objected.

"Eat first."

So we waited, and finally amazing food appeared: za'atar, huge breads, *shakshuka* (an Arab version of huevos rancheros), olives, tomatoes, and fried potatoes. It was delicious. We finished just as the demonstration began. A parade of about eighty people—men, women, and children from the village and Palestinians from other towns—made up the bulk of the marchers. But there were also a number of internationals, mostly Germans wearing Palestinian scarves, and some Israelis—half of whom were obviously queer.

The marchers got as far as the top of a hill. This, I was told, is the "safe zone," and I decided to stop there. Since Sonya and Tal have gone to the front lines, facing off the armed Israeli soldiers, I am babysat by "Shuki," Elisha Alexander, one of the leaders of the Israeli trans community, and his partner, Joanna. They were very caring and very kind. Even though I was armed with alcohol pads in case of tear gas attack, I didn't want to get gassed. This particular gas tells your nervous system that you are choking, but you are not choking, so demonstrators smell an alcohol pad or an onion to change their brain's sensory perception. It's emblematic of the Israeli-Palestinian condition. You have to stick your nose in an onion to stop suffocating. From my spot at the top of the hill, in the shade of a tree and a giant cactus and in the company of some older Palestinian men, I observed the events below. The demonstrators marched down the hill and right up to the wall. Israeli soldiers and sharpshooters were evident from three sides, where they stood behind concrete barriers. The demonstrators held signs, waved Palestinian flags, and sang songs. The children slid down an incline and threw stones. Some of them were young enough to have done this every Friday of their lives. Soldiers started shooting tear gas. I observed a total of five rounds of tear gas canisters, but most of the demonstrators did not disperse. They covered their faces with handkerchiefs and held onions to their noses. The sun was brutal. The Israelis applied sunscreen, water-based only as the oil-based products retain the tear gas on the skin. After about an hour and a half, the demonstration was over. We all walked back together to the center of town, stopping at the village deli, where the internationals bought cans of a sweet coconut drink imported from Thailand. I was led to a group taxi bound for Ramallah, paid my six shekels, and started the next part of my journey—waving goodbye as we tried to weave through the sudden flood of outgoing traffic. It was crowded and chaotic. In thirty minutes it would be empty and calm.

I stayed the night at the Royal Court Suites Hotel, in Ramallah, which is fancy, comfortable, and principally occupied by Palestinian Americans on long-awaited return visits home. The breakfast buffet offered three kinds of labane, fresh yogurt with apples in honey, *zatar*, and olives. At nearly every table, guests with American accents told stories about finding their old house or not finding their mother's house, and how much has changed in forty, forty-five, or fifty years. The place is laid-back. There is one computer with Internet access in the lobby. People use it, then tell the clerk how much time they spent on it, and the clerk either charges or just lets it go.

Sami, my Ramallah contact, turned out to be a young, sweet gay boy, kind, intellectual, and adorable. He had spent the day trying to re-build a park in a village where settlers are attempting to take over a spring. He told me in his truck that the settlers had come down and tried to destroy the park that morning. It was the first time he had ever interacted with them face to face. He was unnerved and exhausted.

"What do you do with your rage?" I asked.

"It's hard," he said.

We stopped to pick up Ramallah's own Taybeh beer and some vegetables and fruit, which were absolutely gorgeous. Bright tomatoes, sharp green onions, rich strawberries. He boycotts all Israeli products. The Palestinian Authority is now officially boycotting settlement products, which Sami said was the only good thing they had done to date. Like most of the queers I am about to meet, he doesn't like Fatah or Hamas and has his own vision for Palestine.

We arrived at the "house" of A, who, like Sami, is an anti-occupation activist. The apartment was more of an office. It looked like a bachelor pad, except that instead of posters of women and football players, there were posters of Palestine, political prisoners, liberation poets, and Che. The very strapping and buff but burdened A had just been arrested and interrogated by Israelis after having secured Norwegian divestment from Elbit, a company busily profiteering in the Occupied Territories. As a full-time activist, he spends a lot of time taking internationals on tours of the wall. A number of European countries are increasing their rates of divestment from Israeli companies, but all of this was news to me, as I had never noticed coverage of it in the U.S. media.

As A talked continually on his cell phone, Sami started a long, laborious process of making a salad. It took two hours. In the meantime, the others arrived: F, a gay man who lived in New York for many years. Hind, a straight woman who was educated at a Seven Sisters school and now works full time for the boycott. And E, a woman educated at a hippie school in the Midwest. B, a soft-spoken woman, arrived late and brought a bottle of wine. The group is highly educated, deeply sophisticated, and able to easily acknowledge the connections between queer and Palestine without using rhetoric. The conversation was so smooth and natural that I couldn't tell who is queer and who is straight. I felt more comfortable with them than I did with their Israeli counterparts: the Palestinians are more familiar. Being with them made me realize that the Israeli anti-occupation queers are a lot more marginal. The Israelis, of course, are twice marginalized, being anti-occupation *and* queer. Being openly queer keeps them on the fringe of Israeli society, but being anti-occupation really makes them freaks. As a result, the realm of politics in which they can operate is prescribed. The Palestinians, on the other hand, are deeply integrated into the struggle of their nation and their families. The queers have enormous conflicts with their families; many are closeted, but not all. Yet they have a secure and recognized role as anti-occupation workers, and so are not alienated politically in that way. It makes a huge difference.

We had a great conversation — alive, honest, and creative — that went on for hours. So many interesting things came up. Their number one strategy, A. explained, is to organize American students. Hind and A told me about recent victories on U.S. campuses. I was only vaguely aware of this activity and didn't know if I was underinformed, as I have been on every aspect of Palestine, or if they were overestimating. Yes, I did know that Hampshire College divested. They are using the South Africa divestment movement of the 1970s and '80s as their model, and certainly I remembered that one well. Activists such as GRIT-TV anchor Laura Flanders cut their teeth on divestment at Columbia in the early 1980s. It's a smart and savvy choice. Hind reported that Berkeley students held a meeting until 3 in the morning and finally voted to divest, but that the president of the university vetoed it. She attributed the veto to AIPAC — the center of the U.S. Israel lobby and public enemy number one in this room. She also talked about great student victories at other schools, including Carleton University in Canada and the University of Michigan at Dearborn. E talked about visiting the University of Michigan at Dearborn when she was studying in the United States. "There are so many Arabs there," she said. "When you walk down the street you don't feel like you are in America. You feel like you are in . . . Arabia."

As we were talking, I started thinking as an American. I believe that many Americans are disturbed and disgusted with Israeli government policies but don't know what to do with their feelings. That certainly described me . . . for decades. We discussed this particular obstacle. Some of the activists have almost written off America as a lost cause. They are focusing on Europe. Others know that making progress in America is key but don't know how to do it. As we talked, certain specific problems come into focus. Palestinians have no human face to Americans. We are, after all, a celebrity culture. And we are not a sophisticated people in the way that we make political choices. Given those two fundamentals, what would make it possible for Americans to move to a place where Palestinians are included in our understanding of people deserving and needing freedom? In that conversation, I heard the acronym PEP for the first time: "Progressive Except Palestine."

From my point of view there were two figures missing in the conversation. The first was an identifiable Palestinian spokesperson who could become the "go-to" person for the U.S. media, someone that people who watch CNN, Charlie Rose, Rachel Maddow, and *Meet the Press* would become familiar with. In a sense, a Palestinian Naomi Klein: an attractive, intelligent media figure whom Americans can identify with and relate to. Someone like the people in this room. I remembered watching Arafat on television; he was so unpalatable to American tastes. Up to then, for me the most effective Palestinian figure in the media was Edward Said, despite his imperious streak, and then Hanan Ashwari. But what about a younger, hipper, sophisticated, funny, attractive U.S.-educated man or woman who knows American culture and can simply make the case, with charm? Maybe someone openly gay? Someone with an American accent. Hind, who would be perfect as this person, explained to me that the movement deliberately does not want to develop such a figure. That it is a "movement" of many and doesn't want to single out individuals in this way. I entirely understood and, of course, agreed. And yet I was torn because I know that Americans favor personalities over principles. This is always the question, isn't it? How dangerous is it to adjust one's politics to fit corrupt situations? It's a question I can't answer, even for myself. But Hind is so smart, articulate, attractive, and persuasive, and she has an American accent from having been educated at Bryn Mawr. I know that she would be the perfect media representative for BDS in New York.

The second thing missing was a credible American celebrity speaking out for Palestine. There is no one famous and reliable who is there to give other Americans permission to move forward on this subject. Like what Richard Gere has done for the Dali Lama. Or what George Clooney is doing for Darfur. We started thinking of possible potential candidates.

"Britney Spears?" Sami suggested and laughed.

Yes, it is absurd, and yet not. We came up with a list of intelligent, credible Americans who have shown interest in Palestine and are so famous that no right-wing organization could discredit them. Our number one choice? Alice Walker. She's famous enough that it can't be taken away. Someone in the room said that Walker had been to Gaza. They weren't sure of her position on Palestine, but hopeful.

Finally, the salad was ready. We each drank a glass of wine and spooned it out. The atmosphere was relaxed. We were comfortable together, trying to problem-solve. E knew from experience that Palestine-Israel is America's low moment of unawareness and, like every Palestinian who has lived in the United States, had many stories of incredibly annoying comments she had to endure from her well-meaning college colleagues.

"'I feel bad for you,'" one said. "'And I think you should have a state.'"

"If you are saying that I should have a state," she retorted years later, "then you know nothing."

We talked about Birzeit University. I had never heard back from Professor Nimr, and I wasn't sure if she just didn't get back to me, or if she *didn't get back to me*. Sami said that a gay group also tried working with Birzeit and had been ignored. So I knew it wasn't just me. We then talked about Judith Butler's recent series of lectures there just a few weeks before, which most of the people in the room attended and loved. She was spoken about with great admiration. Could Judith Butler be the potential celebrity?

"She's a superstar in the academy and a great leader," I said. "But she's not Richard Gere."

"She was amazing," Hind said.

"I was surprised that she didn't bring up gender," Sami said. "She just talked about politics."

That was true. While she did have smaller "queer" conversations, her largest, most public talk did not make the connection.

"Is she a lesbian?" Hind asked.

"She's the most important lesbian intellectual in the United States, maybe the world," I said.

This spurred another round of engaged conversation, again about the pressing question of "gay imperialism," which now was taking on even more definitions. Is "gay imperialism" what's going on when Israel claims to be a fair and democratic country because a gay couple can hold hands on the beach in Tel Aviv? Is it gay imperialism when someone like me comes and makes suggestions about finding celebrity spokespeople so that

Americans can listen? Is gay imperialism at work when someone decides not to come out when speaking to a Palestinian audience, even one that includes queer people? Is gay imperialism coming out, or is it not coming out? What should the rest of us assume about a Palestinian audience?

This line of thought led me to move on to the subject most pressing on my mind: my meeting the following day with Omar Barghouti of PACBI. I explained the situation and my goal: to get a statement from PACBI acknowledging LGBT support of the boycott. I reiterated my reasons: if queer people are turning down queer events in favor of boycott, we want to be sure that we're not repeating the historical error of supporting movements that treat their own queer communities badly. We don't want to be in the closet in our support, and it will be easier to be persuasive with the broader LGBT community in arguing for boycott if PACBI acknowledges queer support. Mutual recognition. And if it can't do that, can it acknowledge support for queer Palestinians in this city? I was still trying to figure out how to integrate it all. I asked for advice.

Hind, perhaps because she was straight, was certain this will be no problem with PACBI. She seemed confident that it would be easy. The queers, however, were not so sure. The frustrating experience of being ignored by folks at Birzeit might be an indication of how straight organizations will respond. At the time, queers in Ramallah were working with John Greyson and Elle Flanders to create a BDS Film Festival that would offer an alternative to the state-sponsored and highly boycottable Tel Aviv LGBT Film Festival. The gay group's strategy was to be in coalition, unofficially, with PACBI. They would do the work, but their names wouldn't be on the coalition. In return, some queer films would be included. That is generally their strategy, to do their work but stay under the radar. My impression was that this is in place so that PACBI can work with them without having the name of any gay organization next to theirs. The projected BDS festival had not been able to get going.

Every person in the room spoke passionately and emotionally about Palestine. All of them were deeply involved in anti-occupation organizations. But some had decided that they, as a group, should not take official pro-boycott positions. Why? It had something to do with their branches in Israel and potential problems with funding, licensing, and Israeli bureaucracy. I wasn't clear on the specifics, but fear of reprisal of some kind was at stake. Hind, who is on staff at a boycott organization, pushes the organizations on this. She thinks the relationship between queer groups and the boycott apparatus should be a two-way street. PACBI, she is sure, will comply with my request and the queers should respond with a pro-boycott statement. The gay people in the room were not confident that PACBI would come through, and they didn't want to make an official boycott statement. It was unclear who was telling whom what to do. And it was intriguingly unclear which party was more endangered by the relationship with the other. I asked Hind to come to the PACBI meeting the next day. I was hoping that her confidence would be persuasive.

The conversation moved on to secular Jews. The hippie-school girl had had it with American Jews who knew that something is very wrong with Israel but were unwilling to take the step of speaking out or acting. I tried to say that this constituency has a lot of promise for the future, but they too need a daddy. They need someone with credibility whom they trust to give them permission to take a step that they already know is right. They need a Jewish Richard Gere. A viable path seemed very possible all of a sudden: students, whom A calls "the leaders of the future," queers, who I feel will be more responsive to boycott and sanctions if they feel that PACBI supports queers, African Americans, whose leadership would be so transformative in this effort. Despite efforts by such individual African American figures as June Jordan and Alice Walker to advocate for Palestine, the mainstream African American communities had not gotten involved. But this too could change. Suddenly I could picture it. A variety of disenfranchised communities coming around to reality on a variety of different paths. I was excited, encouraged, inspired.

It was, by then, late. The salad was finally eaten. F, the guy who had lived in Greenwich Village for seven years, had a question to ask me before we all went to bed.

"What happens tomorrow," he asked, "if you talk to PACBI, and Omar says no?" It's the same question Udi Aloni had asked me on Passover.

"I'm a grownup," I said. "If he says no this time, maybe the next time someone else asks, he will say yes."

That is, after all, how gay politics has always worked, isn't it? The cumulative effort of the generations. But I took his warning to heart.

7. FINDING THE STRATEGY

The two words I repeated over and over again as I left my meeting with PACBI were: *you failed. You failed.* Sarah, *you failed!*

Omar and Hind showed up promptly at 1 at the café of the Royal Court Suites Hotel. This time Hind was a bit solemn, businesslike, not the relaxed, freewheeling person I had seen the night before. And when Omar arrived, the reason for the tonal shift was clear. For the first time since I had left New York, I was in a conversation that was actually uncomfortable. There was none of the frank camaraderie of the lesbians in Tel Aviv talking about their military histories, none of the generous correctives offered by Mizrachi and trans Jews at the Rogatka, none of the relaxed "we're in this together" breakfast at W's house in Bil'in. None of the sophisticated, excited banter of the Palestinian activists the night before. No, I can honestly say that this was the first conversation I'd had that was ... how to put it? Uptight.

Omar is a fierce, intelligent, confident, kind of terse man, married with kids, who has a slightly annoyed snap in his voice when he wants to. I wasn't sure if this articulated condescension was because I was a Jew and an American and therefore too powerful and someone to be deflated appropriately, or because he knew I had credibility only with queers, that straight people do not recognize me, and that therefore my usefulness was limited so I didn't deserve his full respect. But Jew, lesbian, or whatever the problem was, he conveyed his distaste with clarity. This immediately put me in the position—due to the flaws of my own psychology—of trying to find a way to please him, to get the "we're in this together" vibe going so we could solve problems. I started out with a report on my activities, thereby creating him as the authority, which sometimes is what straight men need to relax. I reported on the success of the Rogatka event and suggested that alternative venues become institutionalized so that more people could boycott, knowing they could still communicate.

"No," he said. "PACBI does not have a set of approved venues, nor do we blacklist. We look at each case individually and take their nuances into account."

I nodded, deciding that I was not going to disagree with him about anything. But I did think, *That's fine when you have five boycott visits a year, but what are you going to do when you have fifty?*

Then I raised the question of a Palestinian go-to person in the U.S. media. I then returned to my crass Americanism, suggesting again that, like Israel, BDS could brand a media representative, get a press agent to have this person's name in the database of every reporter in the country. Someone so established as *the* media contact, that every time AIPAC issues a report, this person would be automatically called for a response. This was a tactic I had learned early in my experience doing grassroots politics in America, something I had recognized in the abortion rights movement. When your opponent spends the time and money to create an event for himself, let the press know that you are the other side. Use the media to create space. It conforms to the press's false conception of itself as "objective." My enthusiasm, however, did not sell my idea. So much for marketing. Omar repeated the objection that Hind had voiced the night before: that the movement did not want to develop someone with this kind of power. Individuals should not represent movements. And, of course, he is right. The problem is that there is no mass of Palestinians in the United States to represent. So they end up never being heard, or else being translated by third parties. In the AIDS movement, there were spokespeople, but any activist was qualified to speak to the media. Since the people being victimized by U.S. military aid to Israel are not visible in the United States en masse, it makes sense to create a spokesperson. Omar and Hind then mentioned a few people whose names I did not recognize. Our definitions of "celebrity" were clearly culturally differentiated. One thing we all agreed on was total lack of coverage in the U.S. media. Omar was even having trouble getting into such fundamental publications as the *Nation*.

"I will try with the *Nation*," I said. Note to self: follow up with the *Nation*.

Still, he felt that things were improving.

"It's a very fringe movement in the U.S.," I said. "In the last few months I have spoken to hundreds of people about what I'm doing, and 98 percent of them have never heard of boycott."

"It's not mainstream," he nodded. "But it is no longer fringe."

Then we moved on to the question of the larger celebrity endorser. This sparked a bit more interest, but again, principle predominated strategy. Omar, I then learned, was educated at Columbia University in the 1980s. *Aha, the centerpiece and hotbed of the South Africa divestment movement.* Now I understood. He'd seen the fury and fire of students occupying buildings, holding hunger strikes, building encampments on campus lawns. This was his inspiration and his strategy. Made sense to me.

What then happened was that Omar kind of ranted. I felt that he was hissing at me, and that was okay. He had a right to be angry. And the content of his complaint was as interesting and informative as intelligent, accurate criticism almost always is. First he brought up Naomi Klein — who by now had become a kind of totem ghost, following me ethereally through my experiences, ever hovering but never within reach. He told me about Naomi apologizing for having taken so long to come around to this issue. That she was ashamed. I felt that he wanted me, too, to be ashamed. And the truth is, I was ashamed. I had already realized that months before. So, even though it was an indulgent desire on his part, I gave it to him, since it was also the truth.

"I also feel that way," I said.

"You do?" He smiled.

"Yes." It was the absolute ugly truth.

"As a Jew you have a privilege," he said. These were not his exact words, but the gist of what I believe he meant to tell me. "You have the privilege to speak out on Israel and boycott. Non-Jews don't have this privilege because they are afraid of being called anti-Semitic."

I cannot overstate how much I hate and disagree with this statement. And even as I write this a year and a half later, I am sick of hearing it. As far as I am concerned, most non-Jews *are* anti-Semitic, and this simple assertion of the secret threat of the all-powerful Jew to brand some innocent Christian with the label "anti-Semite" is a good example. They don't seem to be afraid of being anti-Semitic on a wide range of other planes. Only when it comes to criticizing Israel are they suddenly controlled by the thought. I have spent my whole life listening to non-Jews make insulting, distorted assumptions: all Jews are rich, all Jews are smart, Jews operate tribally in a secret cabal, Jews are good at making money (and keeping it: "Jew him down"), Jews make good accountants! We're loud, we're pushy, we know how to succeed, we help our own, and we force the Holocaust down everyone's throat. And most important, we control the media, we control the banks, we control the U.S. government, we run the global show, and so on.

It is clearly true that people who oppose U.S. policy in Israel come up against heavy criticism, sometimes crossing the line into harassment, abuse, and censorship. And the most right-wing groups call them anti-Semites. I observe this, read accounts of this in *Muzzlewatch* every day. Certainly I was experiencing this myself with the still delayed publication of *Gentrification of the Mind*. I had taken out all the Israel content but couldn't get anyone to read the new draft or to even respond. It had been months since the editor had communicated. But this was not an unusual experience. I had experienced this kind of harassment all of my adult life for being out as a lesbian in my work and for articulating critiques of power. I had been censored, blacklisted, fired, demeaned, marginalized, and shunned. That's the price we pay for asking for structural change of power. The fact that there are American or European straight Christians who fear this same experience just tells me that they are so entrenched in their entitlement and privilege that the thought of people being mean to them for telling the truth is more overwhelming than the idea of remaining silent. It's not as if they're going to be imprisoned, denied free movement, or experience physical violence, all of which Palestinians do face. It's just about being demeaned. So what? This "fear" says a lot about privilege in America and almost nothing about anti-Semitism. Of course there are people who stupidly conflate criticism of Israel with anti-Semitism and use this as a smokescreen argument. But its consequences are no more severe than homophobia or racism in silencing people. That is to say, they are unjustified, cruel, dishonest and petty, but not more so than the men who run the American theater or any other institution that excludes and discriminates. To make right-wing Jews so uniquely distinct and all-powerful is a distortion.

Of course, for Omar, powerful right-wing Jews are brutal colonizers, killers, and culture destroyers. But in the American context, they are no worse than any other bullying entity. Being called a "self-hating Jew" is no worse than being called an angry lesbian or man hater or being ignored by the cultural establishment for having lesbian content. However, instead of raising all this with Omar, I decided to use my internal energy to use this very moment to make my tactical big move.

"Well, Omar, here's the reason I wanted to meet with you today."

I explained to Omar that LGBT people were increasingly being asked to boycott queer events and were doing so. I told him that in April, only a month away, I would speak at a Harvard Conference, "Gay Rights Are Human Rights," at the Kennedy School, and that boycott would be among my subjects. That I would love to have something I could show or read to the audience about PACBI's support or recognition of queers. That there is a shift and a division in the human rights movement globally about whether gay people are "human"—that there is an effort to expand international definitions of human rights to full inclusivity, and that this would be a great forum to present boycott as queer-friendly. So was there some way that PACBI could acknowledge queer participation of the boycott?

His first response was "No, there can be no general statement." But then he started to rethink. In fact, he recalled that when John Greyson had started his involvement, PACBI had issued some statements of praise.

"Did those statements have the words *gay* or *LGBT* or *queer* in them?"

He didn't remember.

Okay. Next.

Well, what about some kind of statement of support for Palestinian queers?

"No. These are two separate issues. There is no overlap."

Okay, that was clear.

I started panicking. I didn't want to come away with nothing.

"Well, is there a queer Palestinian spokesperson on boycott who could come to the States?"

"No," he said. "There is no such person. The organizations have not signed on to the boycott."

Right then, I saw on Omar's face an expression I had seen on straight people's (and closeted people's) faces all of my life. The "no queers" unequivocal response.

I failed. I failed. I failed. And then I remembered Udi Aloni in my apartment in New York, and I remembered F surrounded by political posters in A's apartment in Ramallah. Both men, one straight over fifty and Jewish, one young, buff, and Arab, both saying to me, "What are you going to do if he says no?"

"Omar?" I asked. "What can I do for you?"

"You're creative. You're a militant," he said. "I'm sure you'll come up with some good ideas."

I staggered back to my hotel room. I missed my girlfriend. I couldn't call her because my phone didn't work in the West Bank. I felt bad. *I had failed.*

An hour later, Sami came to pick me up to meet with Al-Qaws.

"How did the meeting with Omar go?"

"I failed," I said.

"Really?" he said. "I talked to Hind, and she said it went well."

"I don't know," I said. "I know nothing about Arab or Palestinian culture. I don't know how to interpret what means what."

"She said it was good."

We drove in his truck to "the safe house," which turned out to be a comfortable house with a lush, shaded garden and enclosed porch that the queers in Ramallah had rented to have a place to hang out. It had gone well until neighbors noticed that men and women were gathering together at the house, and they complained. How ironic! The neighbors were upset that men and women were socializing with *each other*. If only they knew! This group was quite different from the one I had met the night before. Although there were some heavily politicized people and intellectuals, there was also a contingent of folks who basically just wanted a lover and some gay friends to hang with. This group included Haneen, the director of Al-Qaws, who had come in from Jerusalem for the meeting; Hiyam, a bright, energetic intellectual lesbian in a hijab who worked as a translator for anti-occupation internationals; R, a kind of disco queen fag with designer sunglasses; E, an effeminate intellectual who just got back from graduate studies in London; P and P, a gay man and his bisexual sixteen-year-old sister; and W and L, a butch-femme couple of the old school. W, a Christian, was about forty and very talkative and engaged; L, about twenty-five, was a tiny blonde femme who did not say a word during the entire visit. They spent the whole meeting with their arms around each other. Sometimes that's what gay organizations do — give you a place to be with others with your lover and have your arms around each other.

It was a beautiful afternoon; we drank tea and coffee underneath an almond tree. I looked up and there were almonds actually growing. Among the plethora of new experiences I was having daily, this was my first time seeing almonds on a tree. Hiyam pulled down a green one in its pod and offered it to me with salt, necessary to bring out the taste. It was delicious, and totally new. How many times in my life had I eaten anything off a tree? We relaxed. I was comfortable again.

I started to tell the whole story, and no one was surprised. There was a reason this underground grouping had offered to be a silent partner in the BDS film festival. So they were neither appalled nor disappointed until I got to the part about PACBI saying that there was no openly gay leader who could tour the United States to talk about boycott. Hey! That was far from the truth. There were many queers in Palestine involved in LGBT organizing who were deeply involved with boycott. And PACBI's assertion was a bit insulting. In fact, offensive.

"We don't need them to speak to the U.S. queer community," Haneen said, brightly. "We just do it directly."

This would be my first of many times I would hear Haneen saying the absolutely clear, reasonable, right, and big-picture thing that clarified what we all now *had* to do.

Of course. This was so obvious, how did I miss this? I had gotten involved in my own version of gay imperialism and forgotten that the most direct and intimate relationship was between U.S. queers and Palestinian queers, not the boycott apparatus per se. That's why all my conversations with Ramallah lesbians and gays and allies had been so easy and comfortable, and only my conversation with the straight boycott apparatus had been so difficult. Because the Palestinian queers and I were in the same community—and I needed to step up and start acting in a way that acknowledged this.

We immediately went into full organizing mode. Who are the American queers who fund Palestinian LGBT organizations in the West Bank and in Israel? Two foundations that I knew quite well came to mind immediately. It made sense for me to go to these two groups and see if we could bring folks over for a tour of LGBT centers, conferences, and university programs. Then I thought of the Harvard Kennedy School LGBT Human Rights initiative. What would be a more appropriate place to bring these organizers than to the Kennedy School's annual conference next year? The ideas just started flowing, but all from the same principle:

1. That there are many Americans who are uncomfortable with U.S. military support of the Israeli occupation.

2. That it made sense to work within subcultures that have community identities and their own recognized leadership: students, queers, African Americans, secular Jews, academics, and artists.

3. That the best way to raise consciousness was through human contact.

After some more tea, we shifted to the presentational part of the afternoon. As in Tel Aviv, I had brought some copies of my book *Ties That Bind*, and gave the same fifteen-minute talk about my work on familial homophobia. And this audience—this gathering of Muslim and Christian Palestinian queer people with no rights, whose country was occupied, who could never go to their own beach, the beach I had just enjoyed—

responded *exactly* the way the Israelis had. They sat there nodding their heads in recognition. And then we have *that* conversation, the one I have had my whole life in every queer place I've ever visited: the conversation about coming out to parents, the cruelty of families, the lack of comprehension, the disappointment, the pain, the fear of one's own parents. And there was nothing in what they said that was profoundly different from what every other gay gathering I've spoken to had said. In some crazy queer way, on this one plane, we were all in it together.

"I'm not a big fan of gay marriage," I said at one point.

"Why not?" one of the young men asked.

"Because marriage sucks," Hiyam answered, laughing in her hijab.

That night, I received a very kind and encouraging note from Omar. He sent me a long list of links to PACBI press releases commenting on actions of support from LGBT people, especially John Greyson. But what was absent from these acknowledgments was support for LGBT people ourselves. For example, one PACBI statement in Greyson's defense reads as follows:

> The attacks on Greyson have ignored his expressed reasons and sought to silence him by saying he would be unwelcome in other countries of the Middle East, including the occupied Palestinian territory, because of his activism around LGBT rights. Smearing Israel's victims as homophobic is not just a racist tactic calculated to create fear, it is a thinly veiled attempt to divert attention from the facts and compelling arguments raised by PACBI, Greyson, Naomi Klein, Ken Loach and many others justifying diverse forms of institutional boycott against Israel.

It is a tricky statement because it uses terms like "LGBT" and "homophobic" but does not come out *for* Palestinian queers.

The truth is that I liked Omar. He impressed me. He inspired me to want to make him understand what queer people are doing—how much we have changed our expectations for ourselves and how much we need reciprocity and acknowledgment, something I felt sure he would eventually be able to understand.

The next morning I left Ramallah. I took a taxi through its broken streets to the crossing at the Qalandia Gate. This was to be my first checkpoint. As soon as I stepped out of the taxi, I felt a tension, desperation, and depression that I hadn't yet experienced in Palestine. I had seen rebellion, brilliance, resistance, bravery, strength, sophistication, but I had not yet experienced what the people there undergo every single day just to get to work. The only American phenomenon I can compare going through a checkpoint to is the experience of getting arrested. They are quite similar.

The gate is a mechanized, cold structure where people line up in corridors separated by metal bars, somewhat like corrals for animals. Once you step in line in one of the corrals, you can't step out. There are no benches; no one can sit down. There are no bathrooms. There are no human authorities; everything is mechanized, so no one tells you how long it will take or what the problem is. We stood still for almost twenty minutes before advancing and then waiting again for the rest of the hour and some that it took to get through. There were long periods of just standing. Not knowing why. Not knowing when it would change. A woman arrived with a sick child who had a surgical tube in his nose. It was impossible to allow her to pass ahead, because there was no person in charge to negotiate with. All we could interact with was a mechanized turning door, divided into four quadrants, like the doors on the NYC subway, but also with metal bars. Whenever it was time to advance, the door would make a loud grating noise and turn one quadrant. Whoever was next in line would jump in — as there was no warning it was about to happen. Then that person would be locked in the tiny quadrant space, waiting for the next turn of the machine to release him into the security room.

Once through the long blockade, we saw signs in Hebrew, Arabic, and English that instructed us to take off our belts and put them and our bags through a scanner. The signs told us to have our papers ready and step into the next room, invisible to the waiting crowd. When it was my turn, I walked into a concrete room, where I saw three Israeli soldiers behind a bulletproof window. They looked like kids I had known. The guys could have been my cousin from Westchester who played trombone in his high school marching band or my first boyfriend, who lived in Brooklyn, smoked pot, and liked bluegrass music. The girl had that sexy Israeli thing that only Jewish girls from the suburbs could pull off in the 1960s and '70s. Energy, stature, large kinky hair, long earrings. But here they were bullies, assholes. They were the people causing the pain. They laughed and joked with each other with sleazy, superior expressions. I, a Jew, stood there in front of them, but they never spoke to me or acknowledged me. I didn't smile at them or acknowledge them. Clutching my American passport, which protected me from being them, I looked for some instruction of how to proceed. But in this final phase, all the signs were in Arabic and Hebrew, so I didn't know what to do. Finally one of the soldiers, who in

America might have grown up to be a high school math teacher and never in his life carried a gun or bullied a child, waved me on with no expression. I stepped out into the other side, East Jerusalem, where I and all the males emerging from concrete rooms — businessmen in suits, young boys with backpacks, old men with wizened faces — stood together and put our belts back on. Then we got onto the number 18 bus, and I watched as it dropped everyone off at their jobs. Offices, hotels, wherever they went to earn a living that day before returning back through the checkpoint at night to get home to dinner. This was the most harrowing moment of my entire trip. This was the moment that might help so many people understand that the checkpoint is not about security. It is only about humiliation.

I arrived at the Damascus Gate and watched the pilgrims on Easter Sunday, saw the stacks of bread for sale to the Christians, and waited for Ezra to drive by and pick me up. I was already intimate with Ezra, although he had never met me, because of Elle Flanders's film *Zero Degrees of Separation*, which shows his love relationship with a Palestinian man being systematically destroyed by the harassment of the Israeli state. His lover was repeatedly arrested, and they were continually in court. He couldn't live freely, and they were regularly harassed. Finally the man couldn't take it any longer and returned to his village in the West Bank to marry a woman. Ezra is a full-time advocate for Palestinians. In recent years he has focused on the rural poor in South Hebron, which is where he was taking me. He is particularly interested in shepherds, people who need land for their animals to graze.

He is a busy, committed, excited man in his late fifties, entirely on the side of good. Every one or two minutes his car phone rang. Regardless of the gender of the caller, he responded with endearments I have now learned: *Motek*, *Chamuda*, and the Arabic *Habibi*. Who was calling so much? Activist friends who recognized his truck as we drove along the highways and side roads. An old lover phoned from Ireland. Ezra, an Iraqi Jew, is an Arab and speaks Arabic. Non-Jewish Arabs called frequently on our trip. He seemed to be entirely integrated into the real community in which he lives. He turned off the main road, down an unmarked dirt path. He knew every side turn in Hebron. We came to a sign "Israelis are forbidden to enter," and he continued happily. We stopped to buy gas in an Arab village. Even though he lives in West Jerusalem, he tries to buy all his goods in Palestine.

For the next five hours Ezra would take me on the most intimate tour of the occupation I could ever experience. We actually went into settlements, some of the most notorious. They were gated communities of white, religious Jews. The houses were homogenous and substantial. The roads were uniform and excellent. There were supermarkets, parking garages, and parks. Some had air conditioning. These were the Stepford wives of Israeli suburban life, the most stultifying, suffocating, uniform gated communities I have ever seen. We saw a small group of settlement children going on a group bike ride, followed by three Jeeps. That is what the Israeli army is, an armed escort for settlement children at play. Ezra conceded that while many people live here for ideological reasons, some just need housing. And yet the lifestyle is so extreme, it was hard to imagine being able to breathe in a place like this if you weren't exactly like them.

In each settlement, we parked, briefly, and stood at the top of a hill or vista. Most of the time there was a barbed-wire locked gate at the edge of the development. Looking beyond it, about two city blocks, we usually saw an Arab village. These were the native communities that settlers encroached upon to create their developments. Ezra took me into village after village. So many people knew him, and they smiled, waved, shook hands, embraced him. Each village, large or small, shared certain qualities: there was not a single good road to be seen. The streets smelled like open sewers. People bought water from trucks. The villages were poor, neglected, crumbling, filled with men of all ages with nothing to do and the women serving them.

"Look," Ezra said, pointing to two young boys standing by the road as we drove by. They stopped and looked. One put his arm around the other as they watched. "That is their activity for today. And this will go on for years."

Over and over we go from comfortable, new, protected, vacuum-sealed settlement to poor, dirty, ill-served, embattled Arab village, each separated by a locked fence patrolled by the Israeli military. I had never seen anything like this before in my life, and I searched for the word to describe it. And then I finally got it. After years of dismissing the word as propaganda or exaggeration. I finally understood it in terms of what I was seeing: apartheid. Two separate systems by which one group dominates and controls the other through brutality, denial of rights, and lack of liberty. They have separate roads, separate water, separate experiences. One has autonomy, protection, and opportunity. The other does not. And these are townships just a few feet away from each other.

"The government issues demolition orders," Ezra said. "Then they tear down people's homes. Once they're gone, the settlement can build."

At Elle's suggestion, I handed over an envelope of cash, about $100 in shekels collected from friends. Ezra thanked me, pulled up to an Arab handyman's roadside shack, handed him the money, and asked him to put a toilet into a village. We then drove to this place, which was far worse than a shantytown. About seventy people lived in hovels made of garbage and dirt. There were a few goats and sheep in a pen. Up on the hill, I could see the splendor of the new settlement. As we drove in, a young man came running out of his shack to greet Ezra. He was laughing and smiling, and he shook my hand. Everyone we met seemed used to Ezra appearing with women and have long ago learned to treat us like men. The boy and Ezra gossiped in Arabic. The boy was wearing an Israeli soldier's shirt, and Ezra begged him to get rid of it. He explained that the soldiers could use it to harass him. The boy agreed, pulled it off his back, and threw it in Ezra's truck. He is a trusted authority, that's for sure.

We drove off and pulled into another roadside business. Ezra emerged with two cans of the sweet Thai coconut drink that I had had in Bil'in. This seemed to be all the rage in Palestine. We drove to a checkpoint. The woman asked Ezra for his papers, and I reached for mine.

"Don't do it," he said. "Don't obey until they make you."

The woman just assumed I was with him, and once his papers checked out, we were waved on.

Soon he pulled off the road again, this time onto a path of dirt and then rock. It was then that I understood why he needed four-wheel drive. We were slowly crawling over terrain not intended for machines: around a hill, into a rocky ravine, along a deserted gully. After about a half hour of this, we came into a clearing, and I saw a Palestinian family. I saw one, two, three, four young boys, and an older teenage boy. I saw their father. Then I realized that they live in caves. Two caves in the side of a hill. I looked up over the hill and saw a Jewish settlement in the distance. As Ezra drove up, everyone came running. Then the woman emerged from the cave, carrying sheets of plastic and some foam mattresses, and handed them to the oldest son. Everyone was happy to see Ezra. We all shook hands, and they led us to a canvas tent set up in between the goats and the sheep. Inside, the tent was stamped "European Community Humanitarian Aid." The oldest son lay the plastic on the dirt, and then the mattresses. Ezra and I sat down. He explained to the father that I am "from America and have come to help Palestinians." They looked at me and nodded. I was sure that this introduction had served many before me.

The family were shepherds and normally would move their flocks to graze in different areas at different times. But now they were afraid that if they left their land, the settlers would take it. So they were overgrazing the same patches, and the grass was not returning. Settlers were coming closer and harassing them. They had no protection and no communication. Ezra decided that they needed a camera. He got on his cell phone and tracked down someone to bring them one. The father wanted electricity and asked Ezra how he could get it. It's possible, Ezra answered. But not immediately. Ezra and his band of activists are, I realized, like an independent aid agency. Whatever cash went into their hands was immediately translated to solving the needs of the poorest people in the land. He had total credibility. The wife brought out tea, and the oldest son poured it. The wife then brought out a very poor quality of bread and a bowl of sheep's butter. We ate and talked. As we drove out about an hour later, we passed some guys working in the fields. They were gathering wild grass to feed their goats. They also knew Ezra. He pulled over, and they offered us a piece of their bread. The bread, made with olive oil, was delicious. I realized then that this was a very male-dominated world, and Ezra received a lot of male attention. He loved it, and they loved him.

We drove past another checkpoint. A small group of Arab children were walking through on their way home from school. The Israeli soldier was being tough with them. They all were probably seven years old. He looked at their papers and acted stern. Ezra yelled out, "They were here before you. They will be here after you."

The soldier said something back, but Ezra didn't hear him. We're both over fifty now. Some things are starting to fade.

I needed to use the bathroom, and we happened to be driving through a settler town that had a public area: bathroom, restaurant. Ezra pulled the truck over, and I asked some hassids where the bathrooms are. They gave me accurate directions. Inside, a religious woman was washing up. I washed up too, and she decided to be helpful, in that awful Jewish way I remember from my childhood, so invasive you just can't breathe. She wanted to pour the water over my hands with a plastic cup. Okay. "Thanks," I say. I didn't want to even try to speak Hebrew. I stepped back out onto the street and saw that Ezra was surrounded by police. He waved at me, and I walked right past him. He turned then, and we both jumped in the truck. A hassid with a video camera filmed me through the window of the truck. What did we do? Not sure, but we drove on. His phone rang. A fellow activist saw us getting harassed. They were everywhere: friends and foes.

He took me then to the town of Karmel. A large Arab village, the streets are full, dusty, smelly. We visited another friend, an Arab man and wife with three developmentally disabled children; two are deaf and have no sign language and no access to treatment. They were poor, and their clothes were filthy. They offered us oranges to celebrate a new grandson's birth. Again I was treated like a man-human while the wife sat to the side. Again Ezra said, "She has come from America to help Palestine." They spoke in Arabic for a while. It was getting late. We were two hours late to meet Sonya in West Jerusalem. I was exhausted. I get it. I finally got it.

I slept in Tel Aviv that night three blocks from the beach. The next evening I drove up with friends to Haifa for my final event—an evening at the Women's Center with two organizations: Isha L'Isha, a feminist group, and Aswat, the Palestinian lesbian organization. Aswat is for Palestinians living in Israel, and it was the only lesbian organization in Israel at the moment. There were thirty-five to forty people in the room. My talk was on thinking strategically, choosing political tactics. I tried to emphasize getting away from grim left-wing language and instead using normal conversational words to convey our ideas and feelings. Overall I encouraged trying out new approaches.

"If something didn't work, don't do it again."

I met their fundraiser, Ghadir, a sharp, focused, frenetic femme who really has the drive to succeed for Aswat. She takes copious notes and asks real questions. One of Aswat's main problems was getting in the media. I suggested approaching it systematically: research all of the media outlets, find out who is who in each place, identify who your potential friends are, and try to communicate with them. Some of the women in the room were interested. They wanted to make progress. Others were obstructionist, always finding reasons why it wouldn't work and not trying to find ways that could. Ghadir tried to help me understand their particular situation as Palestinian gay women living in Israel, which they call "48"—referring to the land that was seized in 1948 when Israel became recognized as a state.

"Israel is a *selective* democracy," she said.

And I realized that this phrase answers a lot of questions. She told me that when the sniper fired into the Tel Aviv LGBT Center the previous year, the broad LGBT community held a huge demonstration. Many straight and gay leaders and organizations spoke from the podium. But Aswat was not allowed to speak. They were told by the Jewish LGBT leadership that Israel "is not ready" for a Palestinian queer group to speak from the stage.

They feared that Aswat would make the connection between hate crimes against gays and hate crimes against Palestinians. And this, the leadership felt, could not be allowed to occur. This was the kind of racism they were dealing with inside the Israeli gay community.

As I listened, I thought, *She must come to America.* That American queers needed to meet her, hear her, listen to her experiences, and come to understand. I knew that if Ghadir and Haneen and Sami could be seen and heard in the United States, American queers could start to understand. Sitting there, I had this vision, that boycott could become the obvious position for progressive LGBT people in the United States. That all they needed to do was meet people like Haneen and Sami and Ghadir. Then more people would "get it." My recognition of my own long-term capitulation to the propaganda I'd been indoctrinated into *floors me.* I thought I had overcome so much, but I had just begun. This was paramount in my mind the next day as I endured the exit interview at Ben Gurion airport. "Who did you visit? Do you speak Hebrew? Why not? Do you belong to a synagogue? Why not?"

I left Israel knowing this was only the beginning.

PART II AL-U.S. TOUR

8. HOMONATIONALISM

Now that I'd had the experience, the relationships could be formed. As a consequence of those relationships, we decided on our first collaborative action: bringing Palestinian queer activists to America. And this tour would take place in a dynamic and quickly evolving world context.

All my life, my "theory" has emerged organically from my actions. I never engaged theory for its own sake, as I find it causes divisions that action would heal. But as we go about the systematic work of activism, doing concrete things that create change, decisions have to continually be made. Selecting one option over another requires awareness of values and ethical framework, and that is when my theory starts to be formed.

At the same time, I am always open to other people's good ideas. And I have often been inspired by their insights and conceptualizations. The trick is to find new words or imaginings that help actions to move forward effectively. In the case of Israel/Palestine there was significant thinking in place that was invaluable for our organizing. And among those resources, Jasbir Puar's articulation of "homonationalism" was a principal inspiration.

It was only when I came back to New York in the spring of 2010 that I found the words I needed to match my feelings and perceptions. It was then that I learned that what Heike Schotten had called "gay imperialism" was part of the larger concept called "homonationalism."

"Homonationalism" is a phenomenon identified by Puar, a Rutgers University professor and board member of the Audre Lorde Project, in her 2007 book *Terrorist Assemblages*. Her term is used regularly in academic and activist circles in western Europe and the Middle East, and received a broader audience through her column in the *Guardian* of London. Homonationalism describes a contemporary phenomenon, most prevalent in northern European countries such as Germany and the Netherlands, where white gays, lesbians, and bisexuals (and in some cases transsexuals) have won a full range of legal rights. Through marriage, parenthood, and family, they become accepted and realigned with patriotic or nationalist ideologies of their countries. Instead of being feared as the threat to family and nation that they were once seen to be, this new integration under the most normative of terms is held up as a symbol of that country's commitment to progress and modernity. Some then identify with the racial and religious hegemony of their countries and join movements opposing immigration or racial and cultural difference. They construct the "other," often Muslims of Arab, South Asian, Turkish, or African origin, as "homophobic" and fanatically heterosexual.

Just a few examples of homonationalism in 2010 and 2011:

—In the Netherlands, 22 percent of the readers of *Gay Krant*, a popular gay magazine, announced their support for Geert Wilders's anti-immigrant Party for Freedom.

—The campaign run by openly LGBT groups in the United States against the "don't ask, don't tell" policy emphasized gay participation in the wars in Afghanistan and Iraq instead of focusing on discrimination in the military as principally a matter of exclusion from employment.

—In London, Safra Project, a queer Muslim organization, asked white gays to cancel a pride march in an immigrant neighborhood partially because of its associations with the English Defense League, a Far Right group.

—In Norway, Anders Behring Breivik, who killed scores of Muslim teenagers at a youth camp, cited American gay writer Bruce Bawer's anti-Muslim essays among his influences.

In no case have homonationalist gays objected to Christian immigrants, even though fundamentalist Christians are leading antigay campaigns in the United States and exporting them with deadly consequences to Uganda and other countries around the world.

Puar's work on homonationalism helped me to see and understand the shifting structures of homophobia and homosexuality in the context of global politics. It was already clear that the LGBT conversation belongs within the framework of global politics, but because both the news media and the paid leaders of American LGBT organizations have not caught up to this, LGBT events are still seen as fragmented bits of domestic news. When I pitched articles on the rise of the Palestinian queer movement to *Harper's* and the *New Yorker*, the editors, who agreed in advance to consider the material, lacked the understanding or context to even be able to respond. I had to work very hard to get a pass from *Harper's*; once they saw what the article was actually about, I never heard back from the *New Yorker*. Even though Puar had published extensively in the *Guardian* of London, none of the American editors whom I contacted knew what "homonationalism" was, since global LGBT politics is not a recognized American journalistic beat. If journalists are busy insisting to their readers that gay marriage with a religious exemption in New York State is the big queer news of the world, there is no way to open their pages to what is happening in queer Palestine. To me, the real story is that while some gay people are adopting nationalist anti-immigration attitudes and joining imperialist militaries, others are working together across national boundaries to break down racial and gender exclusion. The activism of LGBT people on the questions of border, citizenship, and occupation is producing an international dynamic that has consequences for world politics.

Spring 2010 appeared to be an extraordinary moment for these contradictions between the assimilating homonationalistic global LGBT and the anti-occupation queer international. Over the next four months there would be a complex display of international anxiety about Israel and Palestine expressed directly and indirectly through queer players and playing fields. These conflicts would become apparent in Berkeley, Toronto, Madrid, Berlin, Haifa, and the courts of Canada and the United Kingdom and back to Ramallah before the summer closed.

Armed with these new and evolving understandings, I returned to New York at the end of Passover week 2009 and promptly started organizing the U.S. tour of LGBT Palestinian leaders, which we had determined would take place in February 2011.

My first decision was to organize the tour by phone, instead of by Facebook or email, because I wanted to talk things over with people. I wanted to build the tour in such a way that it would take in key people who were influential in different aspects of the LGBT community in the United States, people with credibility among those who knew them. My idea was to approach some varied folks in trigger positions to create a cumulative response, larger than any single element.

So I picked up the phone and called reliable, interesting, diverse people whom I had known or met over the course of my previous thirty years of organizing for justice. Almost everyone I called agreed to participate. The only two people who blew me off were two famous queer theorists. Everyone else — organizers, activists, academics, and combinations thereof — immediately said yes. In the process it became clear to me that folks do so little work on the phone these days that when you actually get in a real interactive conversation, there is a better chance of reaching a positive result.

For the next ten months I kept up individual conversations with each of the coordinators. In most of the cities I found someone to moderate the panel who was responsible for the venue and whatever funding he or she could find. At the same time, in most cities I had to set up a second team to do the on-the-ground organizing—which involved everything from getting the community to the events to taking the speakers to the airport and watching as they went through security.

Since my perception—correctly or incorrectly—was that Palestinian solidarity politics in the United States is associated by many with the didactic margins, I wanted to avoid existing organizations, venues, and rhetoric. I wanted this event to be as free of baggage as possible because my goal was to help give Palestine a human face in the LGBT community in a way that would reach people who were not informed. This meant using conversational language instead of rhetoric. It meant creating events that were fun instead of grim. I wanted Palestine to become a normative conversation for mainstream queers. Besides, I already knew that Haneen, Ghadir, and Sami were funny, warm, savvy, sexy, and totally accessible, very far from the gray, humorless image of the iconic oppressed freedom fighter that has evolved in the American imagination.

I organized six events in diverse, relatively neutral but esteemed venues in different cities, with facilitators who had credibility and gravitas in those communities. I wanted facilitators who could both protect the speakers from any hostility that might come from audience members and instill trust in that audience.

Soon I had a rough draft of the tour. It would start February 2011 in Minneapolis, where the National LGBT Task Force would hold its annual conference: "Creating Change." The task force was once America's leading policy-oriented LGBT organization. Founded in 1973, it worked with Congresswoman Bella Abzug on the first draft of the first gay rights bill in history. Over the years the task force has occupied different positions on the queer continuum depending on how insightful or ineffectual the wildly varied leadership was. At times it seemed like the gay wing of the Democratic Party, but it was then supplanted by more conservative national gay organizations. In recent years they had focused on providing an outlet for activists in the regions through the national conference. The event's director, Sue Hyde, who has a deeply progressive history, was very enthusiastic about bringing the Palestinian queers to Creating Change, and she proposed a Saturday afternoon event. Flo Rozawsky and Jessica Rosenberg of the International Jewish Anti-Zionist Network agreed to do all the community organizing and transport. I wrote the proposal, with myself as the first moderator of the national tour, and awaited approval.

Using Creating Change as a starting point, I then built a rigorous schedule of events continuing with February 6 at the University of Illinois, Circle Campus, moderated by Professor Lynette Aria Jackson, an African American lesbian historian. That would be followed by an event at the Harvard Kennedy School moderated by Tim McCarthy, an Irish American gay man who heads the Carr Center for Human Rights and Social Movements, and the Iranian Harvard professor Afseneh Najambadi. In Cambridge I happened upon the same Heike Schotten, a professor at the University of Massachusetts, whose post on "gay imperialism" had been so helpful. She agreed to do the on-the-ground work for the Harvard event. Next would come a program at the Center for Lesbian and Gay Studies at the City University of New York's Graduate Center, organized by its executive director, Sarah Chinn, and by board member Matt Brim. The program would be moderated by Katherine Acey, an Arab activist who was the founding and longtime director of the Astraea Foundation, which funds lesbian organizing around the world, including Aswat. After that, the tour would go to the University of Pennsylvania for talks moderated by Professors Heather Love, a white lesbian, and Amy Kaplan, a Jewish straight woman, with graduate student Naava Et-Shalom (who had contacted me earlier about a petition against the Law of Return) doing the groundwork. Heather had returned from the Tel Aviv conference as a supporter of BDS and was enthusiastically supporting, building, and facilitating the Penn event. The tour would then end in San Francisco. In the Bay Area, Berkeley student Zohar Weiman-Kelman would bring the event to the Arab Resource and Organizing Center.

The funding was really patchwork. I was able to get $5,000 from Astraea and $5,000 from the University of Pennsylvania, including two round-trip tickets from Tel Aviv. The Arab Resource and Organizing Center could put in $100. Harvard would pay for transport and hotel. CUNY was broke. What was missing was money for per diems, airplane tickets, hotels, operating expenses, and donations to Aswat and Al-Qaws to reimburse the activists for their three weeks of work. I have to find $30,000 more. And the visas? Who was going to be in charge of the visas? A community started to create itself.

The other promise I needed to keep was to try to help Omar get into the *Nation*. Not that I have any sway there. In the 1990s I published the magazine's first-ever article on AIDS, but it was about AIDS and the homeless. The *Nation*'s queer coverage is very territorial, and I haven't even been able to get my books reviewed there in years. Nonetheless, "principles before personalities." I contacted the two people I knew there to inquire how Omar could get a piece on BDS in their pages. I got two conflicting answers. One person told me that the editor in chief, Katrina Vanden Heuvel, was "skittish" about the boycott. The other contact said that Omar had a piece he was currently cowriting with one of the managing editors. Omar said this was not true, so I had been stonewalled.

A former ACT UP staffer who worked at the Open Society Institute, George Soros's foundation, suggested I file an application there for funding for the tour. When I did so, it turned out that the person on the other end had known me from when we both attended Hunter High School in New York in the 1970s. He forwarded the application to the institute's office in Amman, Jordan, and I had an amazing one-hour phone conversation with Hanan Rabani, its director of the Women's and Gender Program for the Middle East Region. Hanan told me that this tour would give great visibility to autonomous queer organizing in the region. That it would inspire queer Arabs—especially in Egypt and Iran—to follow the model of the Palestinians and create their own organizations. For that reason, she said, funding for the tour should come from the Amman office, since the principal benefit would be to the region. *None* of this had occurred to me, but boy was I happy to hear it. To polish it off, she suggested that instead of the $10,000 I had requested, that they give me $15,000. What a coup. I immediately called the Bay Area Arab Resource and Organizing Center and assured the people there that since this money was coming for diasporic queer Arab organizing, we would cover most of their expenses without their having to fundraise. As I kept working, there were so many decisions to make. Ghadir, Haneen, and Sami and I talked via Skype on occasion and emailed almost daily, but still the conceptualizing of the tour was my call. It had to be—they simply didn't know the terrain.

Since I was now the contact person, I ended up speaking for the project regularly and had to engage the problems of "solidarity politics" for the first time. This meant examining my relationship to Ghadir, Haneen, and Sami. Was I there to do exactly what they wanted? Or was I there to advocate for what seemed best to me? Because of a combination of familial homophobia and looming Israeli laws against the boycott, two of the three speakers were concerned about having their full names released or having their pictures taken. This was very disappointing to me, of course, since I had envisioned a big public relations campaign. But we soon worked out a compromise. All of the media was on radio. Restrictions on recording and photographing would be strictly enforced at all venues. "Boycott" and "BDS" would not appear in any of the publicity, though the speakers would address it if the audience brought it up. This also meant that overtly pro-boycott organizations could not be official endorsers.

Another concern that arose was the very present danger of being substituted for the Palestinians. I know that Butler, Klein, and every other Jew who is becoming a spokesperson for BDS and Palestine are fully aware that their own voices are more acceptable to the media than are the voices of the Palestinians themselves. It doesn't undermine the power of their action. But as with *Mad Men* or Michael Moore movies, the critique of supremacy ideology also replicates it. The medium may not be the entire message, but it is a strong component. This happens for a number of reasons. The foremost reason is racism against Palestinians in general, a kind of discomfort on the part of white, non-Muslim journalists and administrators about speaking directly with Palestinians. Jews, ironically, become the substitute of convenience. But also at play is the problem that we discussed in Ramallah, that Palestine does not have accessible, recognizable spokespeople established in the U.S. media. There is no "go-to" person. Palestinians' conscious refusal to develop Palestinian media figures in the United States made this obstacle more difficult to overcome as international expressions of support and hostility to Palestinians expressed themselves daily. These problems of representation were surpassed by pure excitement about Haneen, Ghadir, and Sami's visit. And the long summer between my trip to Palestine and their arrival in New York was filled with expressions, in many cities in the world, of anxiety, hope, and change in the relationship between the queer international and Palestine.

Here are some key examples:

Berkeley

A week after my return, on April 14, 2010, the *Nation* ran a previously planned, very moving piece by Judith Butler about the divestment campaign at the University of California Berkeley campus. The events at Berkeley were high drama. In late March, the university's Student Senate voted 16 to 4 to divest from General Electric and United Technologies because of their roles in the occupation. A week later, the president of the Student Senate, Will Smelko, vetoed the vote. The students had an opportunity to override his action. Butler's piece was an address to her students in the face of this veto, imploring them to vote to override. Rarely do students get pressured from professors in the pages of national magazines, but this vote was worldwide news; Desmond Tutu implored them, Noam Chomsky implored them. And all of the right-wing Jewish organizations turned out in force. Jonathan Kessler of AIPAC told his organization's policy conference, "We are going to make sure that pro-Israel students take over the student government and reverse the vote. . . . This is how AIPAC operates in our nation's capital. This is how AIPAC must operate in our nation's campuses." Berkeley was playing out an international conflict over the legitimization of boycott/divestment/sanctions.

To understand more about the issue of divestment, I returned to the website that Dalit Baum works on, Who Profits From the Occupation? (www.whoprofits.org), because she had been so instrumental in persuading me to use sanctions in the first place. The website analyzes multiple levels of economic profiteering from the occupation.

The first is what they call the "settlement industry." As of 2010 there were 135 settlements in the West Bank, the Gaza Strip, and Golan Heights and dozens of additional outposts. They house more than 560,000 Jewish Israelis. As I witnessed in my own experiences in Bil'in and Hebron, these settlements include housing developments and roads and water systems for the exclusive use of Jews. These violate international law; article 49, paragraph 6, of the Fourth Geneva Convention stipulates that "an occupying power shall not deport or transfer parts of its own civilian population into territories it occupies."

Permanent changes made on occupied land violate the Hague Regulations. And these violations create many opportunities for profiteering. Israeli companies located in settlements use Palestinian resources, land, and labor. Companies profit by sustaining the settlements and connecting them to Israel. And some companies forge real estate deals and construct Israeli infrastructure and housing on occupied land.

Right now there are hundreds of Israeli companies working out of the settlements. Some export their products worldwide. The companies benefit from low rents, special tax incentives, and lax enforcement of environmental and labor laws. Palestinians employed in these industrial zones work under severe restrictions of movement and organization, with hardly any government protections. The companies produce everything from aluminum to wine to halvah, computers, carpets, olive oil, plastics, and translation services, and they are subsidiaries of such well-known companies as General Mills (Pillsbury) and Central Bottling Company (Coca-Cola Israel).

The settlement movement achieves two goals: annexing more land and resources for Israel and cutting off Palestinians from the same. Since the Israeli road system in the West Bank is forbidden to Palestinians, it creates a Jewish-only space on top of the Palestinian space. In this way, the roads and settlements become part of the separation system, which also includes fences, walls, gates, and checkpoints. This brings a lot of money to the Israeli construction industry, including real estate dealers, realtors, contractors, planners, and suppliers of materials, security and maintenance services. Some of these include Bank Leumi, Caterpillar, Siemens, and Volvo.

Then there are companies that provide discriminatory services to the settlements that are forbidden to the surrounding Palestinian neighbors. These services connect settlements to Israel and normalize their status. The companies also provide private security that keeps Palestinians out of the settlements. These companies include Aroma Espresso Bar (which just opened a beautiful franchise on Houston Street in Manhattan, where my cousin works), Ace Hardware, Blockbuster, Mercantile Bank, and Motorola Israel.

Since the 1967 occupation, Israel has used its military rule to the advantage of Israeli corporations and the detriment of Palestinian economic development. All Palestinian imports and exports have been controlled, thereby making Palestinians a captive market for Israeli goods. As I witnessed at the Qalandia Gate, checkpoints and walls have all but destroyed Palestinian labor's bargaining power. Restrictions on movement limit workers' employment choices, and their dependency on security permits makes labor organizing almost impossible.

But the vilest arena of profiteering is that of companies who make money by providing materials and services to control the Palestinian population. Three and a half million Palestinians live under a severe military regime, with no basic civil liberties, and are subject to arbitrary repressive violence by the Israeli military and security forces. In the West Bank, two million people are divided into dozens of fragmented sections surrounded by roadblocks, fences, walls, checkpoints, settlements, and roads for Jews only. Hundreds of thousands of Palestinians are blacklisted and cannot pass any checkpoint. Large areas of the West Bank are forbidden to Palestinians altogether. There is no freedom of speech or right to organize or protest. Military violence, as I witnessed in Bil'in, is the normative reaction by the Israeli state to nonviolent protest. House demolitions, curfews, and arbitrary arrests are a regular part of life. As a result, there is a huge private security industry in Israel. A lot of the repression has been privatized, including guarding settlements and construction sites and maintaining some checkpoints. In addition, the design, construction, operation, and maintenance of the Wall of Separation and other mechanisms of separation are big business. There are now civil engineering firms that supply ready-made watchtowers or razor wire fences, as well as biometric identification systems and surveillance technology. These include Chevrolet and Hewlett-Packard. Finally, there are companies that supply the Israeli army with such equipment as armored bulldozers (Caterpillar) to demolish villages.

For these reasons, in March 2010, the Student Senate at UC–Berkeley voted to pass the following bill:

WHEREAS student research has revealed that according to the most recent UC investment report, within the UC Retirement Program fund and the General Endowment Program fund, there exist direct investments in American companies materially and militarily supporting the Israeli government's occupation of the Palestinian territories, including American companies General Electric and United Technologies; and

WHEREAS General Electric holds engineering support and testing service contracts with the Israeli military and supplies the Israeli government with the propulsion system for its Apache Assault Helicopter fleet, which as documented by Amnesty International and Human Rights Watch, has been used in attacks on Palestinian and Lebanese civilians, including the January 4, 2009, killings of Palestinian medical aid workers and

WHEREAS United Technologies supplies the Israeli government with Blackhawk helicopters and with F-15 and F-16 aircraft engines and holds an ongoing fleet management contract for these engines, and Amnesty International has documented the Israeli government's use of these aircraft in the bombing of the American School in Gaza, the killing of Palestinian civilians and the destruction of hundreds of Palestinian homes, therefore

BE IT RESOLVED that the ASUC [Associated Students of the University of California] will ensure that its assets and will advocate that UC assets do not include holdings in General Electric and United Technologies.

Issued on March 24, the bill was vetoed a week later by Senate President Smelko on the grounds that Israel was being "singled out." He said that the bill was "a symbolic attack on a specific community of our fellow students." By now I know that this kind of statement is not only false, but is also a sign that the speaker is not thinking for himself. It is sort of the emblematic clue that someone is regurgitating what he thinks he is supposed to say. If the person claiming special persecution had actually come to that conclusion himself, he would have examples. He would first prove that no nation in the world in violation of international law is criticized except Israel. This would be impossible to prove because it's not factual. But he would also have to go deeper and argue *why* Israel should be permitted to violate international law *because* some other violators are not being made accountable. There are few examples in moral argument where someone is allowed to proceed with an unjust action simply because there are others who do it as well. This is the weakest argument in this entire debate, and the one repeated the most. People never claim that Israel's action does not violate international law. That's a given. They simply argue that to do so is all right because others do it as well. It is disheartening to see members of the opposition be so careless and knee-jerk. I want them to have good reasons for their positions.

Naomi Klein's statement in support of the students' bill addressed this directly. Klein wrote, "Whenever we take a political action, we open ourselves up to accusations of hypocrisy and double standards, since the truth is that we can never do enough in the face of pervasive global injustice." Simultaneously, at another University of California campus, the UC–Davis Food Co-op received a petition asking for a vote on a boycott of settlement-produced products. The co-op leadership refused to allow a vote to take place.

On Sunday, April 11, *Haaretz* reported that the Israeli Defense Force had issued a new military order enabling the deportation of tens of thousands of Palestinians from the West Bank. Likely to be targeted were people whose identification cards bore home addresses in Gaza, people born in Gaza and their West Bank–born children, or those born in the West Bank or abroad who lost their residency status. Also, foreign-born spouses of Palestinians. The order defines an "infiltrator" as any person present in the West Bank without a permit. It applies to all people: Palestinians, U.S. citizens, Israeli citizens. These restrictions are aimed at clamping down on protesters in the West Bank and Jerusalem, and subjects them to prison sentences of up to seven years.

On April 14, in her plea to Berkeley students to override the veto, Butler wrote, "It does not de-legitimate Israel to ask for its compliance with international law. Indeed, compliance with international law is the best way to gain legitimacy, respect and an enduring place among the peoples of the world."

That day I went to the website of Aswat to see how this Palestinian lesbian organization surviving in Israel presents itself to the world. And I was moved to see that the first thing any visitor to Aswat's site will read is a quote from Audre Lorde, the Caribbean American lesbian philosopher, leader, and "warrior poet"—and my college professor at Hunter College. Aswat takes inspiration from Audre's statement: "When I dare to be powerful and to use my strength in the service of my vision, then it becomes less and less important whether I am afraid." This, for decades, has been the lesbian vision. To do what has to be done to move our world and ourselves toward a place of full humanity on our own terms, regardless of the "risk," in all the ways that can be defined.

This is the same vision articulated by Dalit Baum and Black Laundry's statement that "our own oppression as lesbians, gays and transpeople enhances our solidarity with other oppressed groups." And of course the argument that lesbians have made for more than a century in the forefront of movements for human rights to which they have contributed, and by whom they very much want to be included, are also expressed in Palestine. Butler tells her students, "If you struggle against voicelessness to speak out for what is right, then you are in the middle of that struggle against oppression and for freedom, a struggle that knows that there is no freedom for one until there is freedom for all."

Lesbians who are out in their work and have a vision for international justice have always been invested in the word *all*. Reading this, I think again about who is at stake when we talk about expansive analysis, about inclusive language. Who is humanized by *all*, and abandoned by *some*. In this moment, I see that it is the Palestinian queers who are the living embodiment of the "All" and provide the world with an opportunity to do what Butler calls "what is right."

It's the kind of opportunity that the world too often wastes. The students at UC–Berkeley voted to uphold the veto, and the school lost its chance to divest.

Toronto

Homonationalism was simultaneously playing itself out dramatically in Toronto, where the organization Queers against Israeli Apartheid was threatened with being banned from the gay pride parade. Because of the now common financial involvement of various governments in gay pride, these events had increasingly become platforms for confrontation around homonationalism, and the scandal in Toronto sprung directly out of an evolving international context.

Some background: In New York, where gay pride marches originated, there are now two separate kinds of events—LGBT and queer. There is the corporate-underwritten, permitted LGBT March, and then there are the Dyke March, the Trans March, and the Drag March on the other side of town on other days. A similar division exists in Tel Aviv: one between the mainstream homonationalist LGBT community and the smaller anti-occupation "queerim"; separate marches or, some years, just separate contingents. The Israeli debate coalesced in 2006 when Jerusalem was selected as the location for the second World Pride celebration. These World Pride events not only bring a lot of money to the LGBT tourism of a particular area, but they create a vital but temporary consensus. The LGBT community in Jerusalem has consistently been harassed and continues to face enormous opposition from the religious Right, so on LGBT-only terms, it was a great location. The problem is that Israel's violation of human rights is so extreme that the theme "Love across Borders" was absurd. In addition, World Pride was in direct conflict with the then one-year-old boycott, the only viable nonviolent plan to make Israel conform to international law. The celebration had already been rescheduled once from 2005 because of tensions surrounding withdrawal from Gaza. Yet the delay only heightened the contrast as World Pride took place against the backdrop of Israel's assault on Lebanon and the simultaneous construction of the Wall of Separation. Aswat was one of the groups that boycotted the events, stating, "At the same time that we celebrate our pride, the Palestinians are going to suffer and be under curfew."

The Lebanese LGBT group Helem also boycotted World Pride: "Human rights are universal, indivisible and interdependent, and the rights of gays, lesbians, bisexuals and transgender people should not be placed in competition with the long struggle of the Palestinian people, including Palestinian LGBT people." Twenty-two organizations ultimately joined the boycott of World Pride, including the relatively mainstream Gay and Lesbian Human Rights Commission in New York City.

By 2009, the emergence of LGBT anti-occupation organizations was visible enough that the *Advocate,* a conservative gay magazine, ran an article by James Kirchick criticizing them: "There may be queers for Palestine, but Palestine certainly isn't for queers." The response appeared a short time later in *Monthly Review*: an article titled "Israel, Palestine and Queers," written by our own Haneen Maikey, the director of Al-Qaws, and Jason Ritchie, an American anthropologist. They wrote:

> As in most societies, homophobia is a problem in Palestinian society, but there is not some organized, widespread campaign of violence against gay and lesbian Palestinians. Of course there are occasional acts of violence . . . and the social norms and mores about gender and sexuality that give rise to such violence create a climate in which many queer Palestinians cannot live their lives openly and honestly. At the same time, there are many openly gay and lesbian Palestinians, and . . . they are actively engaged in changing the status quo in Palestinian society by promoting respect for sexual and gender diversity.

At the same time, *Haaretz* joined the conversation with an article by Morten Berthelsen, "Stop Using Palestinian Gays to Whitewash Israel's Image." Berthelsen cited a *Haaretz* poll showing that half of the Israeli population believes that homosexuality is a perversion.

In September 2009, the International Gay and Lesbian Travel Association chose to hold its tourism conference in Tel Aviv, aimed at boosting LGBT leisure tourism to Israel. Helem, the Lebanese LGBT group, asked the association to cancel. In its statement, Helem said that the association's decision was "consistent with globalization's tendency to distance the *final product* from the moral implications of the manufacturing process." Helem asked that the 2005 boycott be respected "until Israel meets its obligation to recognize the Palestinian people's inalienable right to self-determination and fully complies with the precepts of international law." Anti-occupation queers are speaking the language of the LGBT mainstream and are lobbying from within the rainbow. The more that Arab and Muslim LGBT groups gain visibility *within* the queer conversation, the more accountable the broader community will have to become.

This conflict was expressed in San Francisco when the Jewish Film Festival joined with the Consulate General of Israel to create special gay programming for Israel Pride Month in April 2010. The event was also sponsored by San Francisco's LGBT synagogue, Sha'ar Zahav. "Out in Israel" was protested and picketed by Queers Undermining Israeli Terrorism (QUIT), a Bay Area anti-occupation group, and others. The issue was not the censorship of Israeli artists, but rather the orchestrated propaganda campaign to sell Israel to U.S. queers based on certain rights for Israeli gays despite atrocities in Gaza and the West Bank. The protests were rather successful, and only about fifty people attended the films.

At the same time, the Bilerico Project reported the marketing of the first all-Israeli gay porn film, shot on location in Israel and titled *Men of Israel*. Michael Lucas, a former porn star and known nationalist who owns his own film production company, said that one of his major motivations was to promote gay tourism to Israel in the way that gay porn had previously promoted gay tourism to eastern Europe. (*Go to Tel Aviv and have sex with hunky Israeli guys! They're so masculine, they're soldiers!*) Even more ironically, *Men of Israel* was filmed on the site of a destroyed Palestinian village. Palestinian American filmmaker Nadia Awad called this "desecration porn."

But the central arena for these conflicts in the spring of 2010, was — surprisingly — Toronto. In Canada, gay people have legal marriage, and laws allow for asylum for some LGBT refugees. Toronto is also the home of an LGBT Palestinian solidarity organization Queers against Israeli Apartheid (QAIA), a small group created in 2008 that had carried out events and participated in the city's Dyke March and thirty-year-old Gay Pride March. The group's mission statement says, "Homophobia exists in Israel, Palestine and across all borders. But queer Palestinians face the additional challenge of living under occupation, subject to Israeli state violence and control. Israel's apartheid system extends gay rights only to some, based on race." This reminded me again of Ghadir's description of Israel as a "selective democracy." As a Palestinian lesbian, she should know.

Just as students were voting to divest in Berkeley, the Toronto B'nai Brith, the Simon Wiesenthal Center, and a Canadian gay Jewish attorney named Martin Gladstone decided to stop QAIA from marching in the 2010 parade. In the midst of the fracas, B'nai Brith Canada prepared a press release announcing that it had "contacted the Prime Minister of Canada, the Premier of Ontario and the Mayor of Toronto" in an effort to get QAIA excluded from the parade. It was going to the top.

The Canadian context is one in which Jews make up 1 percent of the electorate and are themselves divided on Israel. But 10 percent of Canadian voters are fundamentalist Christians who believe that a major war in the Middle East will make Jesus return to earth. B'nai Brith of Canada's spokesperson, Frank Dimant, was appointed inaugural chair of the department of modern Israel studies at Canada Christian College, a fundamentalist institution. On April 24, Toronto City Council member and mayoral candidate Giorgio Mammoliti gave QAIA 24 hours to withdraw from the Pride Toronto parade "or else." He threatened to introduce a motion at City Hall to withdraw Pride Toronto's funding. When QAIA refused, he did bring the motion to the floor, but in a 24–21 vote the council bounced the proposal back to its executive committee. Why? Because QAIA had not yet officially applied to march in the parade.

This was an extraordinary event in gay history. As far as I know, not only had Pride Toronto never excluded any group, but, more important, no government in the world had ever told a gay pride event to exclude someone. The relationship between the Toronto LGBT community and the Canadian government had become so intertwined and cozy that politicians felt free to police queer events. And even more upsetting, Pride Toronto had listened. A movement built in illegality and rebellion had become so enmeshed with the state that it could not imagine running an event without grants from the government. Hence homonationalism.

Soon afterward, Pride Toronto announced that no one would be allowed to march in the parade under banners with the words "Queers against Israeli Apartheid." A letter signed by Pride Toronto's executive director Tracey Sandilands promised the city that the words "Israeli apartheid" could "be covered under the need to abide by the City's anti-discrimination policies." In other words, the phrase "Israeli apartheid" was declared to be hate speech.

Pride Toronto announced it would vet all messaging in advance of the parade through an ethics committee. But a grassroots, Facebook-driven rebellion ("Don't Sanitize Pride") put a stop to that.

The next step was for the pro-Israel coalition to threaten Pride Toronto's funding. The year before, Pride Toronto had received $175,000 in public funds from the city. The May 22 *Globe and Mail* reported that Pride Toronto's board voted to ban the term "Israeli apartheid" from all of its events. The paper cited a statement by Israeli defense minister Ehud Barak earlier that year that "if the Palestinians vote in elections, it is a binational state. And if they don't, it is an apartheid state." Thus the paper cited evidence that the idea that Israel employs apartheid-like tactics is one that has been recognized broadly. Not just by Nelson Mandela and Jimmy Carter, and certainly not only by a small organization of homosexuals in Toronto.

Four days later, about a hundred people demonstrated in front of the offices of Pride Toronto. At stake, of course, was even more than whether LGBT people should have the right to say that Israel practices apartheid. QAIA is an organization created to support Palestinian queers. To do that, they have to stand for equality for all LGBT people. This global relationship reaching from one queer to another across the forbidden border of Jew and Palestinian, North American and occupied, was so anxiety-provoking that those entrusted to run Toronto's gay pride celebration were willing to profoundly change the history and intention of a thirty-year-old tradition. They were willing to transform a community-based event of free expression of queer diversity to a sponsor-driven event whose parameters were to be decided by funders. The meaning of QAIA was so profound that it caused one of the most significant transformations of self-understanding in the LGBT community since Stonewall. Pride Toronto had transformed itself into something entirely identified with and dependent on the state.

As Martin Gladstone told the Canadian LGBT newspaper *Xtra!* that, "like every other recipient of public money or corporate money, there are compliance issues. Pride has no choice." And in a sense he was right, because once the LGBT community allowed itself to become so dependent on state funding that it couldn't imagine going forward without it, it was doomed.

And yet. In the Jewish Voice for Peace's newsletter, *Muzzlewatch* warned that "Israel's foreign ministry thought it could easily dupe LGBT people as a cover for its agenda to make the world forget the Occupation and settlement expansion, walls, extra-judicial killings and so on and so forth. But they forget that many LGBT human rights heroes, many of them Jewish, are already leaders in the Palestinian equality movement and won't stand for it."

The first response came from Alan Li, an immigrant from Hong Kong who had founded Asian Community AIDS Services. On May 25, he resigned as Pride Toronto's grand marshal. Later that same week, eight founding members of the organization's first event, in 1981, wrote an open letter to the community explaining that they were

> totally opposed to the decision of the current Toronto Pride Committee to ban the use of "Israeli Apartheid" at Toronto Pride events. . . . We remind people of the political riots of Pride in the Stonewall rebellion against police repression in 1969 and community resistance to the massive bath raids of that year. . . . We also remember in the 1980s that lesbian and gay

activists around the world, including in Toronto in the Simon Nkoli Anti-Apartheid Committee, took up the struggle not only for lesbian and gay rights in South Africa but linked this to our opposition to the apartheid system of racial segregation and white supremacy. This global queer solidarity helps to account for how it was that constitutional protection for lesbians and gay men was first established in the new post-apartheid South Africa. Solidarity with all struggles against oppression has been a crucial part of the history of Pride.

Simon Nkoli was an openly gay black South African revolutionary who eventually died of AIDS. His outness and that of other freedom fighters influenced African National Congress leaders to include gay rights in the new South African constitution.

Pride Toronto's capitulation was quickly followed by a series of resignations. Michelle Walker, a cofounder of the Vancouver Dyke March, declined Pride Toronto's Community Service Award. *Xtra!* called upon Pride Toronto to reverse its decision. Jane Farrow turned down the "Honored Dyke" award. On June 4, eighteen former grand marshals and award recipients renounced their honors, including filmmaker John Greyson, winner of the 2009 Arts Award, whose withdrawal from the Tel Aviv LGBT Film Festival after Gaza marked the beginning of LGBT support for sanctions.

Elle Flanders, a Jewish lesbian filmmaker, wrote a piece about the debate from her perspective.

How does a Canadian Jew distinguish between rights for gays and rights for Arabs? Just recently the Knesset passed a law forbidding Arab citizens of Israel from purchasing homes within Jewish settlements (those inside Israel, not the West Bank). Effectively the law states that based on one's ethnicity (not citizenship), one may not buy property in certain areas. If we simply replaced this for "gays," would the liberal Canadian Jew be outraged?

Madrid

On June 9, queer conflicts about Israel and Palestine expressed themselves in an entirely different manner in Spain. Shortly after the Israeli army raided ships attempting to break the Gaza embargo, killing nine people, one Israeli contingent was banned from the July 3 Pride march in

Madrid. These were not Israeli individuals who were excluded, but rather the municipality of Tel Aviv, which, as part of Brand Israel, had intended to finance a float. The president of the Madrid LGBT Federation, Antonio Poveda, issued a statement: "After this attack, and taking into account that there has been no condemnation on the part of the Mayor of Tel Aviv, we decided not to allow the float to participate. We see nothing wrong with Israeli organizations who are clearly in defense of human rights taking part privately in gay pride."

This was escalation from the other queer corner. Israelis who were silent on the occupation were no longer welcome in Madrid. No other nationality in the entire World Pride was subjected to these terms for inclusion. On June 14, I spoke by Skype at a Toronto rally in favor of full inclusion of all LGBT people in gay pride events, including Madrid. Unlike Queers against Israeli Apartheid, the Israelis in Madrid did not respond with an argument for Open Pride, something that the Toronto experience showed resonates with LGBT people. Instead, pro-government Israelis made arguments emphasizing Palestinian homophobia as they whitewashed Israeli human rights violations. Dana International, the Israeli transsexual pop star, spoke at a press conference protesting the Madrid exclusion. She wore an Israeli Defense Force T-shirt. Mike Hamel of the Israeli nationalist organization Aguda argued that "there is a huge economic potential in gay tourism for Israel, and the pride parade is part of this." He added that Israel was petitioning World Pride to have Tel Aviv host the parade in 2013.

Back to Toronto

On Wednesday, June 23, 2010, Pride Toronto withdrew its ban of the words "Israeli apartheid." Instead it would require all participant groups to sign on to the city's nondiscrimination policy. On Sunday, July 4, Toronto's gay pride parade set off with QAIA members taking their place in the line of march without incident, but certainly with larger numbers and more visibility for their arguments than they would have experienced had the B'nai Brith not gotten involved.

The next day, Jerusalem police demanded that their own pride organizers change the parade route because they objected to queer Israelis passing a religious school and ending the march at the Knesset. Mikie Goldstein, chairman of parade organization Open House for Pride and Tolerance, was infuriated. "We are determined to rally for our rights," he said.

So at the same time that pro-Israeli government forces were using an illusion of tolerance in Tel Aviv as an excuse to defeat anti-occupation organizations, Israeli queers were being harassed in Jerusalem. And then being excluded from pride events around the world for either being anti-occupation or silent about war crimes.

What is most interesting to me in these extraordinary events was the letter of protest from the surviving founders of Toronto Gay Pride defending QAIA. They referred to the radical roots of gay liberation as necessary for LGBT progress around the world. They saw solidarity as a global force for change. But what is different between this earlier era's experiences and today is that in 1981 there was no chance of having LGBT perspectives integrated into the general progressive view. Battles about freedom, censorship, exclusion, and inclusion all took place within a community hermetically sealed from without by homophobia. The straight world did not participate and didn't even know that the discussions were happening. Today's queer international has a playing field of higher potential because of all the previous decades of work to make ourselves known to the dominant culture. Today we are poised to be an organic part of a larger freedom vision, and we are almost ready to insist on reciprocity. These battles inside of queer environments can be extended to the realms of international politics. And this is exactly what happened in Toronto. For although most of the letters of support that QAIA received came from other LGBT people or organizations, two nongay organizations participated in the conversation and expanded it: Jewish Voice for Peace and Electronic Intifada. Now, not only were LGBT people speaking to international politics, but international politics was speaking back. And in both cases, Jewish Voice for Peace and Electronic Intifada have openly gay people in significant positions who, rather than prioritizing away their own condition, are organically integrating their sexual politics within their internationally focused organizations.

It is hard to understand how anyone can condone this level of censorship — cracking down on queer groups and excluding them from pride events. It's nonsensical, and nothing positive will be gained by it. Why would the Israeli government go so far as to use the Toronto City Council to kick a tiny pro-Palestinian queer group out of a pride parade? I was reminded of my experience watching Netanyahu lie on television. *He must know he's lying*, I thought. But soon, I read a document that helped me understand the error of my interpretation.

Haifa

That same spring, Isha L'Isha, the Haifa-based feminist organization, issued a fascinating report, "A Wall of Silence: The Limits of Public Discourse in Israel, The Case of Gaza." Like Electronic Intifada and Jewish Voice for Peace, Isha L'Isha has integrated a gender perspective into its anti-occupation politics. Invoking the Israeli responsibility to counter false claims of human rights and a tolerant open society, Isha L'Isha addressed the question of public discourse and the institutions that obstruct it. The group claimed that in Israel, the subject of national security is perceived to be the domain of experts who are a small, exclusive group primarily consisting of retired military personnel. Women, Palestinian citizens of Israel, Mizrachim, the ultrareligious, citizens who have not done military service, people with disabilities, and new immigrants have minimal voice in the Israeli media during escalations of political violence. Despite the many stories from Gaza on the killing of civilians, very little was reported. Israeli antiwar demonstrations received almost no mainstream media coverage. They wrote, "Any knowledge that leads to a complex picture is perceived in contrast to the black-and-white reality and interpreted as dangerous and subversive."

The report then goes on to a very helpful and clear analysis of how the Israeli "silencing mechanism" works. According to Isha L'Isha, the system progresses by creating a clear sense of division into black and white, right and wrong, us and them. Fear and intimidation are broadcast to the Israeli public to make them feel constantly insecure personally and nationally. At the same time, the state constructs a national Jewish self-perception as moral, humane, cultured, and peace-seeking while constructing the stereotype of the Palestinian as the complete opposite.

I am struck by the importance of this last insight. In all matters, people who face and deal with problems, who negotiate, reach toward resolution. To do this seriously, one must view one's opponent as an equal partner in creating change. Since the media and educational system do not present a complex image of Palestinian society, it becomes impossible for Israelis to work with Palestinians for solutions.

So, it was not, as I suspected, that these right-wing Jews knew that they really did feel superior and were coming up with smokescreen arguments to hide behind, but rather that they were reflecting an Israeli mechanism of distortion that does not permit these feelings to be honestly expressed.

Most important, as the Isha L'Isha report points out, every alternative critique, action, and vision that does not line up with the official position of the state of Israel is seen by the hegemony as contradicting the vital interests of state security and, in some cases is seen as treacherous. In this way, many Israelis and many supporters of Israeli policies "refuse to take responsibility for the state of war," what Isha L'Isha calls "the endless war." They cite the Fourth Geneva Convention's definition of a "war crime." "War crimes include, among other things: Mass murder of innocent civilians; the deportation of a large group of people; use of non-conventional weapons; collective punishment; home demolitions as punishment; preventing food supplies, medical equipment and more." The report asks for a feminist alternative vision of the relationships between the state and its citizens, religion and the state, economics and security. And as I am reading, I come across the key statement that has united so many queers opposed to the occupation.

> Make the connection between one type of oppression and another within society, and therefore the solutions we propose are not for one group at the expense of another, but rather ones that the whole society would benefit from. It is a vision that includes difficult coping with knowledge open to complexity, the inclusion of new experiences, unfamiliar ideas and invites voices and experiences of those outside the immediate group.

From the first day that I started opening my mind to these questions, I have found over and over that, in the arena of Israel and Palestine, it is those who are the most disenfranchised from power who are the most ecumenical and inclusive. They are the most creative and most open to a world in which *all* people's needs are addressed. Because they know that unless it is a society for *all*, they are going to be excluded. For this reason the queer anti-occupation voice of Palestinians and Israelis repeatedly proved itself to be the most advanced and therefore inclusive—within a complex debate—toward human reconciliation and justice.

    The report concludes with the stark admission that feminist women in Israel against the occupation are perceived by Israeli society as taking actions that identify "too strongly" with the enemy and that compromise to the point of betraying the interests of Israel. This perception stands in full contrast to the self-perception these women have. They see themselves as committed to values of justice, creating political change that incorporates the aspirations and needs of all sides. Compromise, to them, is not weakness. And that perception is in stark contrast to dominant Israeli and pro-Israeli ideology.

At this point I have solidified my understanding.

The Yiddish word *mensch* is widely recognized. It means being a person in the full sense of the word. To be a person, one has to be able to face and deal with problems. This requires having an intact self and seeing that other people are real. It requires facing and understanding the sources of one's discomforts, being accountable to not project anxieties onto the people who did not cause them. It requires knowing the difference between a trigger and an attack. It means taking responsibility to clearly explain how you feel and then being interactive enough to listen to how the other person feels. As one and the other trade information, each of them should be transformed, even slightly, by the knowledge accrued by listening. It means recognizing that there are two equal parties in the relationship and that they both have feelings, experiences, and rights.

I am blown away by the insight of Isha L'Isha that as long as Israel falsely creates Palestine as an inferior partner, it will never be able to solve problems with Palestine. Since all human beings have, as the Lebanese LGBT organization Helem says, "inalienable" rights, to refuse to engage is pathological. It is a kind of grandiosity born, I believe, from the hidden yet present knowledge that one's own behavior is unjustified. Refusing to engage is to choose the façade over truth, to reject accurate knowledge of one's actual self. And so, the Israeli "silencing mechanism" is a pathological behavior designed to protect a delusion of superiority. And it requires escalated upkeep.

So there are these two opposing forces at play in the arena that interests me most:

There are people in Israel and around the world, at all different levels of society, who want to repeat over and over again that "Israel is being singled out" for criticism. And that that fact, this singling out, is more important than whether or not Israel's actions are just. Even though Israel is actually not being singled out, they claim this because they have internalized the idea that to face and deal realistically and truthfully would endanger them and be treacherous to their larger community. They believe that repetition is safe, and expansion of understanding is unsafe. They feel frightened, but they are the ones who are dangerous. So they alternate between stasis and negative escalation.

Then there are people who are invested in dynamic group action as an impulse for change. The most viable, nonviolent strategy on the table is the one being propelled by a group of secular Palestinian intellectuals and being embraced by their Israeli and global counterparts. And this is the strategy of boycott, divestment, and sanctions. What makes BDS difficult is that it requires a critical mass of people to take the time to understand why it is necessary and how it works. And it is dependent on people outside of Palestine and Israel to carry it out. We have to be the ones to impose sanctions, or else there are no sanctions. It is a strategy devised by the oppressed, but dependent on allies. And as far as I can see, it is the strategy with the most potential for success.

What makes this even more exciting, is that despite the homophobic continuum of Palestine, Israel, and the United States, both this sector of Palestinian secular intellectuals at the base of boycott and the boycott's global participants include a significant number of LGBT people: Palestinians, Israelis, and internationals who approach boycott from a queer politic of inclusion and rights for *all*. This sector is increasingly interactive with PACBI and other anti-occupation organizations, and it is therefore influencing them in their recognition of LGBT communities in Palestine, Israel, and other places all over the globe. It is an unusual opportunity.

Ramallah

In spring 2010, a number of events pushed this relationship to the next level. First, a member of Al-Qaws became a staff person at PACBI. Then a new organization was created in Ramallah: Palestinian Queers for Boycott, Divestment, Sanctions (PQBDS).

The launching statement of PQBDS is fascinating in terms of the tropes and themes unfolding in the coming together of the queer international and anti-occupation politics: "We see the Queer movements as political in their nature; and ones that analyze the intersections between different struggles, evaluate relations of power and try to challenge them." Here it is again: the uniting across oppressions, the plea for the complicated *all*, the humane use of the word *try*. "We call upon the LGBTQI communities around the globe to stand for justice in Palestine through boycott, divestment and sanctions against Israel until the latter ends its multi-tiered oppression of the Palestinian people."

Again, the call comes from *within* the rainbow, using Western-style terms (LGBTQI), although the language is more ideological ("struggle") than an American queer would use. But in a paradigm that is very familiar to queer people who are used to identifying across categories, the statement is positioned as one queer person asking another for support—a resonant request.

The statement goes on to discuss settlements, the Wall of Separation, and checkpoints. And subterfuge: "In the last years, Israel has been leading an international campaign that tries to present Israel as the 'only democracy' and the 'gay haven' in the Middle East, while ironically portraying Palestinians, who suffer every single day from Israel's state racism and terrorism, as barbaric and homophobic."

The statement ends by explicitly asking LGBTQI people around the world to "reject all invitations to speak at and collaborate with Israeli universities and institutions, in accordance with the guidelines for the Palestine Academic and Cultural Boycott of Israel (PACBI)."

Omar's excuse for not aligning PACBI with the Palestinian queer movement, because it was not publicly pro-boycott, was now moot. As one Palestinian lesbian wrote me by email: "I think this gives us a head start with the BDS movement. Lets see if they do the same for us. :)" Of course it's the :) at the end of her message that says it all. The creation of PQBDS is an extremely savvy and sophisticated move on the part of LGBT Palestinians. They are enacting the wish for the *all*, and giving many diverse kinds of people an opportunity to agree. They are reaching out to PACBI in a way that forces it to acknowledge the Palestinian queer movement. They are reaching out to LGBT people around the world who may be new to boycott but who pay attention when other queers talk about their lives. And they are providing an opportunity for anti-occupation groups in Israel and around the world to further integrate boycott politics with the global LGBT. And simultaneously, they are giving voice to the most authentic position capable of contradicting Israeli homonationalism. It is a seemingly simple step, with enormous potential, and a transformative range of meaning.

Four days after their launch, *Bekhsoos*, the publication of Meem, an organization for Lebanese lesbian, bisexual and trans women ran an interview with PQBDS, asking, "This is the first time we hear Palestinian queers from the Occupied Territory and inside Israel publicly speaking in alignment with the Boycott/Divestment/Sanctions campaign (which was launched in 2005). Why now?"

PQBDS: The Palestinian queer community now has enough resources to engage with different discourses and to use different strategies to bring the sexual and gender struggle to the forefront. . . . It was about time to start deconstructing Israel's image as a "gay haven," and put a stop to the use of our name.

Bekhsoos: Sexual and body rights often take a backseat in nationalist struggles. Within the context of the Palestinian struggle today, why is a queer perspective necessary?

PQBDS: Unfortunately we often hear political activists delegitimize sexual and bodily rights, claiming it is not the right timing, and that we must all focus on the national struggle only—as if it is a sterile struggle. We believe that Palestinian Queers can contribute, challenge, and hopefully in the future, break the current struggle's hierarchy and instead suggest to mainstream political movements (including the BDS movement) alternative ways of doing and changing that are based on real engagement between struggles and deep understandings of the intersections between them. . . . We are an integral part of this society.

So here it is: the strategy to create a more progressive, secular, feminist and pro-gay Palestinian movement, coming from Palestinian queers, and using the nonviolent strategy of sanctions. Could any make more sense than this? It has been many years since I have become aware of a political movement with so much potential for progressive change. Not since ACT UP in the 1980s—also a movement of severely oppressed people facing hugely distorting mythologies with no rights. And just as ACT UP was able, ultimately, to change the world, I see that kind of radical potential in the Palestinian queer movement today.

Berlin

All of these resonant events, tendencies, alliances, evolutions, and expansions in the relationship between Israel and Palestine and the global LGBT were to come to a crashing head in the late spring of 2010, when Judith Butler was awarded the Civil Courage Prize by the Berlin Christopher Street Day Committee for its gay pride celebration. Organizers did not get what they bargained for.

It was a rather dramatic occasion. A huge, festive crowed gathered. The host made a gorgeous introduction, honoring the day's awardee. Butler approached the microphone to excited applause. And then she said, in perfect German:

When I consider what it means today to accept such an award, then I believe that I would actually lose my courage, if I were to simply accept the prize under the present political conditions. For instance, some of the organizers explicitly made racist statements or did not dissociate themselves from them. The host organizations refuse to understand antiracist policies as an essential part of their work. Having said this, I must distance myself from this complicity with racism, including anti-Muslim racism.

We have all noticed that gay, bisexual, lesbian, trans and queer people can be instrumentalized by those who want to wage wars, i.e., cultural wars against migrants by means of forced Islamaphobia and military wars against Iraq and Afghanistan. In these times and by these means we are recruited for nationalism and militarism. Currently, many European governments claim that our gay, lesbian, queer rights must be protected and we are made to believe that the new hatred of immigrants is necessary to protect us. Therefore we must say no to such a deal. To be able to say no under these circumstances is what I call courage. But who says no? And who experiences this racism? Who are the queers who really fight against such politics?

If I were to accept an award for courage, I would have to pass this award onto those who really demonstrate courage. If I were able to, I would pass it onto the following groups that are courageous here and now.

1. GLADT: Gays and Lesbians from Turkey. This is a queer migrant self-organization. They work very successfully within the fields of multiple discrimination, homophobia, transphobia, sexism, and racism.

2. LesMigraS: Lesbian Migrants and Black Lesbians, is an anti-violence and anti-discrimination division of Lesbenberatung Berlin. It has worked with success for ten years. They work in the fields of multiple discrimination, self-empowerment, and antiracist labor.

3. SUSPECT: A small group of queers that established an anti-violence movement. They assert it is not possible to fight against homophobia without also fighting against racism.

4. ReachOUT is a counseling center for victims of rightwing extremist, racist, anti-Semitic, homophobic, and transphobic violence in Berlin. It is critical of structural and governmental violence.

Yes, and these are all groups that work in the Transgeniale (Alternative Pride), that shape it, that fight against homophobia, transphobia, sexism, racism, and militarism, and that—as opposed to the commercial Christopher Street Day—did not change the date of their event because of the Soccer World Cup.

I would like to congratulate these groups for their courage, and I am sorry that under these circumstances, I am unable to accept this award.

This quickly became a full-fledged scandal broadcast from mainstream German press and television, *Le Monde diplomatique,* to academic forums and, of course, the queer international. As SUSPECT said in its response:

> Radical movements and individual acts of bravery or brilliance do not come from nowhere, but are the result of collective labor and local and transnational histories of organizing. . . . The globalizing significance of Pride parades in not only corporatizing LGBT politics worldwide, but also drawing the line between those countries that are modern and those that need to either catch up or be punished, invaded, targeted through visa and other anti-immigrant campaigns, or deprived of aid, echoed in our ears.

In clarifying statements, Butler gave a series of concrete examples of homonationalism, on the part of the Berlin Christopher Street Day leadership. Using information gathered by queers of color in Berlin and their allies, Butler pointed to German gay groups like Maneo that actively seek institutionalized racial profiling as police practice. She detailed the denial of gentrification and a provocation of antigay violence, with the blame being placed instead on Muslim immigrant communities threatened with displacement. She pointed to the false distinction between queer and Muslim. She suggested that the German LGBT community focus instead on increases in right-wing violence and homophobia within the church.

A week later, Jasbir Puar posted some behind-the-scenes background to these events on Bully Bloggers, an emerging forum created by academics Lisa Duggan, J. Jack Halberstam, and others.

According to Puar, on June 17, two days before the award, emails started flying among academics and activists about Butler's acceptance of the Civil Courage Award. As a result Butler received many letters about the Christopher Street Day organizers noting that they had supported explicitly anti-immigrant and anti-Muslim positions. After meeting with local groups who updated her on the realities of gay German politics, she determined her response.

Puar addressed some fundamental contradictions in solidarity politics in which "cultural capital accrues to those who represent the 'Others' rather than to those who are represented."

On July 1, Puar published a piece in the *Guardian of London* titled "Israel's Gay Propaganda War." Here she argues that Israel's strategy of "recruiting cultural icons to promote Israeli modernity has faltered" and that Israel is being increasingly contested at LGBT events.

Two days later, Aeyal Gross, the gay Israeli law professor who had originally invited me to speak at Tel Aviv University, published a piece on Bully Bloggers about the history of queer Israeli anti-occupation organizing. Gross described how, in 2001, after the beginning of the Second Intifada, he and a group of friends decided that they could not take their usual places in nationalist gay pride events, "given the egregious human rights violations." Instead, they decided to march in black carrying a banner emblazoned "There Is No Pride in the Occupation." This attracted a lot of press attention and led to the founding of the queer radical activist group Black Laundry. "LGBT activists," Gross wrote, "now find themselves in a double bind." Victories for civil rights are quickly co-opted by the Israeli government. "Gay rights," Gross said, "have essentially become a public-relations tool." In the past, he said, it was widely assumed that LGBT rights would correlate with advances in civil rights and the peace process. "Today, the opposite may be true: LGBT rights are used as a fig leaf, and the larger the area that needs to be hidden, the larger the fig leaf must be." The terms of the "deal" between Israeli LGBTs and the state are "that we will be good, normative and Zionist gays, who are willing to partake in the discourse of Israel as a liberal democracy and collaborate directly and indirectly in the state's use of gay rights. . . . In return we will get sympathy and some support from the state."

I was truly amazed at how much territory this global LGBT, this queer international, this coming together of LGBT politics and anti-occupation politics had covered since I first became aware of the debate that Al-Qaws, Aswat, PQBDS, Maikey, Puar, Butler, Gross, and others were constructing. I had been contacted by the LGBT studies conference at Tel Aviv University only eight months before. In that short time, the bridge was created between the Palestinian queer movement and the boycott movement, major dramas played out in gay pride events around the world, and in every case, the anti-occupation faction was victorious. The boycott's legitimacy has increased so much that the Israeli Knesset was now considering dramatic human rights violations for its Jewish citizens to counteract the boycott's consequences. And the conversation had reached the pages of some of the world's mainstream newspapers.

This was one of the most encouraging progressive developments in grassroots global politics of our day and represented the potential for enormous understanding between people of diverse levels of privilege and experience. The uniting factor was a desire for justice and a kind of deeply human identification across borders real and imagined. The coming together of anti-occupation and LGBT politics was appearing as one of the most exciting and hopeful, promising developments in a contemporary world lacking imagination and hope. Change is always possible. And here it was.

9. AMREEKA

Haneen of Al-Qaws and Ghadir of Aswat arrived in New York on a snowy February 2, one day late due to weather. Sami would fly from Amman to San Francisco ten days after. Because I had met Ghadir in Haifa and Haneen in Tel Aviv and again in Ramallah with Sami, their faces had been in my heart and mind every day of the ten months of planning. As the details of the six-city tour and a team of almost fifty people on the ground had come together, I was thinking about Ghadir, Sami, and Haneen continually, sometimes waking up in the middle of the night with some detail of their trip on my mind. They had become the center of my consciousness. When I saw Haneen and Ghadir come out of customs, I felt filled with love for them. In my view, the four of us had sustained an amazingly healthy, productive, constructive political process. After only meeting briefly in person, we were able to negotiate really difficult political questions fairly easily, due to great mutual respect, a desire to be effective, and maturity in problem solving. So when Nadia Awad (the Palestinian American filmmaker) and I finally saw Haneen and Ghadir emerge from customs at the airport, I felt this huge joy.

We checked them into the Desmond Tutu Conference Center in Manhattan, housed in an old monastery at Twenty-first Street and Tenth Avenue. The icy walk to the restaurant around the corner revealed immediately that Ghadir needed winter boots. But slipping and sliding, we made it and were joined for dinner by Mahdi, a Palestinian architect working in the United States, and Jasbir Puar. Jasbir had asked to join the tour by organizing a special public event for Ghadir and Sami to meet with queer people of color groups on February 18 at the Audre Lorde Project, and she had become an integral part of the entourage. She had just come back from a conference in Amsterdam at which both homonationalism and its critique had surfaced and collided. Whereas the European and the global queer communities were increasingly using homonationalism in their work, the United States remained behind.

The next day we went to Macy's and bought gloves and scarves and warm shoes. Ghadir picked out gray suede boots with tassels that looked great (but that later proved hard to take off at airport security). Haneen and Ghadir met with the Arcus Foundation, and then went with me through the bitter cold to the office of radio station WBAI-FM Pacifica radio, a fifty-year-old People's Radio, to be interviewed by Brad Taylor of the queer show OUT-FM. Brad, an old friend from ACT UP, comes from Texas and still has the drawl. He was busy as a member of the Gaza Freedom March and a long-term supporter of Palestine, working in a group called Siege Busters, organizing to be part of the Freedom Flotilla. They had a great interview—talking about events unfolding daily in Egypt. Brad raised Joseph Massad's criticism of Arab queers working with LGBT frameworks. Although Massad loomed large in every conversation about queer sexuality and Arab peoples, the queer Palestinians had never had direct contact with Massad's work and didn't know how or if his thoughts had evolved to include them.

Brad talked to Haneen and Ghadir about the goals and visions of the queer Palestinian movement in the context of the revolution exploding in Egypt. Their responses were clear: the more open a society, the better for women and queers. They described how the CNN reports in their hotel rooms were troubling: they found the U.S. media's obsession with the Muslim Brotherhood to be distorting and missing the point. It was their first interview and a very successful and reassuring one.

Then we got into a cab and came to my sixth-floor walkup for a cup of tea, and then went back down the stairs to Moustache, a tiny Lebanese restaurant in Manhattan's East Village. There Haneen, Ghadir, Jasbir, Mahdi, Nadia, and I were joined by Nadia's sister, Alia, and by a special guest: the queer filmmaker John Greyson had flown down from Toronto to meet with Haneen and Ghadir. The food was great, and the conversation was exciting. Nadia brought the new PSA she had just written, shot, and edited in a matter of days for PQBDS. John talked to us about the possibility of World Pride coming to Toronto in 2014, and we went through and around some preliminary thoughts and ideas—all I knew was that I envisioned "a float," and I kept saying "and some kind of float." World Pride is an event in which many people march by country. What if there were a Palestinian contingent, placing Palestine in the queer global pantheon? What if in the next three years we could mobilize the queer Palestinian diaspora? And, most important to me . . . what if there was . . . *a float*?

John also brought up a question close to my heart, as the cofounder, with Jim Hubbard, of the MIX LGBT Experimental Film and Video Festival—now in our twenty-fifth year. John reported that as part of Brand Israel, the Israeli consulate was making donations to LGBT film festivals to buy time to program queer Israeli films. Of course we all support queer Israeli filmmakers, and any LGBT film festival programmer should include his or her work if he or she thinks it deserves to be programmed. But none of us wanted the Israeli consulate buying space for work to use the gay community to prove how progressive Israel is. We didn't want the consulate to use our community institutions to promote the illusion of Israel as a gay utopia to deflect attention from human rights violations against Palestinians. As Haneen said, "When you go through a checkpoint, it does not matter what the sexuality of the soldier is."

This question of "pinkwashing" was looming larger and larger in the conversation of queers and the occupation.

While homonationalism is a product of white culture and emerges unconsciously whenever white gay people (and their admirers) assimilate into racist power structures, it is not deliberate government policy. However, nowhere has homonationalism been more consciously harnessed by governments than in Israel, where the maneuvering of gay rights to support racist agendas evolved strategically from marketing impulses. This pinkwashing is a paradigm central to an understanding of queers and our relationship to occupation. It is as fundamental as homonationalism, and here I want to give you a clear documentary history of the practice of pinkwashing, which you can use as an analytical tool.

The phrase was originally coined in 1985 by Breast Cancer Action to identify companies that claimed to support women with breast cancer while actually profiting from their illness. In April 2010, QUIT used the term "pinkwashing" as a twist on "greenwashing," used to describe companies that claimed to be eco-friendly in order to make a profit. The first use of the term in relationship to Palestine is attributed to Ali Abunimah, the editor of Electronic Intifada, at a meeting in 2010 where he said, "We won't put up with Israel Whitewashing, Greenwashing or Pinkwashing."

That night Jasbir talked to us about her work in more detail, and everything seemed to be clicking. She had just come back from a conference on queer sexualities in the Netherlands. She said that while homonationalism and pinkwashing were prominent topics of conversation, at the same time nationalist and racist discourses about the supremacy of Christian cultures over Islamic ones were equally predominant. The more she spoke, the more my earlier thoughts were reinforced about the gay world dividing into two separate impulses over Palestine, Muslim immigration, and nationalism. We were LGBT or we were queer. That night, we had all these talented queer people sitting together making media, making theory, imagining floats, communicating, thinking together, and trading recipes for labane. I had already learned my first Arabic words *Yalla* (let's go) and *Yanni* (I mean), and *Sa-ha* (something to do with drinking alcohol, which we were doing a lot); I now knew how to say *Hallas* (approximately, "shit" or "that's no good" or some negation), *enti* and *inti* (to be said in repetition — *enti inti*, meaning *you* — "you" with emphasis), *Anjad* (truth, really), and the most important word: *wot-everrrr* ("whatever" in an Arabic accent). Never did I learn how to say, "How are you?" "Hello," or even "yes" and "no." But I could run a monologue of "Let's go, I mean, really, you, I mean, shit. *Whatever!*" I also was trying to learn Arabic-English Facebook slang, which included repetition of letters: "Haneeeeeeeeeen. Al-siiiiiiiiiiiiiiigh" and a few numbers, especially 3 and 7, which, I later learned, represented letters whose sounds can't be replicated in the English alphabet.

We also now put "Al" meaning "the" in front of everything worthy of respect. This came from a moment at Creating Change when someone asked me, "Are you *the* Sarah Schulman?" Unable to let me forget it, Ghadir dubbed me "Al-Schulman," *The* Schulman. And she was now Al-Ghadir, and we were now on Al-Tour with Al-Haneen. It was a joke, but also our sign of respect for each other through the teasing.

We also talked more about Joseph Massad, whose work argues that "Western male white-dominated" gay activists, under the umbrella of what he terms the "gay international," have engaged in a "missionary" effort to impose the binary categories of heterosexual/homosexual into cultures where no such subjectivities exist, and that these activists in fact ultimately replicate in these cultures the very structures they challenge in their own home countries. Massad wrote that "the categories *gay* and *lesbian* are not universal at all and can only be universalized by the epistemic, ethical, and political violence unleashed on the rest of the world by the very international human rights advocates whose aim is to defend the very people their intervention is creating." We learned that he had never actually met with the new wave of young queer Palestinian activists, and so John, who was having lunch with him the next day, offered to make the introduction.

The next morning, I picked them up to go to the airport, and we flew to Minneapolis to give a workshop at Creating Change, the twenty-third annual conference of the National LGBT Task Force. Local Palestinian solidarity activists had organized our rides to and from the airport, and we were met by a cowgirl named Ashley driving a blue Oldsmobile. After checking in, we registered for the conference. Haneen's nameplate said "Haneen — Jerusalem, XX." We ate hamburgers, which triggered jet lag. But by the next morning we were having coffee at 7 and on the go. The executive director of the conference, Sue Hyde, made a point of coming by to sit with us and to welcome Haneen and Ghadir. She told us there were twenty-two hundred people at the conference, and she was very attentive and supportive about the time, placement, and location of our workshop, titled "Palestinian Queers/U.S. Queers: What Is Our Relationship?" Haneen and Ghadir also received a very kind email from Joseph Massad inviting them to get together with him while they were in New York. Even though the schedules didn't correspond, the ice had been broken, and a new phase of dialogue had begun.

One weird thing that happened that morning was that a Jewish friend of mine stopped by our table. I introduced her to Haneen and Ghadir and asked her what workshop she was presenting.

"You wouldn't be interested," she said.

"I am interested. Tell me."

"It's on LGBT synagogues and their relationship to Jewish gay organizations."

"Sounds great," I said. "I'm coming."

The last thing I wanted was any paranoia or misunderstanding coming from gay Jews. So at 10:30 I went off to the workshop, which proved to be an interesting discourse about "controversy" and its righteous aspects. Very appropriate. The thirty or so of us went around the circle and introduced ourselves.

"I'm Sarah Schulman. I have been creating queer Jewish literature for thirty years. I'm happy to invite you all to the panel I am moderating today at 3 with two dykes from the Palestinian queer movement. Which is part of a tour that has been endorsed by Sharon Kleinbaum, the rabbi at Beit Simchat Torah, New York's LGBT synagogue." To which a young man from her synagogue nodded and smiled.

And, in fact, about ten people from that workshop did come, as did about one hundred others to hear Ghadir and Haneen speak. Urvashi Vaid, one of my mentors and heroes, also came. And as Ghadir and Haneen spoke over and over again about feminism and how feminism was foremost in both their organizations, Urvashi kept nodding and smiling.

It was a really good event. They told the histories of their organizations. How Aswat, the Palestinian lesbian group, had started in a chat room, and how the six women who were communicating there built enough trust to actually meet. How Al-Qaws, the Palestinian LGBTQ group, had started as a project of the Jerusalem Open House but then realized that they needed to meet in a Palestinian space. And how Haneen became director of Al-Qaws, an organization divided by the Wall of Separation, which means the Ramallah members cannot attend the organization's dances because they can't come through the checkpoint. Even so, four hundred other Palestinian queers already in Israel had just showed up for Al-Qaws's latest dance party in Yaffo. Because mobility and travel are so difficult for them, the queers in the Ramallah chapter of Al-Qaws, of which Sami is a member, bring a more radical politic to the larger organization and enrich it in numerous ways. All of this information was spanking new to 99 percent of the audience. Haneen and Ghadir were great speakers. They were savvy, funny, tough, personal, and driven by integrity.

Of the many stories they told and ideas they expressed, two really stood out for me. One was Ghadir's personal story. After attending the requisite segregated Israeli school system, she had come out as a student at Tel Aviv University, thinking she was the only Palestinian lesbian on the planet. So her entire lesbian sexual life took place with Jewish women. To have lovers and friends, she would go to parties and clubs where she was the only Palestinian. One night she and her lover were going to a party, and her friends asked her to not say that she was "Arab." Since she is trilingual (Hebrew, Arabic, English), she could pass for Jewish, and she followed their requests. But soon afterward she had a crisis and "realized" she could not be lesbian and Palestinian. She packed up her belongings, left without saying good-bye to her girlfriend, and moved back to her city, where she was in the closet for ten years. She got married, had a child and mimicked Palestinian heterosexuality, until one day when she was watching *Ally McBeal* on television. And there was the famous "first TV kiss" between Calista Flockhart and Lucy Liu. She could not get it out of her mind. Soon she got divorced and joined Aswat. She is still not out to her family or to her closest straight Palestinian friends.

This provoked a very interesting conversation about what "coming out" means in a Palestinian context. Both Haneen and Ghadir explained that open conversation about sexuality in general is taboo in Palestinian society. A straight woman would not announce to her parents that she was having sex with her boyfriend. So to say, "I am a lesbian" is to say "I have sex" and would therefore just result in being thought of as promiscuous. What emerged from the conversation is the realization that in English the term "coming out" represents two distinct and separate experiences: the recognition of one's own desire *and* the placement of one's self willfully in vulnerable line with public hostility. For Palestinians, only the first concept is relevant at this point. Because their resistance to the occupation is paramount in all their activities and unites them with their families, it is not essential to come out in this way in the LGBT community.

When I asked them if they work with Israeli gay groups, the answer again was quite sobering. Ghadir described being excluded from the demonstration protesting the killings at the Tel Aviv Gay Center and described this as a "lost opportunity." Instead, she noted, Palestinian feminist groups in Israel, such as Kayan, have welcomed Aswat. Of course, not also without bumps. She described a recent event against "honor killings"—a large coalition in which every group except Aswat was listed by name and definition; Aswat, whose full name is Aswat: Gay Palestinian Women, was shortened for the public statement. When Ghadir called around to other groups on the list she found that some were willing to insist on Aswat's full inclusion by name. Not all, but some. It became clear to the audience at Creating Change what a difficult spot these women are in, and how amazing it is that they have been able to bring together feminism, queer desire and love, and resistance to occupation into a coherent, articulate, and humane politic.

Later, Urvashi invited us out for a drink on the top floor of the Minneapolis Hilton. We brought along Dunya Alwan, of Birthright Unplugged, an Arab American queer woman who has worked tirelessly to expose Birthright—an organization that brings Jews (for free) from around the world to Israel, where they can get the citizenship that Palestinians are denied. With her came Flo, Jessica, and some other friends from various Palestinian solidarity groups who had done so much to bring out the Minneapolis audience. Urvashi, always honest and always willing to hear what others have to say, expressed how impressed she was with the presentations, how moved, yet indicated that she had disagreements with the sanctions movement.

When the drinks arrived, I had my cornball moment of offering a toast. I quoted Audre Lorde, who famously said, "I am a Black lesbian warrior mother poet doing her job, asking are you doing yours?" And I held my glass and toasted: "We, who are doing our job!" It was so unifying to know that we were a room of women, each and every one for whom that statement was true.

Dunya, who was meeting Urvashi for the first time, clearly and concisely conveyed the bare bones of the Palestinian situation, and by the end of the conversation Urvashi had conceded that she lacked basic information. This was exactly the point I had come to. The more I learned about Palestine, the more I realized how little real information is in general circulation in the United States. And with that comes the difficult but necessary self-criticism that I had confused repression of information for information. We ended up hanging out with Urvashi at different stages of the evening, dancing with her at a South Asian dance party, and finally eating pizza together at 2 A.M. in the hotel bar.

The next morning I sent Ghadir and Haneen off to Chicago and Boston, keeping in touch by text and phone. We had bonded. As I watched them drive away to the airport, I missed them already. And an hour later a text came from Ghadir, "We miss you." Something profound had been created.

With all of this hanging out, we'd communicated on the deepest levels. I found myself identifying with Haneen, who reminded me of a twenty-year-younger version of myself. We found it very easy to talk, and Ghadir and Haneen and I had lots of discussions about many complex things. One was this ever-present question of what, exactly, "Zionism" is. I was still trying to figure it out. In the common parlance of people who support human rights for Palestine, "Zionist" is a weird buzz word. It means "people who are pro-Israel" more than it means "people who ideologically believe that Jews must have a nation-state." But to me this was a mistake, because many Jews who support Israel do not necessarily see themselves as Zionists. It's not ideological; it's emotional and sentimental, primarily because they have family in Israel. To call them "Zionists" is to misunderstand, and to speak to someone who doesn't know you're addressing them. I believe that these people can work through their emotional responses by getting more information and having more direct experience of Palestine and Palestinians. To me, when I was growing up, a "Zionist" was a Jew who moved to Israel. The rest of us were not Zionists because we lived here, in the diaspora. A typical conversation from my childhood would be:

"What happened to Joe?"

"Didn't you hear? He became a Zionist and moved to Tel Aviv."

"You're kidding!"

So, for me, "Zionists" are a subset of people who support Israel. And as we know from born-again George W. Bush and his presidency, the most powerful Zionists in the world are not Jewish.

With Haneen and Ghadir, this was an interesting conversation because "Zionist" is a fallback shortcut for "the problem." It was awkward introducing them to the American model, especially the New York model, which includes some Jews from a left-wing tradition that was never Zionist. Only then did I find out that in Israel, as far as Israeli Jews are concerned, "Zionist" is often used to mean "good citizen."

"Hey," I asked them one day. "You guys are perfectly trilingual—Arabic, Hebrew, English—not just speaking but also reading and writing. But the Jewish Israelis I know are only bilingual. How does that happen?"

"We go to segregated schools," they said.

How could I not know this?

And then, how ironic that as a result of segregation the Palestinians know three languages, and the Jews only two.

Before leaving Creating Change, I attended Dunya's panel on pinkwashing, convened with some of the local activists Flo, Jessica, Joseina, and Kate, who were from the International Jewish Anti-Zionist Network. I found this group's name to be unhelpful and inaccurate because I believe that many secular Jews "support" Israel, not because they hold Zionist ideologies; but rather because they have sentimental and emotional relationships to family members who were scattered by oppression and genocide. The women had strong arguments in their defense. We had a good conversation about this. Though they entirely recognized the paradigm I was describing, they felt that those people—sentimentally, but not ideologically, pro-Israel—actually were Zionists and needed to recognize themselves as such. For me, this was not persuasive because I don't think people work that way. They reject a word they don't identify with, instead of "realizing" that that word describes them. Especially when there are real Zionists, people who ideologically believe in Jewish nationalism. The winning strategy, as I see it, is to help Americans understand what Palestinians' lives and hopes and visions are, in informative and humanizing ways. The goal is to shift support from people and policies that maintain the occupation to those that dismantle it. I just don't see this use of the word "Zionist" as being effective in reaching those goals.

What I found to be very persuasive was Dunya's startling PowerPoint presentation about pinkwashing. The slides began with the slogan of the 2006 World Pride Celebration in Jerusalem, "Love Without Borders." The dishonesty is so stark; it is almost hard to grasp how anyone could have thought that would be a good idea in a city that is 56 percent under occupation. The irony of a segregated "World Pride" was not apparent to some of the participants. A poster created by Blue Star PR, an Israeli marketing firm, followed this. The heading read "Where in the Middle East Can Gay Officers Serve Their Country?" The answer? "Only in Israel." The next slide featured a poster by the group StandWithUs. "Why does Israel look like paradise to gay Palestinians?" The answer? "Israel respects life." It really clarified the attempt to depict Palestinians as primitive and Israelis as modern through frame after frame of re-created posters, bus-stop placards, and advertisements. These were especially grating now that I heard queer Palestinians speak for themselves instead of being misquoted in nationalist Israeli propaganda.

Dunya also showed an image that hit me personally. As a Jewish child in New York in the 1960s, I had many opportunities to be solicited for coins to plant trees in Israel. The idea was to help them "make the desert bloom," and although I had never rethought this experience, I still carried with me a benign sense of good at having been part of "planting trees." Dunya showed us a 1930s postcard of a Palestinian village called Saffourieh— a fully populated hillside town with streets, buildings, and gardens. She followed this with an identical photo of the same hilltop today. Only the place is called Tzippori and there was no sign at all that anyone had ever lived there. Instead the hill is covered in trees. I had never thought about where "my" trees had been planted, but certainly the last thing I would have imagined was reforestation to eliminate any sign of destroyed Palestinian villages.

Dunya's presentation was also devoted in part to donations of money to Frameline, the San Francisco LGBT Film Festival, by the Israeli Consulate. This was the second time in a week that the subject had been raised, and I was full of questions. How much money were they receiving? Who is the person at the consulate with such an intimate understanding of our LGBT community institutions? Had anyone spoken with KC Price, the executive director of Frameline? No one could answer any of these questions. It seemed obvious to me that Frameline is a community venue. We make the films, we buy the tickets, we are friends of the filmmakers, performers, and producers. My film *The Owls*, cowritten with the director Cheryl Dunye, had just played at Frameline. Didn't we have a right to sit down with the leaders and find out what they are thinking, how much money is involved, and find out how we could help them keep our festivals from being used for values we don't hold? This was an interesting coming together of two distinctly different political experiences. As an AIDS activist, I had always felt at home in the queer community. As an Arab and Palestinian rights activist, Dunya had been marginalized. Now was our chance to bring this all together and take our place as a central constituency inside the community.

At this point I sat down and with help from the anti-occupation global activist community, amassed a year-by-year documentary guide to pinkwashing so that the history and context of this emerging paradigm could be more easily understood and confronted. And the first thing that became clear, while doing this work, was that pinkwashing was a direct product of Israel's remarketing campaign: Brand Israel. (See the appendix.)

The next leg of the tour followed in the same vein. Lynette Jackson, an African American lesbian professor of African history at the University of Illinois, Circle Campus, moderated the Chicago event. She managed to pull out 150 people on Super Bowl Sunday at 2 P.M.! How did she do this? It was the Zeitgeist. The next talk at the Harvard Kennedy School, organized by the director of the Carr Center for Human Rights and Social Movements, Tim McCarthy, drew more than a hundred people. This is a highly unusual turnout for the Harvard Kennedy School, whose events usually draw only from its own. The response was thanks in part to the work that Heike Schotten, a philosophy professor (specializing in Nietzsche) did on the ground. But also because there was a revolution going on, *right that minute*, in Egypt. And because of this, the United States was waking up to a new kind of interest and identification with Arabs. The raging democracy movements in the Arab world would certainly benefit Palestine, and the constant media coverage revealed the multiplicities of Arab societies as well as America's embarrassing role in propping up despised dictators. Which, in Egypt's case, had been to the benefit of the most reactionary Israeli forces.

But there was another factor behind the large, enthusiastic crowds, the hundreds of Facebook supporters and the excitement that greeted Haneen and Ghadir wherever they went. Even more compelling than that is the hunger of a huge progressive queer community in the United States that is disgusted by marriage and military and that longs to return to the radical social transformation implicit in a feminist critique of gender and sex roles. These types of freethinkers who thrived during the heyday of ACT UP and Queer Nation and the Lesbian Avengers have been kept under a rock by the huge budgets of the marriage and military lobbies, but those visions were still potent and were now being offered a forum in which to coalesce and respond, and so they did.

By the time Haneen and Ghadir and Nadia returned from Boston, we had all decided that our next project would be to create the first U.S. LGBT delegation *to* Palestine. And it would be up to me to pull together a dynamic, influential group to achieve the same synergy there that we had created here. So the projects for the future were lining up: film festivals, World Pride, delegations—our agenda for action was emerging and defining itself.

Through Madhi's relationship at Yale with a professor there, gay historian George Chauncey, a dinner was set up at the apartment Chauncey shared with Ron Gregg, a cinema studies professor at Yale, for Haneen, Ghadir, Mahdi, and Nadia to meet Rashid Khalidi, the Edward Said Professor of Modern Arab Studies at Columbia. Khalidi had not made the queer connection before, so we realized that the cumulative Zeitgeist was reaching straight Palestine in America. The other invited guests were Khalidi's wife, Mona; their son Ismail and Ismail's girlfriend, a Chilean graduate student; Tony Kushner; Kushner's husband, Mark; and Joan Scott of the Princeton Institute for Advanced Studies. Haneen, Nadia, and Ghadir got off the train from Boston, I raced into Manhattan from teaching on Staten Island, and we all made it to Chauncey and Gregg's apartment on time. Kushner had canceled an hour before, and in his place were Alisa Solomon and her wife, Marilyn Niemark.

The conversation was tough at first. People didn't know each other, and Haneen, Ghadir, and Nadia—who had just run back from Boston—were exhausted. But when we started laying out what we had been doing, how dynamic the events were, the global networks that we have, how effective our organizing, I really felt some excitement from the Khalidis. Even though all of this was under the radar, because it was taking place in the queer sphere, they could see that some kind of paradigm shift was occurring. The Khalidis, especially Ismail, a playwright, had a lot of great ideas for the queer Palestinian movement, and I think there was general agreement that human contact is the key to transformation.

"Delegations," Rashid Khalidi said. "More delegations." Which was very much what we had already been thinking. And he emphasized strongly that more African Americans needed access to information about Palestine. I started to think of numerous queer black leaders who would be perfect for our delegation. Respected figures with real credibility who had not yet taken a public position on Palestine and would benefit from being part of an LGBT delegation.

The people in that room had very varied relationships to the questions of sanctions. Joan Scott opposed the academic boycott, I supported sanctions and divestment but favored solidarity visits within the PQBDS guidelines, and Alisa Solomon supported the Israeli actors' boycott of settlement theaters; whatever position people held, it was clear to me that the sanctions movement was a dynamic one. Some people criticized Omar Barghouti, but other people praised him. But that night it became clear to me that Omar was a significant leader, because he had created a movement that we'd all felt we had to respond to. Even our tour, in some sense, had been a response to his initial lack of flexibility on queer issues. I realized over the course of that evening what an important leader Omar really was — not necessarily by uniting people, but still by articulating moral and political challenges that thinking people felt obligated to grapple with and respond to. That is a very special kind of leadership, one that helps others define for themselves who they are.

Staggering under the weight of real politics and good scotch, we all stumbled home, happy but overwhelmed by the range of contacts, conversations, and ideas we had been able to share in such a short time. And I think we were all moved by how far this conversation had come in just a matter of days.

The next morning I picked up Haneen and Ghadir at the Tutu Center, and we walked along the Hudson River, looking at the new Frank Geary building that sits like a cloud on the Westside Highway. As the light of the day progresses, the building is constantly changing shape. It's alive, like the city that surrounds it. We were refreshed by the cold February sea breeze as Ghadir lives on the Haifa sea and, like Manhattanites, is used to being by water. We passed the luxury high-rises, recently sprouting up on West Street, a new style of architecture that Haneen had not yet seen: emblematic of our American moment, the glass walls give a false sense of transparency, but actually the lives of the wealthy that take place inside are entirely invisible. I showed them the piers, the old gay hunting grounds, but the gentrification made a lot of my stories unimaginable. They had to take my word for it. But by now we were friends, so they did. We took photos together with the river in the background. I felt very comfortable with both of them. Haneen has a great political mind. She is a leader, and she is a big-picture person, as I am. She makes her own decisions and is savvy, tough, and fair. Ghadir is someone you can sit around with for hours talking, playing, being silly. Politically she is more disarming stylistically but has enormous integrity and a will of steel. We went out for expensive sushi, and then I took them to be interviewed by Michelangelo Signorile for his Sirius Radio Queer Show. On the way, I explained that Mike was one of the masterminds of the ACT UP Media Committee, that he was a former celebrity journalist who had invented the political strategy known as "Outing" and that he had been willing to prep for the interview by reading the GLQ quarterly special issue on Palestine and Israel, edited by Gil Hochberg, of which Haneen was a contributor.

But I did not remember to prepare them for the studio's location on the thirty-sixth floor of the McGraw-Hill Building. Again, more photos ensued.

Mike's preparation was so thorough that he did not waste Haneen or Ghadir's time giving background or having to justify their experiences. He asked questions about the consequences of "Israeli brutality" and fully grasped that for Palestinian queers, the occupation was a full partner with the homophobia and sexism that obstructs them. And he also completely understood that an occupied society cannot progress in the way that an open society can. It was exhilarating to have the basics be so obvious. Again, my admiration for Mike grew, as did my deepest affection for Haneen and Ghadir. In the short time that I had known them, I had witnessed over and over again the pure ignorance that accompanied 90 percent of the people they encounter and how gracefully but effectively they deal with it. In the American context, information about Palestine and its queer dimensions have to be fought for. You simply cannot get it passively. Given all the censorship, understanding Palestine has to be a commitment.

We walked down Fifth Avenue in the brisk winter early evening to the City University Graduate Center at Thirty-fourth Street and Fifth Avenue, which longtime New Yorkers refer to as "the former B Altman's department store." And we had a chance to look up at the Empire State Building across the street. There, waiting for us, was Kathy Acey, who was to moderate that evening's event sponsored by CLAGS (Center for Lesbian and Gay Studies). I knew that the room we had reserved was too small, as word from other cities was starting to spread, and people were writing on Facebook, building what used to be called "word of mouth." With no media attention beyond our two radio interviews, it was amazing how many people in the country knew about what we now habitually called "Al-Tour."

The room at CUNY started to fill up quite early. I saw Lisa Duggan, an NYU professor; John Francis Mulligan, with whom I had worked for five long years on trying to get gay people into the Saint Patrick's Day Parade; my East Village friends; and pals from the MIX Festival, Jack Waters, Peter Cramer, and Kate Huh. And lots and lots of strangers. It was an excited, mixed crowd. There were pioneers Alix Dobkin and Jim Fouratt. There were my young friends Morgan Goode and Mik Kinkead. Leslie Gevirtz from the LGBT synagogue. And many queer Arabs, some of whom had come from as far as New Haven. Tunisians and Egyptians, most of whom I did not know but was exhilarated to meet. So many queer communities were being united by this event. The word had gotten out and reached many diverse corners. Once again the talk was almost all new information for the audience. Kathy's questions focused less on politics than on the nuts and bolts of organizing.

Q: How do you reach people when they are on the other side of a wall, and can't come to you?

A: Haneen goes back and forth to them.

Q: How do you organize queer women when some are living in very traditional circumstances and can't go out?

A: Meetings are held in the daytime, and a lot of work is done on-line and by telephone.

And, as ever, over and over Haneen and Ghadir emphasized feminism, feminism, feminism. Which they embodied completely.

The dramatic high point of the evening came, however when an older man stood up and announced himself as Israeli. Then he started to berate Haneen and Ghadir about how lucky they were to have Israeli passports, and how they shouldn't bite the hand that feeds them. It was an intense moment for the audience who had become well aware that in Israel, he would have the power of the state, military, and police behind him, but here he could just be a bully without an apparatus.

"You print a passport and write on it that I am Israeli, but that doesn't make it so. I am Palestinian," Haneen said. "That passport is my right, it is not a privilege."

"Thank you for your comment," Ghadir said. And then tore into him about the illegality of the occupation and her strength as a Palestinian woman.

For many of us, as Americans, it was our first experience of watching a face-to-face confrontation between colonizer and resister.

"How will we have peace?" he asked, finally.

"We don't want peace," Haneen said. She wanted freedom and justice.

I remember once witnessing another young woman exhibit extraordinary courage and political leadership. In that case, decades ago, it was the twentysomething Irish heroine Bernadette Devlin on television explaining that a "ceasefire" really meant return to status quo. And that instead what she wanted was a negotiated transformation of that status quo as the pathway to the end of violence. And decades later she had come to New York to stand with the Irish queers and refuse to march in a segregated St. Patrick's Day Parade. Some people never forget what they already know. I had understood her clearly when she was young and when she was middle-aged, and now those words and actions came back to inspire me again.

It was only when the event came to an end that I learned what had happened in the lobby. So many people had shown up to hear our speakers that 220 people had to be turned away. Turned away! And all this without a shred of major media attention. I was devastated that, as organizers, we not only had not accommodated them, we had not even known they were there. But I was elated that we had created a true grassroots phenomenon, without any corporate inflation or promotion. That in fact the queer community that I had last seen emerge during the AIDS crisis—that interracial, anti-imperialist, cross-generational radical community—*still existed* and could still be coalesced by activating their community relationships. They hadn't all been eaten alive by marriage and the desire to kill Muslims in the U.S. army.

About thirty of us piled into a Korean kitsch palace on Thirty-second Street with papier-mâché waterfalls, and then Haneen and Ghadir came over to my place, and we smoked pot and took in the enormity of what we had accomplished together. Sitting in my crappy apartment with Fox Base Alpha on the stereo (no iPod yet for Sarah) and eating whatever was in the near-empty refrigerator (baked frozen spanakopita and honey with almonds that I had brought back from Greece two years before), it was so comfortable, so relaxed and intimate and real. Without any awkward effort we had naturally found each other and connected.

The next morning I picked them up and put them on a train to Philadelphia where once again, even though the event was at 3 P.M. on a Friday afternoon, they had a full house. Moderated this time by Heather Love and by Amy Kaplan, the straight Jewish literary critic and longtime ally of Palestine, Haneen and Ghadir were also hosted by Naava et-Shalom, that same graduate student who had phoned me just ten months before with proposals that had seemed preposterous then but had now clarified as reasonable, once I'd taken the time to understand. That night, exhausted, at a cozy dinner at Heather's apartment, Ghadir shifted the conversation away from herself and Haneen by turning the tables.

"Tell us, what is it like to be queer in America?" she asked. What followed was story after story around the table of the profound familial homophobia, prejudice, and diminishment that these professors, students, and friends had faced in their own lives. Later, Haneen and I ate hamburgers and had drinks at La Guardia airport as we waited for her flight to San Francisco, and we talked again about what was so overwhelmingly obvious. Namely, how oppression wastes people's gifts and obstructs their contributions and how it forces people to spend their lives fighting for things that no one should ever have to fight for.

And then they were off to California!

The Bay Area events were organized by a large coalition created by the Arab Resource and Organizing Center (AROC), a group I came to know through Zohar Weiman-Kelman. Working with AROC had its ups and downs for me and for AROC since I was unfamiliar with Bay Area–style organizing. One emblematic disagreement we had was about where to house Haneen, Ghadir, and Sami Shalami, the brilliant and sweet young man I had met in Ramallah—who was now on his way to San Francisco from Ramallah, visa in hand, via Amman. I had decided to house them at The Inn on Castro, a *Birdcage*-like bed-and-breakfast at the corner of Castro and Market, run by an incredibly sweet and attentive gay male couple. Homey, with unforgettable group breakfasts, The Inn attracts queer visitors from all over the world, as well as transsexuals scheduled for surgery at the local San Francisco General Hospital and their partners, friends, and supportive family. Many times I had had great visits there and amazing breakfast conversations. Even though the Castro district is "over," it is an easy place to navigate, safe for women at any time of night or day, and two blocks from both A Different Light Bookstore and Café Flore.

AROC strongly disagreed with this choice. They communicated to me very clearly that the Castro district was for rich white men and that our guests should stay in Oakland, where most queer Arabs lived. I was adamant that, as great as Oakland is, I was not taking a twenty-three-year-old gay man from Ramallah and putting him in a hotel in Oakland for his five precious days in California. This kind of conflict showed a very different orientation about decision making. We'd also had conflicts about endorsements, posters, and moderators. Back in June I had suggested Angela Davis, but they felt she wasn't "strong enough" on Palestine. They wanted Jewel Gomez, who had never taken a position on Palestine and who, in fact, declined. I recommended a number of people they had never heard of, and then they felt that I was only promoting "famous people." This stimulated a conversation about what "famous" means. I argued that the moderators I had chosen—Lynette Jackson in Chicago, Kathy Acey in New York, Amy Kaplan and Heather Love in Philly—were all recognized by their communities as people who were reliable and consistent. This community-based trust and recognition was the opposite of "famous," which is something produced when corporations get behind individuals to inflate and promote them through commercial media.

However, these disagreements had no effect on the events in San Francisco, which were overwhelmingly successful. AROC did an amazing job with the entire program, including the coup of finding Cherríe Moraga to moderate a packed event of hundreds at Mission High School in San Francisco. As one of the authors of *This Bridge Called My Back* and one of the founders of the lesbian-of-color movement, she was a meaningful and moving choice. And they also created a multigenerational set of moderators in Oakland, led by AROC's Alia Saud—which was also moving and successful. Sami proved to be a great addition to the traveling show. Not only did he represent the West Bank and Al-Qaws, but his brainy, loving approach to synthesizing political analysis and humane experience deepened the effect of the events. The Bay Area events proved to us that yet another by-product of the success of this tour was that it was coalescing the queer Arab community in the United States, giving it even more focus, visibility, and organizing successes.

Maggie Sager, a Bay Area journalist, covered the San Francisco event for *Mondoweiss*. Her article brought the moment to life for readers in other countries, for I now realized that Hanan Rabani of the Soros Open Society, one of our funders, had been 100 percent correct in her prediction that this tour would inspire queer Arabs around the world. The number of Facebook friend requests and repostings made it clear that these events were being celebrated and enjoyed globally.

Sager wrote in her coverage:

When pressed by an audience member as to which situation they would prefer: a perfectly egalitarian queer-friendly society still under occupation, or a free Palestine that still suffers from sexism, patriarchy and homophobia, the three became visibly angry. Ghadir looked at the audience and asked, "Please raise your hand if you would like to live one day under occupation." Sami went on to contend that freedom transforms the mind, giving people the best opportunity to examine their previously held attitudes. . . .

While their discussion did not focus solely on Israel's abuse of LGBT liberation struggles in perpetuating conflict, I took away from it a deepened understanding of just how much more the West unfairly expects of Palestinians than anyone else. We expect Palestinians to not throw stones at Israeli Defense Forces jeeps who come to teargas their protestations against the illegal confiscation of their entire villages while we wouldn't bat an eye at a man who shot a robber attempting to take his television set. We expect them to not elect representatives that reflect their religious sentiments though no one is surprised when the Christian right attempts to influence our political system and we ally ourselves with the likes of Saudi Arabia; and we expect Palestinian society to wholly unshackle itself from the bonds of misogyny, racism and bigotry before we acknowledge their entitlement to basic human rights, despite our own shortcomings.

By the time Haneen, Ghadir, and Sami stepped off the plane from San Francisco at the Newark airport, we knew we had an underground national phenomenon on our hands. And when I saw Sami again, in his white framed eyeglasses, baggy jeans, and suitcase full of books purchased in secondhand stores in San Francisco, I felt like I was being reunited with the courageous young brother I never had. I was filled with love and pride and a fierce desire to protect him and show him the best possible experience. Back at the hotel we were joined by the rest of the entourage, and we all hung around and talked.

Nadia Awad had by now completed all three videos for PQBDS, and she played them for us on her laptop. The first showed a gayish British man — suave, masculine, determined. He looks the viewer in the eye and speaks determinedly.

"You buy free range chicken, bring your own bags to the shop, don't wear leather. Then why do you buy wine made under military occupation?"

The second PQBDS video shows an older Arab woman, dressed traditionally, working on the land.

"This," the female narrator says "is a feminist."
The following image is a young Palestinian girl.
"This is a leader."
And then the narrator concludes,
"Occupation is violence again women."
Each of the three closes with the tag "Palestinian Queers for Boycott/ Divestment/Sanctions." The videos were making their way around the Internet, despite being repeatedly knocked off various servers. But the quality of the work was so high; PQBDS was getting an impressive media presence, even though Nadia was making this work alone in her Brooklyn apartment. She and Mahdi were also now starting a queer Arab group in New York, planning to meet at the LGBT Center.

While the team was in San Francisco, Jasbir and I were facing the reality that we were going to have huge, overflow crowds at their final event, a panel at the Audre Lorde Project in New York. And we had to have a plan. The Audre Lorde Project is a queer people-of-color organization that had recently moved from Brooklyn to share a building on West Twenty-fourth Street with three other queer organizations. These groups had been moving away from the LGBT Center, which had been the Ground Zero of community meetings for almost three decades. The center is a renovated school where ACT UP famously met, but was increasingly becoming a so-cial service center and twelve-step-program provider as trans and people-of-color constituencies increasingly found other meeting spots. The common space at Audre Lorde Project held only about seventy-five people, and we knew it would not be large enough. So Jasbir did two very savvy things. First, she got the other three groups meeting in the building to co-sponsor: Fierce, a queer youth-of-color organization that had been formed in response to the gentrification of the West Village pushing young gay and trans kids off the piers; the Sylvia Rivera Law Project, the legal arm of the trans movement; and Queers for Economic and Social Justice, an organization running groups for queer people in the shelter system. Then she went to key groups devoted to people of color in the community and got them to endorse. First SALGA (South Asian Lesbian and Gay Organi-zation) signed up; and Pauline Park, a longtime trans woman in leadership in the community, brought along GPINY (Gay Pacific Islanders of New York) and Q-Wave. Now the whole building was in on the planning, and Queers for Economic and Social Justice opened up their entire loft for the event, with the other groups offering two overflow rooms with video feed.

I had to teach on Staten Island that day, but Haneen, Ghadir, and Sami met in the morning with Jasbir to plan out the evening's agenda. By the time I had raced back from the ferry to Twenty-fourth street we knew it was going to be a sensational night. Well, one of the video feeds didn't work, and — as was explained to me numerous times by numerous people from the Audre Lorde Project — "people of color don't come on time" (something I have learned over time to be true and not true). But eventually the place was filled to the brim and packed with people on three floors. I would say the audience was 95 percent queer people of color. Five white men showed up (including Brad Taylor of WBAI and Siege Busters), and there were about twenty white women, including Judith Butler; she sat demurely in the last row but was happy to be introduced to Haneen, Ghadir and Sami, who were delighted to meet her. I also finally got to tell her that when she was last in Birzeit, queer Palestinians had been sitting in the audience waiting for her to "come out" and had been disappointed that she didn't.

"Come out?" she said, surprised. "I thought that was a given."

Aha, all speculation had been wrong. Judith had not "decided" not to come out. She just didn't think that she had to. But, as Ghadir told her later, "In Palestinian society, you can't assume anything."

The event was the crowning glory of "Al-Tour." Jasbir's moderation was pitch-perfect as Haneen, Ghadir, and Sami — experiencing what they said was "overwhelming" support, clearly explained why occupation is a queer issue. They articulated, clearly, humanely, and sincerely how much they needed the occupation to end, and that bringing it to an end was as important as their needs for queer liberation and feminism. Again, they explained that Western ideas of the gay trajectory were not always helpful or applicable to Palestinian queers. As Haneen explained, "This idea of visibility and being seen in public, which has been part of the Western gay liberation movements, has become a 'universal goal' that all LGBTQ are asked to follow. In this sense, the coming-out narrative has become oppressive in and of itself, as it functions as a standard by which to tag people: those who are out 'healthy, strong, mature' and those who are not 'weak, immature, backward.'"

Similarly, she addressed the American LGBT obsession with determining words to call ourselves. "I find it ['queer'] useful for the time being but I am not attached to it or any other term. I am happy to move along with language. I am not looking for a term to marry. When it comes to language, I believe in short affairs."

And they were very clear that queer Palestinians need the rest of the

LGBT world to support BDS so that economic pressure can be applied as a nonviolent strategy for change.

In every possible way, Haneen, Ghadir, and Sami made clear that it would be impossible to separate their experiences as queers from their experiences of being occupied. And as far as Israel's claim to be a rescuer or shelter from Palestinian homophobia, as Sami so succinctly put it, "There is no pink door leading to a secret pathway through the Wall for me."

It was moving, unifying, and in every way clarifying. And I had my own personal moment of completion when Ghadir said from the podium that the success of Al-Tour was owed to "Al-Schulman" and what she called "the Schulman Effect"—the synchronicity and chain of events caused by organization bringing together the right combination of different people propelling above the usual operation of things. This, of course, is exactly what I had wanted to achieve and had worked so painstakingly for so long to do: bring together disparate but absolutely vital people in the national queer community who, by working in their own ways at the same time, would create a third force more powerful than any one tendency working independently. In that moment I felt that my more than thirty years as a political organizer—from the abortion rights movement, to ACT UP, to the Lesbian Avengers, to the MIX Festival, to the Irish Lesbian and Gay Organization, to the ACT UP Oral History Project—had finally clicked in a kind of instinctual knowledge of how to make this work, and it had worked. I had a very special feeling, one that I had never had before in my life.

Afterward we had a party at Jasbir's place. By then we had all taken up scotch, since Haneen's drink of choice was "scotch with one ice cube" and Jasbir also is a scotch drinker, so this became the signature drink of Al-Tour. I got home at 2 A.M.

That night we all had emails from Butler recognizing that articulating the queer side of BDS, as Al-Qaws and Aswat had done, was crucial for all of us doing this work. The next morning, before going to the airport, Judith, Jasbir, Haneen, Sami, and Ghadir had breakfast together; they were planning Judith's next trip to Birzeit and how she would bring Haneen up on the platform with her. They also talked about working on our delegation idea, and Judith said she would issue a statement. I decided not to go to that meeting; honestly I think I was so emotionally overwhelmed, I couldn't do it. Instead I sat alone in a restaurant and did what New Yorkers do when they need to escape reality: I read the entire Sunday *Times*.

Finally I picked them up at the hotel, and we crammed all their suitcases into a taxi: Sami had two huge suitcases filled with books. Haneen would bring him the gay ones later, as they would not make it through the checkpoint from Jordan. No cab was big enough for all his books, so Haneen, Ghadir, and Sami had to sit scrunched together with about fifty pounds of books crammed on their laps. We made it to the Newark airport and I stood on a balcony and watched the three of them go through customs. I was ever vigilant in this regard. We never knew when something could happen, but they made it and waved at me from the other side. I had no idea when we would ever see each other again. This was February 20. The tour had been perfect. Two days later, the backlash would begin.

10. BACKLASH

Winter 2011 in New York City was long and rough. It snowed continually. Mayor Bloomberg had fired so many sanitation workers that snow never seemed to be plowed or removed. But in Israel/Palestine, it was sizzling hot.

I had received a second invitation to Israel, from someone I really liked, to speak to a queer youth organization. "We receive no state funding," my friend assured me. I wrote back, asking her to go through PQBDS. If that group agreed that there was no state funding, I would be delighted to come. But PQBDS's research showed that the group had funding from three government sources and also worked with the army. So I had to decline. Another friend was invited to be a judge at the Tel Aviv Lesbian and Gay Film Festival. "They have no state money," he assured me. "They're broke." But the festival's website showed it received significant funding from governmental sources. It became clear that some Israelis don't even realize where their funding comes from, as the queer community and the state are so interconnected. More and more gay people were being invited to Israel, and there needed to be a way for people to find out exactly what they were agreeing to, so they could make an informed decision about whether or not they would break the sanctions.

On February 19, 2011, Omar Barghouti was denied a visa to come to the United States and had to cancel his book tour for *Boycott, Divestment, Sanctions: The Global Struggle for Palestinian Rights*. This drew almost no media attention. I read about it in *Muzzlewatch*. Here was one of the most significant leaders of Palestinian civil society being barred from the United States, and yet there was no *New York Times* mention or television coverage. It was as though nothing had happened.

Haneen, Sami, and Ghadir left New York on February 21, 2011. On February 23, PQBDS issued an open letter offering to serve as a resource for any queer international invited to Israel. I had learned by this time that "open letters" and "calls" are an organic part of Palestinian politics. The document is profoundly meaningful in this context, where expression and mobility are so impaired.

The formation of PQBDS and the meaning of this letter entirely transformed the landscape from the period of a year and a half before, when I had been invited to Tel Aviv University. Now there were queer Palestinians publicly and strategically organized to ask the rest of their global LGBT community to work with them to help them win basic human rights as queers and as Palestinians. They made themselves available for dialogue, conversation, engagement, and relationship. And the decisions to either boycott or violate the boycott were now more deliberate and informed for our community.

On February 24, there were two very significant and opposing documents in my in-box. The first was a public statement by Judith Butler in support of Al-Tour. The second was a note from a friend about a strange occurrence taking place in the West Village. Al-Tour had gone so well, with no backlash whatsoever. It was inevitable that something had to happen, but the person responsible and the venue he picked were entirely unpredictable.

Michael Lucas, the producer of the "desecration" porn film *Men of Israel*, issued a public statement one week after the end of our tour, threatening to organize an economic boycott against the New York LGBT Community Center if it did not ban an organization called Siege Busters from meeting there. Siege Busters, a group organizing to join the Freedom Flotilla to literally break the siege of Gaza, was holding an event at the center as part of Israeli Apartheid Week. I found the note weird, and I didn't really understand what Michael Lucas had to do with our LGBT center or New York in general.

On February 25, however, through some kind of mysterious nonprocess, the board of the LGBT center and the center's director, Glennda Testone, decided, in fact, to do what Lucas wanted. They banned Siege Busters and canceled the group's event.

No group had been banned from the New York LGBT Center for twenty-five years, and that exception was the North American Man/Boy Love Association, an organization committed to abolishing age of consent laws for homosexual sex. Within minutes of the center's decision, Lucas (born Andrei Lvovich Treivas in the Soviet Union) issued the following statement:

"We prevailed! Congratulations to everyone who stood with me in support of Israel. With your help it took only eight hours to accomplish our mission."

The center then issued a statement: "We have determined that this event is not appropriate to be held at our LGBT Community Center, which is a safe haven for LGBT groups and individuals." Once again "our community" was being defined as people who support the siege of Gaza. Once again "safety" was defined by the comfort of those who want to censor and exclude. Once again a community was splitting along homonationalist versus queer allegiances, with Palestine at the core of the division. Only this time, it was in the City of New York.

As we started to try and understand who had made this decision and why, it only got more confusing. At first the center claimed that Siege Busters was "not a queer group" even though it included such long-term queer activists as Brad Taylor, who has run WBAI OUT-FM for decades; Laurie Arbeiter, a former Lesbian Avenger; Sherry Wolf, a former member of ACT UP; and Naomi Brussel, active in the Queer Left since it was articulated in the 1970s. Once that argument fell apart, the center then claimed that Siege Busters was "not about a queer issue." But the center had many diverse groups meeting on everything from life drawing to French conversation, and one group, "New Yorkers Say No to War," had met there for four years. All the center's excuses were lame, and we started trying to figure out what was really going on, while building support for an open center.

A petition to reinstate free speech at the LGBT center was signed by more than fifteen hundred people. Letters came from Urvashi Vaid, Joan Nestle (cofounder of the Lesbian Herstory Archives), the National LGBT Task Force, and Rabbi Sharon Kleinbaum of the LGBT synagogue asking for a return to the open LGBT center that we had all loved and treasured for thirty years. Glennda, the director, was from the first generation of community leaders to not come from grassroots-organizing backgrounds, but rather from corporate—and she not only was board orientated at the expense of community concern, but also didn't know who anyone was. It took her forever to get back to many of the most respected and beloved community-based leaders who had contacted her. She treated icons of the community with complete disregard, disrespect, and lack of acknowledgment. She simply didn't understand why we were upset, and apparently she didn't care.

We were able to determine that Michael Lucas's boyfriend was a former chair of the center's board, so we suspected he had direct connections to corporate or major donors. But we were never able to find anyone who admitted to threatening to withhold money unless Siege Busters was censored. In fact, not one dollar of pro-Israel gay Jewish money was withheld from the center because of free speech. Ironically, the only money withdrawn from the center was on our side, when two major donors stopped giving because groups supporting Palestinian queers were excluded. So even though Michael Lucas had threatened the withholding of Jewish money, this never actually materialized.

We could never get a clear reason from Glennda as to why she had taken such a dramatic action, and so quickly, except that "Siege Busters is controversial." It was a wall of vague avoidance engulfing our beloved center and using Palestine as a turning point in the shift from community accountability to solid corporate model.

Unwilling to give up the LGBT center, a wide range of old-timers started to push for a community meeting to bring the issues into the open.

On February 28, Pete Seeger came out for boycott, divestment, and sanctions. That same day, the PQBDS open letter appeared in *Risala*, PACBI's magazine. That signaled an enormous change in PACBI's recognition of queer Palestinians since my tense meeting ten months before with Omar in the empty hotel restaurant in Ramallah.

On February 27, the LGBT center released the following: "We won't be making any more statements at this time."

On March 2, I got an email from Glennda: "Hi Sarah, I apologize for not reaching out sooner. Can we please set up a time to talk? Thanks, Glennda." I responded immediately with my phone number, but she never called.

On March 4, the Audre Lorde Project, Queers for Economic Justice, FIERCE, and the Sylvia Rivera Law Project all asked the LGBT center to reinstate Siege Busters.

I started to realize that there was a strange new configuration at play. The leaders of the LGBT center, most of whom were not Jews, appeared to believe, *without evidence*, that there was a contingent of rich, vengeful, punitive gay Jews—whose names no one seemed to know—that were funding all our LGBT institutions. That, if we continued to have free speech and open debate in our community, these unnamed punitive rich Jews would take their Jew money and shut down the community.

The same issue came up during the organization of the delegation. Working with friends in Palestine and the United States, I had already started on my second task: organizing the first LGBT delegation to Palestine. Working with the hosts, Al-Qaws and Aswat, and the guide, Dunya from Birthright Unplugged, we chose dates in 2012 and determined that we would have space for sixteen delegates. Thinking about Rashid Khalidi's excitement about delegations, I started conceptualizing how it would be organized along the same lines as the tour itself. We would bring together influential people from different sectors of the queer and LGBT communities who would create a cumulative impact, and whose experiences would carry throughout the U.S. queer world.

Eleven months later, seventy people had said "no," and sixteen people had said "yes."

The situation with Frameline, the San Francisco LGBT Film Festival, was starting to clarify. It had received $2,500 dollars from the Israeli consulate. This was out of a $1 million budget! We offered to fund-raise to replace the money, if it would turn down the consulate. It refused the offer. But in a Skype conversation, Frameline's executive director KC Price told Elle Flanders that he had been subjected to the same strategy that Michael Lucas had used with the LGBT center. He had received communications from people claiming to be "long-term donors" to Frameline who threatened to remove their money if Frameline declined the cash from the Consulate. But when he checked up on the names, he found that none of them had actually contributed money. It was a fraudulent threat from right-wing Jews who had *no history with Frameline*, exploiting these stereotypes about Jewish donors to scare the group's leadership. I invited KC and Outfest in LA (a festival that actually has an evening sponsored by the Israeli state airline, El Al) to the delegation. They both declined. I went to MoMA's film department, Sundance, and the Tribeca Film Festival to urge the leaders there to join the delegation so they could see firsthand what they were being used to keep in place. Some politely declined. Some didn't respond. The question of LGBT film festivals and makers being used by Brand Israel (the official Israeli government re-branding program — see the appendix) came up when the lesbian iconic filmmaker Barbara Hammer appeared in the middle of this debate. After being offered a fellowship by the American Academy in Jerusalem, Barbara had come to learn about the boycott only at the last minute. After corresponding directly with Omar and having long conversations with me and others, she decided to decline the money, join the boycott movement, participate in our delegation, and send out a public statement.

That week I also received a letter from the University of California Press. Finally, after a year of silence, after I had taken out all of my content about Israel, and after an anonymous reader had intervened significantly in the proceedings, the press was willing to publish my book on AIDS and gentrification. Life went on.

On March 7, *Haaretz* reported that a bill to "punish anti-Israel boycotters" passed the first round of Knesset voting. The boycott bill, supported by a vote of 32 to 12, would levy harsh fines on Israeli citizens who supported the boycott. The draft law also called for imposing sanctions against foreign nationals, organizations, and states that supported economic, academic, and cultural boycotts. Clearly the boycott was having an effect. If it was irrelevant, the Israeli government would not be responding so harshly. Judith Butler had to suspend her intended semester at Birzeit.

On March 12, I attended an event sponsored by Adalah-N.Y. on queers and BDS, held at the Judson Church and featuring Judith Butler, John Greyson, and Jasbir Puar. The auditorium was packed, and many of the people there were under the age of thirty; hundreds of people were turned away. I'd heard that Butler had recently spoken in Toronto and that four hundred people had been turned away. Interest in the relationship between BDS, Palestine, and queers was growing daily, and Butler's decision to throw her considerable prestige and accomplishments behind this discussion was paying off considerably. Jasbir was the moderator, and she very clearly and strongly contextualized the conversation in relation to both Al-Tour and the ongoing censorship at the LGBT center. John then presented some wonderfully engaging and provocative clips of films he had made in support of boycott, particularly shorts aimed at Elton John and Justin Bieber, who were breaking the boycott by performing in Israel.

Butler used calm, simple language and clear, purposeful ideas. She systematically went through the basic moral and historical arguments behind the fundamental questions at the core of BDS. As I listened, once again I learned basic concepts from her that helped me grasp the complexities of this movement. And once again I was disappointed to learn that there were fundamentals that I had still not come to understand. It was only at this talk of Butler's that I realized that Israeli Independence Day—the day my grandmother stood on the street waving her Israeli flag, cheering the survival of her people, and mourning the extermination of her own brothers and sisters—is *the exact same event* as the Nakba, the Palestinian day of grief, recognition of loss, and reformulation of purpose toward an autonomous future. These two events were so far apart in my mind that

I had never realized before that they were the two sides of the looking glass. The panel raised some key points. Portraying BDS as "pro-Palestine and anti-Israel" makes it sound like a football game, with false assumptions of equality of positions and equal playing fields. What will be justice for the Jews will also be justice for the Palestinians. Justice is a universal. Israel's borders themselves are shifting and changing and must themselves be understood as weapons, as tools of occupation.

The Jewish right of return ensures that Jewish people hold priority at all times so that non-Jewish citizens can't effectively function within Israel. There is a long history of anti-Zionist Jews, including Communist Jews in New York City. Israel has never and does not now represent all of the Jewish people. Not one group at the expense of another. We cannot affirm rights of mobility and expression without equal access to those rights. Dialogue can solve nothing until colonialism is reversed. Doing business with Israel, as it stands, ratifies inequality.

Each one of these ideas entered into my soul. "Justice is universal." In the end, really, it is that easy.

That night a bunch of us went out for drinks and hours of digesting and discussing the rush of events and ideas that were surrounding us. I thought a lot about the question of redemption of the Jewish people. Butler wants us to recognize our just impulses, historically and actually, and not allow ourselves to be corralled or replaced by unjust entities, regardless of their power. It made me think about my own identifications and agendas for myself among Jews. I think of this journey of grappling with Israel, with Palestine, with BDS and my desire to have this make sense in a queer context; I had at one time experienced that as a "Judaic" journey. But was that really so? What do I have in common with nationalists, racists, and liars?

I can come up with real reasons why they are the way they are, but I feel as though I have spent my life "understanding" why dominant cultural people are oppressive, analyzing their personal needs to justify the inflation of their powers. Is my ability to deconstruct their behavior so that it is understandable the same thing as a relationship? Obviously not. Udi Aloni is my kind of Jew. Judith Butler is the kind of Jew I strive to be. But I identify even more strongly with Haneen, Sami, and Ghadir—their faith in change, their willingness to go out on a limb because they have their eyes on the prize, the commitment to the big picture and to active cooperation with others beyond personal aggrandizement. I see Butler as trying to articulate a way for people like us to be Jews and be historically consistent. What is my role in this conceptual effort? I then realize that of all the many events that I participate in every year, the many talks, readings, and plays I attend, and the many talks, readings, and conversations I give and join in, very few are ahead of where I am at. This is because of the gap between public intellectual culture and private thought for progressives in America at this moment. Rarely do I walk into a room where my assumptions are acknowledged and the speaker then advances my understanding. But Ghadir, Haneen, Sami, Jasbir, John Greyson, Elle Flanders, and Butler had all done that for me. I didn't have to repeat. I could relax and learn and evolve. They had created a public discourse that I desperately needed to have. And when I finally was able to articulate this experience, I felt real joy. Not the joy of explaining well or watching someone else come forward, but the joy of truly being enlightened by another person who understood what I understood and then more.

The only thing that bothered me about this amazing evening was that aside from John Greyson inclusion of PQBDS's videos in his presentation—there were no Palestinians represented on the platform. This problem of substitution that I had perceived from the first day of my involvement was still ever present. Palestinian queers were *still* not an integrated part of the public conversation. Now that Haneen, Sami, and Ghadir were back in the Middle East, it was falling on the Palestinian queers in New York to figure out how much they were willing to fight to be included and when and where. Some Al-Qaws folks in New York decided to start a queer Arab group in NYC. They'd held their first meeting at the center, but once Siege Busters was excluded, and the center took a position in favor of the siege of Gaza, the Queer Arabs clearly couldn't continue to meet there. The Audre Lorde Project invited them to join its own space. I had thought that the exclusion of Palestinian voices from these conversations had to become a thing of the past. But at that moment, I dramatically underestimated the willingness of "progressive" people to exclude individual Palestinians.

My friends, of course, were very well schooled in this and even questioned whether Palestinians on the platform would be listened to. As one queer Palestinian in New York wrote to me:

> Since this panel was about BDS, I would say that there is a substantial value to having non-Palestinians speak. It reinforces the idea that BDS is a diverse and international network of people (fighting for justice, equality etc) and it also speaks to Americans who would have a hard time listening to a Pal-

estinian (regardless of how Americanized and eloquent the Palestinian is.) That is an issue I've experienced at university where certain students would be dis-interested by an event organized by Arabs but would then suddenly show interest when other "white" people (especially known names, professors etc) have already taken part. I don't know if it is a fear of association with Arabs or fear of being labeled as such, but I do know that this perhaps perverse "use" of Palestinian views and values by non-Palestinians works on certain crowds.

While tactically this was clearly the case, politically I found it unacceptable, even though I had followed this path for most of my life: listening to Jews alone instead of equally listening to Palestinians.

However, my American "queer" desire for public Palestinian voices in the New York landscape required that Palestinians living in New York subject themselves regularly not only to this pervasive ignorance but to threats of increasingly horrific Israeli legislation that could be used to punish them were they to return home. I clearly had no right or ability to make these decisions for them. At the same time, I *did* know that I could neither allow myself to be substituted for them nor to refuse to speak when they could not. It was one of these moments where the limits, the absurdities, and the promise of solidarity politics all converged.

Finally, the leaders of the N.Y. LGBT Center announced that they would hold an open meeting. I am relying on notes from Tom Leger's live blogging for the trans FTM journal *Original Plumbing*. The room was not packed—I would say about 80 percent capacity—and I got my first live glimpse of Glennda, a corporate femme in four-inch heels. Tom described her as "a sexy soccer mom." The event was emceed by Ann Northrop, former facilitator of ACT UP, and there were quite a few former ACT UP-ers in the room. In fact, leaders from many stages of LGBT history were there: Andy Humm of the Coalition for Lesbian and Gay Rights, the group that won passage of the Gay Rights Bill in New York City in 1986; Urvashi Vaid, former executive director of the National LGBT Task Force; Lisa Duggan from New York University; Jasbir from Rutgers and the Audre Lorde Project; Leslie Cagan who had organized the one million strong for the historic antinuclear rally in Central Park in 1982; Alissa Solomon, former theater critic of the *Village Voice*; Pauline Park, chair of the New York Association for Gender Rights Advocacy; and many more. People who had given their lives to this community and to the building of progressive change in this country had shown up. Obviously many serious people felt that the transformation of our center from an open space to a politically controlled environment was a significant subject that merited their attention.

In her opening statements, Glennda was very vague but seemed to be saying that the issue on the table was "space use guidelines." Out of nineteen board members, only two were in the room. It felt from the top that the center leadership was not going to be honest and didn't really care. Then this strange man stood up to speak. He had had massive plastic surgery—his face was somewhere between Faye Dunaway and Cher. His skin was pulled tight, his lips were swollen—and then he identified himself. This was Michael Lucas! He looked like Zoolander. With him were three other gay Israeli men, whom I had also never seen before. These were the people who had transformed a thirty-year tradition of free speech at our community center. Also supporting Lucas was an older gay man named Stuart Applebaum from the Jewish Labor Committee; I didn't know him, either. There were two Orthodox Jewish lesbians sitting behind me, holding hands. And there was an older man with a yamacha to my left. I had never seen any of these people before in my life. It is hard to believe that a handful of right-wing Israelis and gay Orthodox Jews had enough power to transform the LGBT Center. It wasn't possible. The only explanation was fear of Jews unknown and unseen.

Glennda then told us that the code of conduct for groups meeting at the center is "don't be violent, don't be naked, don't steal things." So . . . ?

I saw a queer Palestinian friend come into the room. He was the only Palestinian queer in the room—the contested but silent body. He was hanging out in the background, trying to assess the mood. I also saw Andrew Kadi, a straight Palestinian, and Hannah Marmelstein, a queer woman who is a committed experienced activist for boycott. At this point, Tom Kirdahy, a board member, stood up and made a long speech about how the center has to "be a safe space"—that phony word again, *safe*. And then he asserted that Jews would not feel safe with Siege Busters in the building. Of course he is not Jewish, and there are three queer Jewish members of Siege Busters in the room. I stood up and said that I was Jewish and that this debate had nothing to do with anti-Semitism. Alissa Solomon stood up and said that she is Jewish and that the center was not protecting anyone by censoring. The older man with the yamacha yelled out at her, "Are you a member of Siege Busters?"

"No," she said. "I am not now and have never been a member of Siege Busters."

This was insanity.

The center's motive for censorship was still entirely unarticulated. Some-one asked Glennda directly if this decision was made because of donors threatening to withdraw their funds. She said that there was such a threat but that it was "a minor part of the feedback."

Following on the theme of "safety," Michael Lucas stood up and made his pitch. "Jews are made unsafe by Israeli Apartheid Week events taking place."

An Israeli man next to him added, "If groups would meet here that would favor Palestinian right of return, I would feel unsafe."

I looked at my Palestinian friend standing in the corner. He was the one who was unsafe, but no one seemed to count him in their category of "people."

I have always hated the "safety" discourse. Feeling "safe" is not the para-mount goal of life; it's being able to move forward constructively even if one is afraid. Total safety is impossible unless other people's rights are en-tirely infringed, and it's not a desirable state for an adult. How "safety" of the most dominant became the agenda of the LGBT community center is beyond me.

In the end, the center promised to set up a task force, which I immedi-ately volunteered to be on. The center never kept their word. The most accurate statement of the day was made by Pauline Park, a trans woman activist in New York State politics. She stood up at the meeting and pub-licly clarified the meaning of these events.

"The center has taken a partisan position on the Middle East by banning Siege Busters," she said. "They have transformed a center from a place for all, into a place for some."

We left despondent. The Queer Arab Group defected to the Audre Lorde Project space, and lines were drawn even more deeply—but on whose be-half? This still remains unclear. The president of the board, Mario Palumbo (who identified himself as "half Lebanese"), had closed the meeting with the assertion that he would not support any queer group meeting at the center with the word "apartheid" in its title. How he has the moral right to make that decision for the New York City community is never explained. But somehow, for the moment, we all know that justice is not the factor.

That night my Palestinian friend wrote me about his experience witness-ing that meeting: "I am still somewhat in shock over what people said and how this went. This debate (Zionist/non-Zionist American) is still somewhat new to me. I see the importance of having Palestinian presence in this community because these people need major education, yet I found myself incapable of standing up and speaking on behalf of Palestinians and Arabs. Despite feeling completely alienated and uncomfortable, I am glad I came as this was a learning experience. Al-Sigh."

I'm now having conversations about Israel and Palestine multiple times every day. Since I happen to move through very diverse contexts regularly, these talks take place everywhere: the hallway of my building, at work, in a theater, in auditoriums around the country, on the subway, et cetera. It is often provoked by the question, "What do you do?" or "What are you working on?" or even just "What's new?" And yet I rarely get into arguments.

There are memorable exceptions, however. One night I was at Brown University at a theater conference at a table with a Jewish woman who works on "art and peacemaking." I had no idea what this is, but linking the two seemed spurious to me at the outset. Jim Hubbard was in the final six months of editing *United in Anger*, and of course much of the ACT UP footage is filled with explosive political actions that were highly theatrical, expressive, creative, and innovative. ACT UP was a political movement that expressed itself formally and innovated graphic design as tactics for social transformation. But I had never experienced art as useful for peace.

"What's the relationship between art and peace?" I asked.

Turned out, this woman had been part of projects of Israelis and Palestinians making art together. I wasn't sure what to picture here: highly sophisticated, international Palestinian art stars collaborating with Israeli artists at the Venice Biennale? Why would they? Or was this more in the arts-and-crafts realm, Palestinian kids coming through the Qalandia checkpoint to make murals with Jewish kids coming from swim practice?

It had just started to become clear to me that some Jews thought that the progressive position to take was one based on "dialogue"—a false equation, a nonexistent "equality," a substitute for political change. It wasn't because they were ideologically against real change; it was simply a culture of ignorance about the breadth and depth of Palestinian experience and the nonviolent strategy of sanctions. The week before I was to meet the "art and peacemaking" woman, three Palestinian friends were over for dinner. They described the experiences they had all had at different colleges of Jewish students asking them to "grab a coffee" and then having conversations that were either about (1) how inviting Palestinian speakers to campus was offensive or (2) how their families were affected by the Holocaust or suicide bombers or (3) expressing goodwill about the two of them agreeing to disagree.

"They don't hear us," Mahdi said. "They are not listening. They don't want to know what we think."

So what is the goal of art making for peace? Who is this process supposed to change? Is it supposed to make injustice acceptable to the subordinate? Or are those of us who are ignorant and not listening supposed to realize, by making art, that we need to listen? Or is it the working together that gives us — who dominate — the opportunity to listen and change our self-perception? I knew there was a difference between peace and justice. And I didn't understand how art making itself could lead to social transformation. Artists are some of the most reactionary, selfish people I know. Instead of providing venues for more artists to express their dominance, we should be looking for a way for American society to find out what Palestinians are feeling, thinking, and what they want. At least just so we know.

"They want to use us for therapy," Mahdi says.

But back to the "art and peacemaking" woman. I listened to her talk about what I am coming to think of as the kitsch of peace. There are millions of dollars and human hours being spent on these "therapeutic" reconciliation projects, dialogue groups, and other kinds of get-togethers, initiated mostly by Jews, designed to make us all feel better, when some of us should not be feeling better. It's not about how we feel, it's about what we do. And most of us don't have enough information or knowledge to understand what our responsibilities are, so we don't do much.

"You know," I said, "I'm sure some people are working toward a solution by *not* making art together." By this, I meant the desire for autonomy, to not be sucked into Israel, Jews, and Israelis at every turn around every corner. To live independently, freely, without having to explain anything or help a Jew or Israeli or anyone else be a better person. To not to have to take care of the world. But she didn't understand my meaning.

"I know," she said, shaking her head with the gravity of disappointment, as though this was the worst thing imaginable. That a Palestinian would not want to make art with Us, Us, Us.

"Maybe," I said out of frustration, "maybe the best way for artists to contribute to peace is to boycott Israeli state-sponsored institutions and contribute to nonviolent social transformation by *not* making art."

The second I said it, I knew there was going to be trouble, because I didn't take the time to set this up. I didn't smile for an hour, slowly explaining, slowly introducing information that I knew the others at the table didn't have, as I had not had it. I just jumped, and of course it backfired big-time.

A non-Jewish man at the table, from a theater company in the U.S. South, was enraged. He was so angry he hissed.

"I knew some Egyptian artists who were visiting us, and they wouldn't go to see a show because there were Israelis in it, and they were boycotting."

"The boycott is not against individuals," I said, knowing that I had screwed this up and that it was all my fault. But I was also annoyed that he didn't know why Egyptians would not feel like going to see Israeli artists.

"Yeah," he said. "But they were under orders of the Muslim Brotherhood."

I know from how Haneen, Ghadir and Sami reacted to U.S. television coverage of the Egyptian revolution that our information about the Muslim Brotherhood is distorted, designed to frighten and decontextualize. "Muslim Brotherhood" is the new 'shorthand for the Islamophobic ideal that no Arab would have an authentic sincere reason for not wanting to support an Israeli artist. Instead they are all supposedly in a cult of religious fanaticism that turns Muslims into zombies robotically intent on destroying Christendom and whatever Jews are on its side.

This seems to be one of the most profound obstacles toward informed American conversation about Palestine. Americans don't have even the most basic information about Palestinian society, how multidimensional it is, and who our progressive political partners are.

Whenever I am with Palestinians I hear one phrase over and over again: "Palestinian civil society." It's used so often, it's like a throwaway. But almost no American I run into knows what this means.

Technically "civil society" refers to the arena of uncoerced collective action around shared interests, purposes, and values, not enforced by the state. "Civil society" commonly includes charities, development nongovernmental organizations, community groups, women's organizations, faith-based organizations, professional associations, trade unions, self-help groups, social movements, business associations, educational and artistic collectives, coalitions and advocacy groups—that is, all the elements of a dynamic multidimensional society. So when you read the July 9, 2005 call for boycott from PACBI, the heading at the top was "Palestinian Civil Society Calls for Boycott, Divestment, and Sanctions against Israel until It Complies With International Law and Universal Principles of Human Rights." It was signed by a wide range of groups including the Dentists Association, the Federation of Trade Unions, Teachers Union, Farmers Union, Engineers Association, the Lawyers Association, all the political parties in the Occupied Territories, global refugee groups, Environmental Education Centers, the Consumer Protection Society, and the YMCA of East Jerusalem.

In other words, the sector of Palestinian society that is asking for support of this boycott is filled with professionals, leaders, and intellectuals. Yet the texture of who makes up Palestinian civil society is murky in the minds of most Americans, who have no idea of how Palestinians live or how varied their society is. As a result they become constructed in the American mind as people to be lectured to, to be used for our own therapeutic needs, to be "partnered" with as a way of fixing both of us. But never, ever, as people to be listened to and to learn from.

These prevalent misconceptions are often explained as "willful ignorance." But speaking from my own history of ignorance, the degree to which it is actually willful is hard to articulate. The human process of refusing to know is not and cannot be freely chosen. It is an unconscious choice, produced by a confluence of factors including the privilege of the prison of ignorance.

On June 2, 2011, the New York LGBT Center issued the following statement:

> The Lesbian, Gay, Bisexual & Transgender Community Center today announced a moratorium, effective immediately, on renting space to groups that organize around the Israeli-Palestinian conflict.
>
> "We must keep our focus squarely on providing life-changing and life-saving programs and services to the LGBTQ community in New York City" said Executive Director Glennda Testone.... "Make no mistake, everyone is welcome at the Center; but these particular organizing activities need to take place elsewhere."
>
> ... said board president Mario Palumbo, "we are first and foremost a community services center and need to ensure that all individuals in our community feel welcome to come through our doors and get what they need to live healthy, happy lives."

Once again I marvel at the use of words like "life," "community," and especially "everyone." Since this rule is most directly going to affect Jews and

Arabs, it's clear who the LGBT center considers to be human, and who they exclude.

Some months later, I spoke to the center's coordinator for Lesbian Movie Night and asked to show *Zero Degrees of Separation* by Elle Flanders, about an Israeli/Palestinian lesbian couple. She said "yes" and briefly interacted about programming, but she soon disappeared and refused to answer email or phone calls. So queer Jews and queer Arabs are not only not allowed to organize at the center, we're also not allowed to fall in love.

11. UNDERSTANDING

On a Friday in April 2011, I received an email from Laura Flanders, the anchor and producer of GRIT-TV, a cable news program. Omar Barghouti had finally been allowed to enter the United States. Even though he is the most visible leader of the most viable strategy for nonviolent change in the Middle East, he was roundly ignored by the U.S. media. Laura was, in fact, the only television anchor interviewing him. No Jewish leader would debate him. The *New York Times* was silent on his visa restriction, his book, and indeed, his movement. Laura invited me to appear with Omar for twelve minutes on the following Monday. As a result of those twelve minutes, I have, on tape, the most startling conversation.

> LF: Were you surprised, Omar, to have Sarah come over and talk with you about BDS from an LGBT queer perspective? Had you made that connection? Suspected that there would be support in this community?
>
> OB: No, support? No. We were aware of Sarah's politics and principles so we were not surprised, and there's nothing in the BDS movement that excludes anyone, and it was very important to make that connection that this includes queer activists as well. Sarah's contribution to this connection has been really key in bringing this forward.
>
> LF: It's not just a connection of adding people to the coalition though, you're deepening the understanding of what some of the issues are as you discuss this.
>
> OB: Absolutely. Because BDS is not just about ending the occupation and apartheid, it's about building a better society. A better society by definition must be inclusive and must recognize people's rights, individual rights and people's identity, be it gender, sexual identity, any other form of identity should not prevent them from getting equal rights. So we must absolutely be consistent with ourselves and say equal rights for all includes everyone. . . . When South Africa was saying, "Oh, we have more gay rights than any African state," does that make apartheid good? I mean, what's the argument there? So I think the issues have to be ad-

dressed together. I'm against those who say let's delay women's rights. Especially if it comes with women's rights debates. Let's delay women's rights till after liberation. Nothing comes after liberation; either we start now in parallel or nothing will come after we end apartheid and occupation.

There it was.

LF: Now I want you to restate that as well because there are always gonna be people that say, "What are you, dreaming? We've got to deal with, can't even get food and water in Gaza; you want us to take on LGBT equality too?"

OB: I think it goes hand in hand that people have rights, and when we say we want to end Israel's oppression, multitiered system of oppression — denying refugees their rights, racial discrimination in Israel, and occupation — we must immediately in the same sentence say people have equal rights in every form and way.

Omar had changed. And I had changed.

SS: I want to say that the lesson here that I've learned in the last year is that Palestinian society is a multidimensional society and that the BDS movement represents secularity, feminism, increasingly progressive attitudes toward gay people and that this is the sector of Palestinian society that we should be supporting because BDS is the most viable, nonviolent strategy for change.

I stumbled home in a kind of shock. We had succeeded.

Despite Brand Israel, despite the silence of the *New York Times*, despite the LGBT center, despite the anti-Semites and the Islamophobes, despite all that and more, Omar and I had both been motivated by a love and need for justice to transform ourselves so that we were now reaching each other.

We had changed each other for the better. And we did it with the help and support of a huge cast of characters: Haneen, Ghadir, Sami, Jasbir, Judith, John, Dalit, Mahdi, Nadia, Hiyam, Shucki, Yotam, Hind, Zohar, Rabbi Sharon, Sonia, the cowgirl who picked us up at the airport in Minneapolis, Rashid Khalidi at George Chauncey's house, the queerim at the anarchist vegan café in Tel Aviv, the straight Palestinian woman who shared a salad in Ramallah, Lynette Jackson in Chicago, Lily and Alia in Oakland, the family in Bil'in who fed us za'atar before being teargassed, my cousin in Tel Aviv who wrote me a fake letter of invitation, Elle Flanders in Toronto, the dyke who wired up the video feed at the Audre Lorde Project, et cetera, et cetera. The "world," the queer international, the global brotherhood and sisterhood of those who love justice — somehow we had all worked together and created a new reality.

And now I know that there is a significant Palestinian "civil society" that supports a nonviolent strategy for change and is feminist and now pro-gay. And now I know that there is a significant and growing sector of the LGBT community in the United States that recognizes queer Palestine as part of us, something inseparable and organic. We've done something of value, and we've done it together.

eyeless in Gaza

CONCLUSION
There Is No Conclusion

Conclusion for Now

When the bulk of this manuscript was completed I continued to learn important facts and insights, and my process will continue long after it is published.

—When I flew El Al to start my "solidarity trip," I was violating the boycott because El Al Airlines is a "state-sponsored institution."

—What we in New York know as "Israeli Folk Dance," a popular fad in the 1950s, '60s, and '70s, is the Palestinian *dabke*. And the word *Sabra*, meaning a Jew born in Palestine/Israel, is in fact Arabic. A sabra is a prickly pear cactus. It's tough on the outside, sweet on the inside, and indigenous to Palestine. It is impossible for a country founded in 1948 to have an organically evolved folk dance. People who disagree with me say that Israeli "folk dance" came from Eastern European dance. But my grandparents were Eastern European and, believe me, I never saw them folk-dance.

—"Checkpoint" is an English translation of the Hebrew word. The Arabs call them "barriers."

—I joined the advisory board of Jewish Voice for Peace.

—Regarding my distinction between "Jews" and "Israelis" and my surprise that the film *Still Alive in Gaza* made clear that the Palestinians in Gaza did not make this distinction, filmmaker Nadia Awad writes: "It should be noted that after Gaza, soldiers spray painted lots of very disgusting graffiti along the lines of 'don't fuck with the Jews,' type stuff and also the army has made a point, at least through the second intifada, of spray painting the Star of David over tanks/bulldozers before they proceed. The Star of David is a visual reminder of trauma for many Palestinian kids, something that has been exploited to cynical effect. Second, by not saying 'Israeli,' they are keeping the lack of normalization and lack of acknowledgment of the

Israeli state consistent. How can there be Israelis if there is no Israel? The use of the word 'Israeli' in the Palestinian political lexicon is, in my opinion, a post-Oslo thing."

—I saw b. h. Yael's video *Deir Yassin Remembered*, proving that Israeli atrocities against Palestinians were in place by 1948.

— Yael introduced me to Ella Shohat and I was blown away by the clarity of her vision. I came to understand how fundamental the Arab Jewish identity is to undoing racism toward Arabs of all religions.

—Omar Barghouti got published in the *Nation*.

—A friend explained to me one day that the problem with using the Bible to justify Jewish possession of "the land" is that Jews wrote the Bible. I realized that this was the beginning of Brand Israel (see the appendix for a history of Brand Israel).

—PQBDS's first global campaign forced the International Gay and Lesbian Youth Organization to cancel their meeting planned for Tel Aviv. Queer groups in Turkey, Britain, Lebanon, Ireland, and Serbia all supported Palestine.

—In June 2011 I met with KC Price, the executive director of Frameline, and asked him to hold a public conversation about Frameline's acceptance of Israeli government funds. I offered a number of different possible scenarios, and he said he would get back to me. He insisted that Frameline is "neutral." He never got back to me.

—In November 2011, after three months of intense negotiations and the submission of more than 190 pages of documentation, the *New York Times* published a nine-hundred-word op-ed piece of mine called "Israel and Pinkwashing." It was posted 4,555 times on Facebook within three days, was among the "most emailed" articles of that day's paper, was chosen by the *Atlantic* as one of the five best columns of the day in a national forum, reprinted in the *Herald Tribune* and *Haaretz*, and reposted on blogs around the world. I received eighty-seven emails telling me that I am "evil," "racist," and a "Jew-hater" and that I should move to Saudi Arabia or Iran. I received five letters from conflicted Jewish queers who simply could not accept that the Israeli government was using them in this way. But I also received hundreds of emails and postings of support and appreciation. Many were shocked to see the *New York Times* acknowledge pinkwashing and Brand Israel. A month later, Benjamin Netanyahu publicly declined to publish an opinion piece in the *Times* expressly because it had published critical views including that "of the CUNY Professor," and I consider that to be one of the most significant accomplishments of my life.

— The first LGBT delegation to Palestine took place in January 2012, with the following participants: Dr. Tim McCarthy, core faculty and director, Human Rights and Social Movements Program, Carr Center for Human Rights Policy, Harvard Kennedy School; Dr. Jasbir Puar, associate professor of women's and gender studies at Rutgers University and board member of the Audre Lorde Project; Dr. Juliet Widoff, primary care physician, Callen/Lorde LGBT Community Health Services; Dean Spade, assistant professor, Seattle University School of Law, and founder of the Sylvia Rivera Law Project; Kendall Thomas, director of the Center for the Study of Law and Culture, Columbia University; Rabbi Sharon Kleinbaum, senior rabbi, Bet Simchat Torah, the LGBT synagogue; Dr. Pauline Park, chair of the New York Association for Gender Rights Advocacy; Darnell L. Moore, project manager for Hetrick-Martin Institute's new school development project in Newark, New Jersey, and visiting scholar at the Center for the Study of Gender and Sexuality at New York University; Richard Kim, executive editor, the *Nation* magazine; Katherine Franke of the Center for Gender and Sexuality Law, Columbia University; Vani Natarajan, humanities and area studies librarian, Barnard College; Barbara Hammer, filmmaker; Lisa Weiner-Mahfuz, coordinator, Roots Coalition: Queer People of Color Network; Dr. Roya Rastegar, independent film curator and visiting fellow at the Center for the Study of Women, UCLA; Troy Masters, founder and publisher of *Gay City News*; and Tom Leger, publisher of *prettyqueer.com*. Nadia Awad and an all-Palestinian crew filmed the delegation. MIX is her fiscal sponsor, but I leave it to the filmmakers and delegates to tell that story.

— In March 2012, I was a speaker at the "One State Conference" at Harvard's Kennedy School, in which prominent Palestinian and Israeli intellectuals like Diana Buttu, Leila Farsah, and Ilan Pappe called for one democratic binational state, some asking for two rights of return, and others positing the re-welcoming of Arab Jews into "the Arab world" as the key to a united binational state.

— Also in March 2012 I received a leaked "internal document" of the San Francisco Jewish Federation that revealed extensive internal communication with the Frameline festival about the creation of propaganda to support Frameline's acceptance of Israeli government funds. These included phony tweets and planted articles. I sent the document to *Mondoweiss*, which reported on its contents.

— Jim Hubbard and I inaugurated The Pop-Up BDS Film Festival by boycotting the Tel Aviv LGBT Film Festival and instead touring anti-occupation venues in Israel and pro-queer venues in Palestine in April 2012 with the Middle Eastern premiere of our feature documentary *United in Anger: A History of* ACT UP.

— The Lisbon LGBT Film Festival became the first to officially turn down Israeli funding, which it had had since 2005. The change was the result of a three-year campaign by groups including "Panteras Rosa" and John Greyson's withdrawal of his films, even though he'd won the festival's main prize in 2009. "Sergio Vitorino of Panteras Rosa said in the organization's official statement: 'Israel uses queer events to Pinkwash Apartheid, diverting attention from its oppression of Palestinians as well as the real homophobia confronted by the LGBT community inside Israel, and by LGBT Palestinians living under brutal military occupation . . . we can now proceed with celebrating the true message of the festival, one of equality and tolerance.'"

Here it is, two years since I first sat under that tree in the safe house in Ramallah, eating green almonds with salt with Hiyam, Haneen, and Sami. We had come together out of some kind of faith in a better future, not knowing each other, but ready to learn, as we truly have, that we are together on the side of justice.

Up until that moment, I had always thought that an almond was a dried brown seed that came in a plastic bag. But my imagination was being awakened. I learned the truth, that almonds grow on trees, and that I could reach up and pull a green almond off the branch, still not knowing that it was the salt that was needed to bring out its taste. And I would find the answer to a question I'd never asked before: What does salt on green almonds taste like? Answer: It's fresh, unknown, and delicious.

It is only in our most honest, sincere recognition of each other's humanity that the great potential of life — connecting with other people and relating to them as equals — can be understood and truly tasted. And it is with this enrichment of knowledge and experience that we are able to envision and then create a just future.

When we reach for this, it comes.

APPENDIX
Brand Israel and Pinkwashing

A DOCUMENTARY GUIDE

Not only do Palestinian queers face these injustices on
a daily basis and undergo Israeli oppression like any other Palestinian, but also
our name and struggle is often wrongly used and abused to "Pinkwash" Israel's
continuous crimes against the whole Palestinian population.
— Palestinian Queers for Boycott/Divestment/Sanctions

2005

The Israeli Foreign Ministry, Prime Minister's Office Finance Ministry, concludes a three-year consultation with American marketing executives and
launches "Brand Israel," a campaign to "rebrand" the country's image to appear "relevant and modern" instead of militaristic and religious.[1] An article in
Jewish Week explained the marketing maneuvers:

> "Americans find Israel to be totally irrelevant to their lives and they are tuning
> out . . . particularly 18–34 year old males, the most significant target," explained
> David Sable, CEO and vice president of Wunderman, a division of Young and
> Rubicam that conducted extensive and costly branding research for Israel at no
> charge. Starting off with a free trip for architectural writers, and then another
> for food and wine writers, the goal of these "and numerous other efforts" was to
> convey an image of Israel "as a productive, vibrant and cutting-edge culture."[2]

In July 2005, The Brand Israel Group (BIG) presented its findings to the
Israeli Foreign Ministry.[3]

2006

Because it was important for Israel's branding concepts to have internal
consistency and external appeal, the Foreign Ministry held additional focus
groups in Europe and Israel. It hired the firm Marketwatch to determine the
current perception that Israeli citizens held of their own national brand.[4]

That same year, the Electronic Intifada reported that Saatchi and Saatchi was also working for Israel, free of charge.[5]

In October, the *Jerusalem Post* reported:

The Foreign Ministry is promoting Gay Israel as part of its campaigns to break apart negative stereotypes many liberal Americans and Europeans have of Israel. The initiative flies in the face of the swelling protests set against Jerusalem's Gay Pride parade set for November 10. But even as its organizers are receiving anonymous threats of holy war against them, gay activist Michael Hamel is traveling in Europe and North America working on publicizing Gay Israel. A portion of his work, he told the *Jerusalem Post* by phone as he sat drinking coffee in a California airport, has the support of the Foreign Ministry. "We are working very closely with them," said Hamel, who heads the AGUDAH, Israel's LGBT organization. . . .

Speaking on condition of anonymity, a Foreign Ministry official told the *Jerusalem Post* this week that efforts to let European and American liberals know about the gay community in Israel were an important part of its work to highlight this country's support of human rights and to underscore its diversity in a population that tends to judge Israel harshly, solely on its treatment of Palestinians. Still, it is a topic that is so touchy he did not want his name used. But David Saranga, who works in the New York consulate, was more open about the need to promote Gay Israel as part of showing liberal America that Israel is more than the place where Jesus once walked. The gay culture is an entryway to the liberal culture, he said, because in New York it is that culture that is creating "a buzz." Israel needs to show this community that it is relevant to them by promoting gay tourism, gay artists and films. Showing young, liberal Americans that Israel also has a gay culture goes a long (way) towards informing them that Israel is a place that respects human rights, as well, said Saranga.[6]

2007

Foreign Minister Tzipi Livni appointed Ido Aharoni to head Israel's first brand management office and awarded him a $4 million budget in addition to the already established $3 million in annual spending on *Hasbara* (Hebrew for "explanation," or propaganda) and $11 million for the Israeli Tourism Ministry in North America.[7]

Israel began wooing young males with niche marketing to heterosexual men. Saranga initiated a project with *Maxim* magazine, a photo shoot titled "Women of the Israeli Defense Forces," which shows model-like Israeli women who had served in the army, in swimsuits.[8]

Follow-up study revealed that *Maxim* readers' perceptions of Israel had improved as a result of the piece. Saranga was pleased but knew he had a lot of work ahead of him. "Rebranding a country can take 20 years or more," he said. "It involves more than just generating more positive stories about Israel.

The process has to be internalized and integrated, too. Israelis must share in and believe in what we promote."[9]

2008

Saranga told PR Week that the two groups Israel was targeting were "liberals" and people ages sixteen to thirty. Gideon Meir of Israel's Foreign Ministry told Haaretz that he would "rather have a Style section item on Israel than a front page story."[10]

Aharoni's office hired TNS, a market research firm, to test new brand concepts for Israel in thirteen different countries. It also funded a pilot program of public relations efforts called "Israel: Innovation for Life" in Toronto. Aharoni predicted "the execution of a program that will support the brand identity. This might include initiating press missions to Israel, or missions of community influentials; it could include organizing film festivals, or food and wine festivals featuring Israel-made products."[11] This resulted in the "Spotlight Tel Aviv" program at the Toronto International Film Festival, boycotted by John Greyson, Naomi Klein, and others.

PACBI published a sample contract that Israeli artists signed with their government when the artist was "invited" to an international event. The contract text reveals that it is the Israeli government that is inviting itself to international events. The artist is paid with a plane ticket, shipping fees, hotel costs, and other expenses paid by the Israeli government. The contract does not assume *any* funding from the "host" country. In return, the template states, "The service provider is aware that the purpose of ordering services from him is to promote the policy interests of the state of Israel via culture and art including contributing to creating a positive image for Israel."

Yet . . .

"The service provider will not present himself as an agent, emissary and/or representative of the Ministry."[12]

2009

The 2009 EastWest Global Nation Brand Perception Index lists Israel at 192 out of 200, behind North Korea, Cuba, and Yemen and just before Sudan.[13]

The International Gay and Lesbian Travel Association (IGLTA) announced an October conference in Tel Aviv with the goal of promoting Israel as a "world gay destination."[14]

Helem, a Lebanese LGBTQ organization, responded with a call for a boycott.

For some time now, Israeli officials and organizations such as the Aguda, who are cooperating closely with IGLTA, have been promoting LGBT tourism to Israel through false representations of visiting Tel Aviv as not taking sides, or as being on the "LGBT" side, as if LGBT lives were the only ones that mattered. It is implied that it's okay to visit Israel as long as you "believe in peace," as if what is taking place in Palestine/Israel is merely a conflict between equals, rather than an oppressive power relationship. Consistent with globalization's tendency to distance the "final product" from the moral implications of the manufacturing process, LGBT tourists are encouraged to forget about politics and just have fun in a so-called gay-friendly city. . . .

Even more importantly, Tel-Aviv's flashy coffee shops and shopping malls, in contrast with the nearby deprived Palestinian villages and towns, serve as evidence that the Israeli society, just as the Israeli state itself, has built walls, blockades and systems of racist segregations to hide from the Palestinians it oppresses. The intersection of physical and societal separations and barriers have justly earned the term apartheid, referring to an historically parallel racist regime in South Africa against the indigenous Black population of that country. Leisure tourism to apartheid Israel supports this regime. It is not neutral, and it certainly is not a step toward real peace, which can only be based on justice.[15]

That same year, the Zionist organization StandWithUs told the *Jerusalem Post* that it was undertaking a campaign "to improve Israel's image through the gay community in Israel."[16]

The Foreign Ministry told *Ynet* that it intended to sponsor a Gay Olympics delegation "to help show to the world Israel's liberal and diverse face."[17]

2010

Efforts to win the battle of the narrative were launched at January's Herzliya Conference organized by the Interdisciplinary Center Herzliya (IDC); Columbia University's Lauder School of Government, Diplomacy, and Strategy; and the IDC's Institute for Policy and Strategy, which brought together representatives of the Foreign Affairs Ministry, Haifa University, the Prime Minister's Office, Reut Institute, and private communications companies for discussions. The talks reaffirmed the need for rebranding.

Conference findings included the following:

— Many criticisms of Israel will stop when policy toward Palestinians is changed.

— Israel correlates with the terms "daring and independent" but not "fun and creative."

— Fifty percent of people in Western countries are disengaged and do not have an opinion on Israel, and they can therefore be won over by marketing.

— "Narratives of victimhood and survival adapted by Israel over the years are no longer relevant for its diplomatic efforts and dialogue with the West. Nowadays Israel's opponents capitalize on using the same narratives to achieve and mobilize support."

— "People respond well when addressed in a familiar language that uses well-known terms and are susceptible to simple, repetitive, consistent messages."[18]

— "In order to succeed online, one has to detach one's self from strictly official messages and to develop an online personality."

The Ministry of Foreign Affairs allocated 100 million shekels (more than $26.2 million) to branding.

"The Globe found that the activity will focus on the internet, especially on social networks. This is following research performed by the Ministry of Foreign Affairs in which it found that surfers will show sympathy and identity with content that interests them, regardless of the identity of the political affiliation of the publisher."[19]

Three hundred forty million shekels (about $88 million) was spent on an international marketing campaign to brand Tel Aviv as an international gay vacation destination. The campaign would be run in Germany and England through ads on gay community websites and magazines, and on designated Facebook and Twitter pages. The campaign was designed to promote Tel Aviv as "the New Capital."

A 2010 article from Ynet stated that "Etti Gargir, director of the VisitTLV organization, said that the Tourism Ministry and Tel Aviv Municipality invested NIS 170 million (about $44 million) each in the project."[20]

Tel Aviv Municipality submitted an official application to host the International Gay Pride Parade in 2012.[21]

The Tourism Ministry reported that it supports targeted marketing campaigns likely to increase tourism to Israel."

By 2010, the term "pinkwashing" was already in general use by queer anti-occupation activists. In April, Brand Israel launched Israeli Pride Month in San Francisco. It was not a grassroots expression by Israeli queers living in San Francisco but an event instigated, funded, and administered by the Israeli government. QUIT, an actual queer organization, used the term "pinkwashing" in its campaign to counter the cynical use of queers by the Israeli government to promote its Brand Israel project as "proof" of its commitment to human rights.

2011

An article from Ynet stated that "the increased discount flight capacity from England and Germany increases the capability of Tel Aviv to compete with other cities in Europe."[22]

For the first time, the Israeli stand at the International Tourism Fair in Berlin and encourage gay tourists to visit Tel Aviv. According to Tel Aviv Council Member Yaniv Weizman, $94 million of Israeli government money was invested in 2010 in promoting gay tourism to Tel Aviv. The money came from the Tel Aviv Municipality and Tourism Ministry.[23]

In July, the Anti-Defamation League hosted StandWithUs's Yossi Herzog to speak on gay rights in Israel and gay presence in the Israeli Defense Force.[24]

2012

Tel Aviv was selected as "Best Gay City" in a competition organized by American Airlines.[25]

Notes

An earlier version of this guide first appeared as "A Documentary Guide to Pinkwashing," by Sarah Schulman, posted November 29, 2011, on *Pretty Queer* (http://www.prettyqueer.com/2011/11/29/a-documentary-guide-to-pinkwashing-sarah-schulman-new-york-times-oped/).

1. Nathaniel Popper, "Israel Aims to Improve Its Public Image," *Jewish Daily Forward*, October 14, 2005.

2. Gary Rosenblatt, "Marketing a New Image," *Jewish Week*, January 20, 2005.

3. "Branding Israel B," unpublished documents from the William Davidson Institute of the University of Michigan. Case 1-428-823, April 8, 2009, Yaffe Center for Persuasive Communications.

4. Ibid.

5. Rima Mirriman, "Israel's Image Problem," Electronic Intifada, December 6, 2006.

6. Tovah Lazaroff, "Foreign Ministry Promoting Israel," *Jerusalem Post*, October 26, 2006.

7. "Branding Israel B."

8. "Chosen Ones: Israeli Defense Forces," *Maxim*, July 9, 2007.

9. "Branding Israel A," unpublished documents from the William Davidson Institute of the University of Michigan. Case 428-725, April 8, 2009, Yaffe Center for Persuasive Communications.

10. Bill Berkowitz, "Israel Looking for an Extreme Makeover," IPS/Inter Press Service, January 12, 2008.

11. David Brinn, "Israel Eyes Toronto for Marketing Test Site," *Jerusalem Post*, March 17, 2008.

12. Omar Barghouti, *Boycott, Divestment, Sanctions: The Global Struggle for Palestinian Rights* (Chicago: Haymarket Press, 2011).

13. Eastwest Communications, East West Global Index 200, Nation Brand Perception Index, 2008.

14. YouTube, "Tel Aviv World Gay Destination," high-definition video.

15. "Call for Action: Tell IGLTA That Apartheid Israel Is Not for LGBT Leisure Tourism," *Helem*, September 8, 2009.

16. Mel Bezalel, "Gay Pride Being Used to Promote Israel Abroad," StandWithUs/The J Post, June 8, 2009.

17. Itamar Eichner, "Foreign Ministry to Sponsor Gay Olympics Delegation," *Ynet*, May 5, 2009.

18. "Winning the Battle of the Narrative," Working Papers of the Tenth Annual Herzliya Conference, January 31–February 3, 2010.

19. Tali Shapiro, "We'll Take Over the World? Ministry of Foreign Affairs Allocates 100 Million Shekels for State Branding," *Pulsemedia*, August 17, 2010 (translation of *Israeli Globe* article).

20. Danny Sadeh, "Campaign Branding Tel Aviv Gay Destination Underway," *Ynet*, July 21, 2010. This figure is disputed by Esther Hecht of *Hadassah* magazine, who writes that "the deputy director of the Tel Aviv tourism association" told her that the budget for gay tourism in 2011 was 210,000 shekels or $56,000. The latest figure Hecht offers comes from the Tourism Ministry, which claims Israel's annual outlay in promoting gay tourism is one million shekels, approximately $267,000.

21. "Tel Aviv Wants to Host International Gay Pride Parade," Ynetnews.com. March 1, 2010.

22. "Israel Promotes Gay Tourism in Berlin," Ynetnews.com, March 9, 2011.

23. "Tel Aviv Wants to Host International Gay Pride Parade."

24. Jewish American Heritage Month, "Yossi Herzog: Serving Openly Gay in the IDF," http://www.jewishamericanheritagemonth.com, August 6, 2011.

25. "American Airlines Presents Best of Gay Cities 2011," http://www.gay cities.com/best-of-2011/vote.php?page=10, accessed November 20, 2011.

INDEX

9/11, 18

A Film Unfinished, 44, 45

Abunimah, Ali, 54, 135

Acey, Katherine, 107, 146, 147, 150

ACT UP (AIDS Coalition to Unleash Power), 49, 53, 65, 72, 73, 128, 134, 144, 146, 152, 164, 167

ACT UP Oral History Project, 25

Adalah-NY, 161

African Americans, 85, 145

AIDS (Acquired Immune Deficiency Syndrome), 26, 49, 65, 87, 120

AIPAC (American Israel Public Affairs Committee), 18, 60, 61, 81, 87

Aharoni, Ido, 180, 181

Alameddine, Rabih, 11, 17, 51

Alexander, Elisha "Shuki," 79, 173

Aloni, Udi, 49, 58, 59, 64, 66, 68, 75, 85, 90, 162

Al-Qaws (For Gender and Sexual Diversity in Palestinian Society), 38, 46, 49, 54–56, 62, 90, 91, 107, 116, 126, 131, 136, 138, 150, 160, 163. *See also* Maikay, Haneen

Alwan, Dunya, 139, 140–43, 160

Amman, 108, 133, 149

Amreeka, 43

Anti-Semitism, 3, 9–12, 17; fear of, 9, 88, 89. *See also* Austria-Hungary; Belgium; College of Staten Island; Frameline; France; German Democratic Republic; Germany; New York LGBT Community Center; Poland; Russia

Apartheid, 62, 96, 111, 112, 117, 118, 120, 138–40, 172, 173; as hate speech, 118, 119, 120

Arab Americans, 81, 143–47. *See also* Alwan, Dunya; Awad, Nadia; Dabis, Cherien

Arab Jews, 11, 13, 14, 68, 69, 75, 95, 96–98, 176, 177. *See also* Mishali, Yael; Nawi, Ezra; Shohat, Ella; Yael, b. h.

Arafat, Yassar, 82

Arendt, Hannah, 11

Arcus Foundation, 107

AROC (Arab Organizing and Resource Center), 107, 108

Ashwari, Hanan, 82

Astraea Foundation, 107

Aswat (Palestinian Queer Women), 37, 46, 55, 99, 100, 107, 114, 115, 131, 133, 136, 138, 139, 160

Audre Lorde Project, 103, 133, 152, 154, 159, 163, 166. *See also* Lorde, Andre

Austria-Hungary, 13

Aviv, Nitsan, 64

Awaad, Hind, 64, 80–87, 91, 173

Awad, Nadia, 117, 133, 134, 144, 151, 152, 173, 175, 177

Bacha, Julia, 45

Bard College, 18

Barghouti, Omar 27, 31, 32, 37, 46, 62, 84–90, 93, 108, 127, 145, 156, 160, 172, 173, 176. *See also* BDS; PACBI

Barkan, Ronni, 64

Baum, Dalit, 28, 29, 30, 31, 32, 35, 36, 76, 110, 114, 173

Bawer, Bruce, 104
BDS (Boycott/Divestment/Sanctions), 23, 24, 26, 27, 29, 31–34, 46, 48, 49, 53, 55, 58–60, 62–64, 73–76, 80–87, 90, 91, 93, 100, 109–13, 115, 116, 126–28, 131, 145, 152, 154, 160–63, 168–70, 175, 177. See also Awaad, Hind; Barghouti, Omar; Jews and; Nonviolence; PACBI; Toronto
BDS Film Festival, 84, 91, 177
Belgium, 9, 10
Bekhsoos, 127, 128. See also Meme
Ben-David, Lilach, 64
Ben-Gurion, David, 61
Ben-Yehuda, 61
Berkeley, 28, 32, 81, 109, 110, 112–14
Berlin, 41–48, 61, 128–32
Berlinale (Berlin International Film Festival), 41–48
Bil'in, 37, 38, 45, 55, 56, 61, 66, 77–79, 86, 97, 110, 112, 173. See also Khatib, Mohammed
Birthright, 139
Birthright Unplugged, 139, 160
Birzeit University, 51, 52, 83, 84, 153, 154, 161
Bisexuals, 69, 71, 73
Black Bus, 42
Black Laundry, 28, 35, 114, 131
Brand Israel, 24, 25, 54, 61, 121, 135, 143, 160, 173, 176, 179–85; "Spotlight Tel-Aviv," 24, 25
Brim, Matt, 107
Boycott National Committee, 62
Buber, Martin, 41
Budrus, 45, 46, 48
Bully Bloggers, 130, 131
Butler, Judith, 28, 32, 34, 36, 40, 41, 49–51, 58–60, 83, 109, 110, 114, 128–31, 153, 154, 157, 161–63, 173

Canadian Anti-Occupation Activists, 81, 117. See also Flanders, Elle; Greyson, John; Klein, Naomi; QAIA (Queers Against Israeli Apartheid); Yael, b. h.
Canadian Jewish News, 24
Chauncey, George, 144, 173
Checkpoints, 25, 77, 93–95, 97, 98, 111, 127, 135, 155, 175. See also Qalandia Gate
Chinn, Sarah, 107
Chomsky, Noam, 107
Cinema, 41–48, 84. See also Bacha, Julia; Berlinale; Dabis, Cherien; Dunye, Cheryl; Greyson, John; Hersonski, Yael; Hubbard, Jim; MIX; Toronto International Film Festival; Wadimoff, Nicholas; Zuria, Anat
CLAGS (Center for Lesbian and Gay Studies of the City University of New York), 107, 146, 148
Clinton, Hillary, 56
Cohen, Matan, 64
College of Staten Island, 9, 11, 17, 18
Cuba, 27

Dabis, Cherien, 43
Dagan, Adi, 64
Dana International, 121
Davis, Angela, 150
Desiring Arabs, 66
Devlin, Bernadette, 148
Diaspora (Jewish), 7, 12, 13, 14, 24, 41, 140, 141. See also Right of Return
Disapora (Palestinian), 40, 41, 61, 134. See also Abunimah, Ali; Amreeka; Awad, Nadia; Dabis, Cherien; Kadi, Andrew; Right of Return
Dixon Place, 48
Duggan, Lisa, 130, 147, 164
Dunye, Cheryl, 40

East Jerusalem, 56, 61, 63, 95

Egypt, 43, 108, 134, 143, 169
Eichman, Adolf, 11
El-Al, 67, 160, 175
Elbit (Norway), 80
Electronic Intifada, 54, 59, 122, 135, 180
Erato, Hamutal, 64
Et-Shalom, Nava, 40, 41, 107, 149

Facebook, 76, 105, 118, 143, 147, 150, 176
Fatah, 45, 80
Feminism, 66, 123–25, 128, 136, 138–44, 147, 173. *See also* Isha l'Isha; Kayan
Film Festivals, 116, 135 142, 143, 144, 160, 176, 177. *See also* BDS Film Festival; Berlinale; Frameline; Lisbon LGBT Film Festival; MIX; Tel Aviv LGBT; Toronto International Film Festival
Flanders, Elle, 36–39, 49, 51, 58, 84, 95, 97, 120, 160, 162, 170, 173
Flanders, Laura, 81, 172
Frameline, 142, 143, 160, 176, 177
France, 3, 9, 10, 11
Franke, Katherin, 177
Freedom Flotilla, 120, 134, 157. *See also* Seige Busters

Gay marriage, 93, 105, 107, 144
Gaza, 18, 19, 23, 25, 43, 63, 70, 83, 110, 112, 113, 115, 120, 123, 134, 175
German Democratic Republic, 8, 9, 10
Germany, 10, 11, 26, 40–48, 103, 128–32
Ghadir, 99, 100, 106, 108, 109, 117, 133–55, 162, 173
Gissen, Amir, 24, 25
Gladstone, Martin, 117, 119
GLADT (Gays and Lesbians from Turkey–Germany), 129
GLQ, 146
Goldhagen, Daniel, 11
Goldin, Nan, 41
Gordon, Neve, 28, 34, 51
Guardian of London, 34, 103, 105, 130

Gregg, Ronald, 144
Greyson, John, 23–25, 28, 29, 35, 36, 84, 90, 93, 120, 134, 135, 136, 161, 162, 173, 178, 181
Gross, Aeyal, 25, 131

Haaretz, 49, 50, 58, 113, 116, 167, 176, 181
Haifa Women's Center, 37, 99
Halberstam, J. Jack, 130
Hamas, 19, 45, 80
Hamel, Mike, 121, 180
Hammer, Barbara, 160, 177
Hampshire College, 81
Harvard, 25, 89, 90, 92, 107, 143, 177
Helem, 115, 116, 125, 181
Hersonski, Yael, 44, 45
Hiyam, 91, 93, 173, 178
Hochberg, Gil, 146
Hodes, Linda, 5
Holocaust, 1, 3, 6, 9, 10, 11, 13, 15, 16, 30, 44, 45, 46, 47, 168
Homonationalism, 103–33, 135, 158. *See also* Puar, Jasbir
Hubbard, Jim, 23, 25, 135, 167, 177
Hude, Sue, 106, 137
Human Rights, 89, 90, 92, 136

IDF (Israeli Defense Forces), 71, 113, 121
International, the, 65, 66, 136; "Gay International," 66. *See also* Massad, Joseph
International Jewish Anti-Zionist Network, 107, 141
International Law, 110, 113, 114, 124, 148
Iran, 108
Isha l'Isha, 37, 55, 99, 123–25
Islamaphobia, 3, 17, 104, 136, 169; America, 39, 104, 134, 148; European, 10, 11, 42, 104, 129, 130; opposition to, 18, 39, 128–30; Russian, 14. *See also* College of Staten Island
Israel, 34, 67–77, 86–102, 161, 176; Ash-

kenasis, 9; and BDS, 27, 29, 34, 49, 62–64, 95, 98, 161; cinema, 42–45, 135; consulates, 24, 116, 135, 143, 160; democracy, 99, 117, 127; emigration from, 13, 17, 55; foreign ministry, 25, 119, 179–82; immigration to, 11, 13, 68; LGBT people and, 8, 23, 55, 68–73, 79, 81, 95, 99, 94–98, 112, 113, 116, 120–22; LGBT tourism, 115, 116, 117, 180–83; military, 23, 70, 72, 123, 175, 180; Mizrahi's, 68, 69, 86, 123; modern dance, 5; 1967 war, 4; *queerim*, 73, 79, 81, 115, 173; repression of Yiddish, 3; "right to exist," 60; security, 67, 68, 93, 123, 124; separation wall, 25, 37, 45, 77, 78, 112, 115, 126, 137, 138, 147, 154; settlements, 25, 49, 55, 56, 77, 80, 95–98, 110, 112, 127; supremacy ideology, 30, 50, 55, 61, 123, 125; tree planting, 3, 142. *See also* Checkpoints; Gaza; Pinkwashing; Tel Aviv

Israelis: academics, 25, 28, 30, 34, 63, 73, 76, 131; anti-occupation activists, 28, 30, 31, 35, 37, 62–64, 69, 71, 76–79, 81, 95, 97, 99, 122–24, 127, 131; settlers, 96, 98. *See also* Alexander, Elisha "Shuki"; Aloni, Udi; Baum, Dalit; Gissen, Amir; Gross, Aeyal; Isha l'Isha; Kama, Amit; Mesoloelot; Mishali, Yael; Nawi, Ezra; Rogatka; Shapira, Tal; Soloviov, Sonia; Tel Aviv University; Weiman-Kelman, Zohar

Jackson, Lynette Aria, 107, 143, 150, 173
Jewish Voice for Peace, 59, 119, 122, 175
Jewish Week, 179
Jews, 14, 18, 30, 52, 53, 67, 74, 85, 140, 162, 165; Ashkensasi, 9, 68, 69; and BDS, 25, 26, 27, 29, 49, 61–63, 74, 86, 109; dialogue, 167, 168; communists, 9, 162; harassment of Jewish critics

of Israel, 29, 30, 59, 60, 86, 98, 176; money, 159, 160, 166; as scapegoats, 6, 61, 113, 125, 182; trauma, 15, 44, 45, 70, 71. *See also* Arab Jews, Butler, Judith; Diaspora; Flanders, Elle; Holocaust; Israelis; Judaism; Klein, Naomi; Timmerman, Jacobo; Zionism

Jordan, June, 85
Judaism, 12, 14, 15, 16; and forgiveness, 15, 16; sexism, 42, 55; ultra-orthodoxy, 42, 43; values, 50, 60, 113
Juhasz, Alexandra, 46, 47

Kadi, Andrew, 165
Kahn, Yael, 64
Kama, Amit, 62, 73, 75, 76
Kandiyoti, Dalia, 23, 24, 25, 27
Kaplan, Amy, 107, 149, 150
Kayan, 139
Kershner, Isabel, 38
Khalidi, Ismail, 144
Khalidi, Rashid, 144, 173
Khatib, Mohammed, 61
Kim, Richard, 177
King, Martin Luther, 54
Kirchik, James, 116
Klein, Naomi, 25–29, 35, 36, 51, 58, 60, 81, 88, 93, 109, 113, 181
Kleinbaum, Sharon, 137, 158, 173, 177, 181
Kovel, Joel, 18
Kushner, Tony, 59

Leger, Tom, 164, 177
Lesbian Avengers, 49, 72, 73, 144
Lesbian vision, 114
LesMigras (Lesbian Migrants and Black Lesbians–Germany), 129
LGBT Delegation to Palestine, 144, 145, 154, 159, 160, 177
LGBT synagogues: Beit Simchat Torah, 8; Sha'ar Zahav, 117, 137
Li, Alan, 119

Lisbon LGBT Film Festival, 178
Lorde, Audre, 114, 140
Love, Heather, 38, 39, 107, 149, 150
Lucas, Michael, 117, 157–59, 165

Madrid, 120, 121
Mahdi, 133, 134, 144, 151, 168, 173
Maikay, Haneen, 74, 91, 92, 100, 106,
   108, 109, 116, 131, 133–55, 162, 163, 173
Maimonides, 15
Marmelstein, Hannah, 165
Massad, Joseph, 66, 136, 137
McCarthy, Tim, 107, 143, 177
Meme, 127, 12. See also Bekhsoos
Mesoloelot (Tribads), 55, 68, 72
Minneapolis, 107, 137, 140
Mishali, Yael, 75
MIX: NYC LGBT Experimental Film
   and Video Festival, 23, 49, 135, 147
Mondoweiss, 150, 177
Moore, Darnell, 177
Moraga, Cherrie, 150
Motherhood, 70
Muzzlewatch, 59–62, 89, 119, 156

Najambadi, Afseneh, 107
Nakba, 63, 161
Naor, Dorothy, 64
Natarajan, Vani, 52, 53, 177
The Nation, 87, 108, 176, 177
National LGBT Task Force, 158; "Cre-
   ating Change" Conference, 106, 107,
   137, 139, 140, 171. See also U.S. Tour
   of Palestinian Queer Activists
Nawi, Ezra, 36, 48, 95–99
Nazis, 2, 9, 10, 11, 44, 45
Neiman, Ofer, 64
Netenyahu, Benjamin, 25, 55, 60, 61,
   122, 176
Netherlands, 103, 104, 135
New York LGBT Community Center,
   152, 157–59, 161, 163, 164–66, 170
New York Times, 38, 156, 172, 173, 176

Nimr, Sonya, 51, 52, 83
Nkoli, Simon, 120
Nonviolence, 23, 54, 79, 115, 126, 128,
   154, 163
Norway, 104

Oakland, 149, 150
Occupation, 6, 12, 14, 41, 50, 70, 71,
   76–102, 110–13, 116, 119, 147, 169, 173;
   and homosexuality, 41, 69, 81, 83, 84,
   116, 117, 119, 124, 131, 132, 135, 138, 139,
   146, 151–53, 158, 173; silence about,
   6, 30, 71
Omer, Mohammed, 61, 62
One State Solution, 41, 177
OSI (Open Society Institute), 108, 150
Outfest, 160. See also El-Al

PACBI (Palestinian Academic and
   Cultural Boycott of Israel), 23, 27,
   30–31, 36, 37, 39, 48, 52, 53, 55, 62,
   84–87, 90–93, 126, 127, 159, 181
Palestine, 77–102, 111, 156, 169; borders,
   48–57; cinema, 43, 45, 84; education, 43, 51, 83, 84, 99, 138; home
   demolition, 12, 96, 112, 124; Palestinian Authority, 80; resistance, 37,
   38, 45, 51, 53, 54, 56, 61, 79–81, 83, 84,
   86–94, 113, 116, 128, 139, 147, 148, 151,
   164; shepherds, 95, 97, 98; trauma,
   43, 44–45, 71; villages, 37, 38, 45, 56,
   61, 77–79, 96, 97, 99, 117, 142. See also
   BDS; Bil'in; Checkpoints; Diaspora
   (Palestine); East Jerusalem; Occupation; PACBI; Palestinian Queer
   Movement
Palestinian Queer Movement, 31, 36,
   37, 46, 64–65, 80–84, 90–93, 95, 99,
   100, 103, 105–9, 114, 115, 116, 117, 119,
   124, 126, 127, 128, 131, 133–55, 163,
   165, 167, 173, 174. See also Al-Qaws;
   Aswat; Hiyam, Ghadir; Maikay,
   Haneen; Mahdi; PQBDS; Shamali,

Palestinian Queer Movement (*cont.*)
Sami; U.S. Tour of Palestinian
Queer Activists
Palestinians, 33, 44, 45, 46, 60, 62, 65,
70, 89–102, 106, 110, 111–13, 163, 164,
169, 175; as refugees, 6, 41, 43, 110,
123, 126; travel, 61, 93; in U.S. media,
53, 80, 82, 83, 87, 104–9, 134, 141, 142,
154, 176, 179–85. *See also* Awaad,
Hind; Al-Qaws; Aswat; Barghouti,
Omar; Dabis, Cherien; Hiyam,
Ghadir; Maikay, Haneen; Massad,
Joseph; Omer, Mohammed; Pal-
estinian Queer Women; Shamali,
Sami
Park, Pauline, 112, 164, 166, 177
PGBDS (Palestinian Queers for Boy-
cott/Divestment/Sanctions), 126–
28, 131, 134, 145, 151, 152, 156, 157, 159,
163, 169, 170, 176, 178, 179
Pinkwashing, 23, 72, 93, 116, 117, 119,
121, 122, 127, 130, 131, 135, 141, 142, 154,
176, 179–85. *See also* Queer Imperi-
alism; StandWithUS
Poland, 3, 13, 44, 45
Poved, Antonio, 121
Price, KC, 143, 160, 179. *See also*
Frameline
Puar, Jasbir, 103–5, 130, 131, 133–35, 152–
54, 161, 162, 164, 173, 177. *See also*
Homonationalism

QAIA (Queers Against Israeli Apartheid), 115, 117, 118, 119, 121, 122
Qalandia Gate, 93–95, 101
QEJ (Queers for Economic and Social
Justice), 152, 159
Queer, 23, 24, 92, 93, 100; and BDS,
23, 24, 30, 31, 38, 62, 64, 75, 83–85,
89–93, 100–109, 116, 126–28, 145, 156,
157, 161, 172, 174; community, 105–8,
116, 126, 127, 136, 143, 147, 150; government funding, 23, 73, 115, 118, 119;

and immigration, 104, 117. *See also*
Homonationalism
Queer Imperialism (gay imperialism),
38, 39, 65, 75, 83, 84, 92, 136, 153
QUIT (Queers Undermining Israeli
Terrorism), 117, 135, 183

Rabani, Hanan, 108, 150
Ramallah, 23, 31, 36, 49, 55, 62, 79, 80,
84, 86, 90–92, 126–28, 138
Rastegar, Roya, 177
Reach-Out, 129
Reut Institute, 60, 182
Rice-Gonzalez, Charles, 48
Richie, Jason, 116
Right of Return (Jewish), 40, 107, 162,
177
Right of Return (Palestinian), 40, 41,
177
Rogatka, 54, 62, 73–75, 86
Rosawsky, Flo, 107, 139, 141
Rosenberg, Jessica, 107, 139, 141
Rosin, Yeoshua, 64
Russia, 2, 13, 14

Safra Project, 104
Sager, Maggie, 150, 151
Said, Edward, 41, 82
Sandanistas, 27
Saranga, David, 180, 181
Schaeffer, Emily, 64
Schotten, Heike, 38, 39, 103, 107, 143
Seige Busters, 134, 157, 159, 163, 165
Shamali, Sami, 55, 56, 80, 82, 83, 90, 91,
100, 106, 108, 109, 133, 138, 147, 150–
55, 162, 173
Shani, Ayala, 64
Shapira, Tal, 64, 77–79
Shayshon, Eran, 60
Shohat, Ella, 69, 175
Signorile, Michelangelo, 146
Singer, Isaac Bashevis, 3, 6; Nobel
Prize speech, 7, 9
Skype, 59, 108, 121

Smelko, Will, 100, 113
Solidarity Politics, 27, 29, 30, 33, 35, 36,
    38, 39, 45, 48, 49, 52–54, 64–66, 71,
    77–79, 106, 108, 117, 119, 120, 127, 137,
    139, 164
Solomon, Alisa, 144, 145, 164, 165
Soloviov, Sonya, 35, 37, 38, 51, 52, 54,
    62, 64, 66, 68, 74, 77, 79, 99, 173
South Africa, 23, 24, 26, 27, 62, 81, 88,
    120, 172, 182
Spade, Dean, 177
St. Patrick's Day, 49, 148
StandWithUs, 142, 182, 184
Still Alive in Gaza, 43, 61, 175
Stop the Wall Campaign, 55
Suspect, 129, 130
Sylvia Rivera Law Project, 153, 159, 177

Ta-ayush, 48, 97
Taylor, Brad, 134, 153, 158. See also
    Seige Busters
Tel Aviv, 23, 25, 38, 64, 68, 70, 72, 99,
    115, 121, 139; Tel Aviv LGBT Film
    Festival, 23, 84, 156, 177; Tel Aviv
    University Sex Acher Conference,
    25, 26, 38, 39, 63, 64, 68, 72–74, 107,
    131
Tenne, Ruth, 64
Terrorism, 6, 72
Terrorist Assemblages, 103
Testone, Glennda, 157–59, 164–66, 170
Thomas, Kendall, 177
Timmerman, Jacobo, 8
Toronto, 23–25, 36, 115–20, 181
Toronto International Film Festival,
    24, 25, 35
Transpeople, 73, 75, 76, 79, 86, 103, 114,
    115, 121, 127, 129, 149, 152, 164, 166
Trotsky, Leon, 66

Tutu, Desmond, 110, 133

United in Anger: A History of ACT UP,
    167, 178
United Farmworkers, 26
United Kingdom, 104
United States, 58, 104; fundamentalist
    Christians, 104; Israel policy, 13, 14,
    19, 55, 56, 74, 81–83, 85, 87, 88, 89, 92,
    112; military, 39, 104, 129; racism, 39,
    104. See also Christian Zionism
University of California, Davis, 113
University of Pennsylvania, 107
U.S. Tour of Palestinian Queer Activ-
    ists, 93, 104–7, 135–55

Vaid, Urvashi, 137–40, 158, 164
Vanden Heuvel, Katrina

Wadimoff, Nicholas, 43
Walker, Alice, 83, 85
Weiman-Kelman, Zohar, 32, 35, 36,
    107, 149, 173
Widdoff, Juliet, 177
Wilders, Gert, 107
Who Profits from the Occupation, 28,
    110. See also Baum, Dalit
Wolfson, Yossi, 64
World Pride, 115, 116, 121, 134, 142, 144

Yael, b. h., 176
Yakim, Moni, 64
Yiddish, 2, 3, 6, 7, 13, 33, 125

Zionism, 3, 12, 13, 14, 32, 33, 36, 59, 61,
    62, 67, 140, 141, 166; Christian Zion-
    ism, 14, 17, 104, 117, 118, 141; holo-
    caust as justification for, 11; Queer
    Zionism, 32, 33, 157–66
Zuria, Anat, 42, 43

Sarah Schulman's seventeen books include the novels *The Mere Future, The Child,* and *Shimmer,* and the nonfiction works *Gentrification of the Mind: Witness to a Lost Imagination; Ties That Bind: Familial Homophobia and Its Consequences;* and *Stagestruck: Theater, AIDS, and the Marketing of Gay America.* She is a codirector of The ACT UP Oral History Project and a Distinguished Professor of the Humanities at the City University of New York, College of Staten Island.

Library of Congress Cataloging-in-Publication Data
Schulman, Sarah, 1958–
Israel/Palestine and the queer international / Sarah Schulman.
p. cm.
Includes bibliographical references and index.
ISBN 978-0-8223-5358-4 (cloth : alk. paper)
ISBN 978-0-8223-5373-7 (pbk. : alk. paper)
1. Jewish-Arab relations. 2. Arab-Israeli conflict. 3. Sexual minorities —
Political activity — Israel. 4. Palestinian Arabs — Government
policy — Israel. 5. Palestinian Arabs — Israel — Social conditions.
I. Title.
HQ76.2.I75S38 2012
956.05′3 — dc23   2012011640